TAKEN AT NEW ORLEANS, 1861, THE DAY BEFORE THE "SUMTER" SAILED

JOHN McINTOSH KELL

RECOLLECTIONS

OF A

NAVAL LIFE

INCLUDING THE

CRUISES OF THE CONFEDERATE STATES STEAMERS
"SUMTER" AND "ALABAMA"

BY

JOHN M^cINTOSH KELL

Executive Officer of "Sumter" and "Alabama"

WASHINGTON
THE NEALE COMPANY, PUBLISHERS
431 Eleventh Street
1900

COPYRIGHT, 1900, BY
THE NEALE COMPANY
WASHINGTON, D. C.

Dedication

TO BLANCHE, MY WIFE

"Now few are the good things life can hold,—
And the one I prize all others above
Is neither fame, nor a wealth of gold,
But the trust and joy of a perfect love."

Preface

It would scarcely seem *au fait* that a book should make its appearance (no matter how unpretentious it may be) before a criticising and oftentimes censorious public without a preface. Yet I have usually found prefaces either explanatory, apologetic, or regretful. The book will be its own explanation, I have no apologies to make; but my regrets are many and great. Ten years ago I made up my mind and began to write this book for the pleasure of my family and friends. In my busy life weeks would often pass without my writing a word. Having a natural aversion to the pen was often an excuse for my neglect, and the fact was ever before me that a most delightful and perfect book in Admiral Semmes' "Service Afloat" had been given to the world, from which mine could not differ in facts, data, or detail, and could never approach in beauty of diction or language. My life has been one of deeds, not words, and what I have done in the strictest sense of duty and high integrity of purpose shall never be apologized for. To me there has never been a "New South." The blood of heroic sires and gentle mothers in the veins of the present generation have made her what she is—a remodeled country, built upon the grandeur of the past and the holiest memories a people ever inherited! The Will of God could not be stayed or averted. Might prevailed; but behind the frowning Providence of disaster and defeat for His own wise plans and purposes, God has at last smiled upon the South, and she has many compensations from His hand. My regrets are that many who were with us when I began to write will never con these simple pages, for many, indeed most, of the friends of my youth have passed before me "on that road from which no traveler e'er returns."

PREFACE

To their children and my own posterity I leave in these pages the truth of history and hope they will not be without interest to the young. To my brothers, the "United Confederate Veterans," I give the narrative of our times, the "times that tried men's souls," that left us nought save honor, a love of country, the sacred memory of valiant lives and deeds, and a hope in God!

JNO. McINTOSH KELL.

Sunnyside, Georgia, May 3, 1898.

RECOLLECTIONS OF A NAVAL LIFE

PART I

CHAPTER I

I BELIEVE it was Job who so pathetically exclaimed, "O, that mine adversary had written a book!" (which wish I could never explain satisfactorily to myself). Not being solicited by my enemies, but by my family and friends, for their pleasure, hoping it will give pleasure to others also, I venture to record some of the incidents of travel in my long and eventful life. If I may be forgiven the egotism (as I am an "author quite unknown to fame"), I will here introduce myself as an American of Southern birth, a Georgian, proud of my native State. I was named for my maternal great uncle, General John McIntosh, famous for deeds of heroism in the war with the Spaniards in the early history of Georgia.

When I was four years old my father died, leaving to my mother's care five little children. My childhood was spent upon our plantation, "Laurel Grove," McIntosh County, often varied by visits to Sapelo Island, the residence of my mother's first cousin, Hon. Thomas Spalding, whose son Randolph, a few months my senior, grew up with me in the intimacy of brothers. Our grandmothers were sisters, Marjory and Hester McIntosh. Marjory married James Spalding and Hester (my grandmother) married Alexander Baillie, and died leaving an infant, my mother, who was reared by her aunt, Mrs. Marjory Spalding, for whom she was named.

8   RECOLLECTIONS OF A NAVAL LIFE

My boyhood was passed as the Southern boy of that day, in the healthful, manly sports of hunting, riding, boating, and fishing, varied by school attendance in Darien, the county seat of McIntosh County, which was settled by my ancestors, Clan McIntosh, and first named "New Inverness," for their distant home in Scotland. My first teacher was Mr. Bradwell, who was famous in the seaboard counties as a teacher of great merit and ability. Shortly after, Dr. James Troup, the friend and physician of our family, was elected to the Legislature, and going up in his carriage to Milledgeville (for it was before the days of railroad travel), stopped at "Perry Mills" during the examination of a school kept by one Musgrove, a Scotchman. Being pleased with his mode of teaching, especially mathematics and English grammar, on his return to Darien Dr. Troup persuaded my mother to allow him to take me with his son and daughter and place us there at school. This school, however, was of short duration. The poor old Scotchman got on a big "spree," and remaining so for some time, we were sent home. My next teacher was Mr. Pincheon, who conducted a large and prosperous school in Darien till he was called to take charge of the Chatham Academy, in Savannah. To this school I was sent in company with my cousin, Henry K. Rees, now Episcopal Evangelist of the State of Georgia, an earnest worker in his Master's vineyard, honored and beloved in his profession. From this school I returned home and remained a year.

In my sixteenth year I was sent to Savannah into the counting house of Andrew Low & Co., with a view of entering mercantile life. I cannot say that it was to my taste, and after the winter's work I went home for a visit. I found the U. S. Brig *Consort* on a survey of our coast. This vessel was under the command of Captain Glynn, soon succeeded by Captain Ramsey; and here there came a change over the spirit of my boyish dreams at this impressionable age, and I resolved to serve my country as a

RECOLLECTIONS OF A NAVAL LIFE

naval officer. My frequent visits to the ship and the visits of the officers to my home (my sisters being young ladies in society at the time), and the notice the officers took of me as a lad, was no doubt very suggestive of the profession; but I think being born almost within sound of the billows and in sight of the "deep blue sea," I had an innate love for it which grew with my growth and strengthened with my strength, and which will remain with me while life lasts.

At my earnest entreaty my mother (though it must have cost her widowed heart many a pang) applied through our immediate Representative, Hon. Thos. Butler King, who obtained for me an appointment as midshipman in the United States Navy, dating from September 9, 1841.

His letter, which I found among her papers, reads:—

HOUSE OF REPRESENTATIVES, WASHINGTON.
September 11, 1841.

MY DEAR MADAM: After many and repeated efforts I have at length obtained a midshipman's warrant for your son. He now belongs to his country. That he will bear himself gallantly and honorably in the service to which he belongs I do not doubt. That he may attain its highest and brightest honors is the sincere wish of your faithful friend

And obt. servant,

THO. BUTLER KING.

To Mrs. KELL,
    Darien, Ga.

My first orders were to join the Sloop of War *Falmouth*, then fitting out at the Brooklyn Navy Yard, and under the command of my relative, Captain James McKay McIntosh. In obedience to orders I took passage on a sailing vessel for New York from Savannah. Upon the voyage we experienced some rough weather; but having once taken a trip in a brig from Darien to Georgetown, South Carolina, with the family of Mr. John Green, a rice planter of our county (which gave me my first experience of sea life), I felt quite at home on the voyage to New York and did not suffer from seasickness.

10   RECOLLECTIONS OF A NAVAL LIFE

Upon my arrival in New York I found a letter from Captain McIntosh, telling me to take passage in a bay steamer for Bridgeport, Conn., where he was residing with his family. I did as he directed, and ·arriving at Bridgeport about the hour of noon, proceeded to the hotel. My first introduction to Northern manners and customs took place here. I noticed very closely everything that took place, and was much surprised to find young white servant girls attending at the table. The dinner was a revelation to me. Down the center of the table was a row of pumpkin pies. After getting fairly under way with the meats and vegetables, I noticed the girls handing around in pitchers a foaming beverage, which I innocently mistook for champagne, and prepared my palate for a luscious quaff. Holding my tumbler on high to be filled, I soon took a full mouthful, but quietly set it down again, and gazed around me to see the effect on other people. They seemed to enjoy it, but it was my first taste of hard cider, and I was thoroughly disgusted and disappointed. Not so with the pumpkin pie, however; I enjoyed that with the zest of a hungry boy of sixteen. After dinner I sought the residence of my cousin, Captain McIntosh, and made the acquaintance of his beautiful young wife and two pretty little children. Among the features of the little town was pointed out to me the home of P. T. Barnum, one of its residents. One evening while there we were invited to tea. I noticed the absence of all Southern breads, such as waffles, muffins, wafers, etc., and that all the breads were sweet, commencing with doughnuts, which I liked on first acquaintance. In ·two or three days the captain and I went to New York, and then began my life on board a "man of war."

The *Falmouth* was a first-class sloop of war of that date. I at once fitted myself out in the jaunty midshipman uniform, further providing myself with bedding and all the necessary articles, and took up my quarters with my messmates, to "be rocked in the cradle of the deep." Every-

RECOLLECTIONS OF A NAVAL LIFE

thing was pressed forward getting ready, as we were shortly to set sail for what was then known as the "Gulf Squadron," and to take with us as passenger the newly-appointed minister to Quito, Mr. Black. My letters, at this time full of boyish enthusiasm, were preserved among my mother's treasures, and are a great source of amusement to my children now. After landing our minister we had a pleasant and interesting cruise through the Windward Islands, touching at Santa Cruz, St. Thomas, Martinique, and finally shaping our course for Pensacola, the rendezvous of the Gulf Squadron.

On arriving at Pensacola we entered upon a round of gaiety. I saw for the first time here the celebrated Madame Le Vert, who was in the zenith of her fame and popularity. I have seen many more beautiful women, but never saw one more full of grace and vivacity or more charming as a conversationalist. After remaining in port a month or more we sailed for Vera Cruz, coming to anchor under the island of Sacrificios, this being the only safe anchorage from the violent northers that blow across the Gulf of Mexico, and distant some miles from the city. The city of Vera Cruz presented a true picture of Spanish architecture, the houses being built of adobe or unburnt brick, plastered and whitewashed, with tile roofing.

The city was not attractive, and the fort opposite presented a very formidable appearance—built of coral from the reef upon which it stood. Old Vera Cruz, fifteen miles northwest of the present city, is said to be the spot where Cortez disembarked in 1518. Our first precaution after anchoring was to moor ship securely, with our two bowers and sheet anchors so planted as to resist these violent northers, also sending down our lower yards and housing topmasts. In a few days we had reason to congratulate ourselves upon being so well prepared, for we experienced one of those storms in all its fury, making it dangerous for a man to hold his head even above the rail of the ship. We were quite ready and relieved after this severe experi-

RECOLLECTIONS OF A NAVAL LIFE

ence to receive the order to "get ready for sea." In those days (it being before the day of steamers) men-of-war were allowed to carry silver from one country to another as an accommodation to merchants, at the same time allowing a percentage for this service to the captain doing such favor. Our captain had taken on board a quantity of silver bars to be carried to parties in the city of New Orleans. After a pleasant passage we arrived and anchored off the mouth of the Belize, our ship drawing too much water to cross the bar. A little steam tug came alongside, to which the silver was transferred, and I, with other officers, was detailed to take charge of the silver and deliver it to the houses to which it was consigned. My first impression of New Orleans was remarkable in this particular. We landed in the French part of the city, where French was the prevailing tongue, while across the street dividing the American and Creole or French population English was used entirely. After attending to our mission and enjoying a day in the city we returned on board ship and shortly after set sail for Pensacola.

Chapter II

PENSACOLA in those days was the paradise of midshipmen. They, with their seniors, the lieutenants, gave themselves up to the gaieties of this seaport town. It was always noted for the pretty girls that had their homes there, and of course they were always "belles" when the Gulf Squadron was at its rendezvous. Like the Norfolk girls, they were very full of "sea knowledge." My friend, John N. Maffitt, in a charming little story of his, makes an old veteran officer say to a middy: "Mr. Forbes, a leopard cannot change its spots, neither can a Norfolk girl be otherwise than beautiful and d—d dangerous. At school their first class reader is 'Dorsey Lever.' Every Sunday they study the 'Navy Register,' and when standing on the 'Bridge of Sighs' with 'spooney' midshipmen by their sides they become instructors of astronomy, nautical romance and the abstruse science of knotting and splicing." Well, her Pensacola sisters can equal the Norfolk girl, and "sighing sailors, beautiful senoritas, scowling rivals and love-sick middies" filled the tropical air of that old town in my young days, and "music, moonlight, love, and flowers" were the living inspiration!

After refitting we proceeded on our way northward, stopping at Savannah, Georgia, the seaport town of the captain's native State, where he was received with great cordiality, and our ship visited by many of its inhabitants. The captain took advantage of the occasion to visit his old home near Darien, Georgia, and to my great delight I accompanied him, and visited my home and family after many months of absence. We were quite the observed of all in our bright uniforms, and I felt the great importance of my position as an officer of the Government, though

14 RECOLLECTIONS OF A NAVAL LIFE

only a midshipman! We enjoyed our week's visit to the fullest extent, and took stage coach for the city of Savannah, passing through the Counties of McIntosh, Liberty, etc. Experiencing some runaway tilts in the coach and four, we capped the climax late in the evening by the driver going to sleep and upsetting the stage in a marsh while driving over a causeway. Fortunately for me, I had the seat with the driver, and soon extricated myself by jumping clear of the wreck. Not so, however, with the inside passengers; they had to climb through the upper windows of the coach. The rotundity of the captain made this rather a hard job for him and he lost no time in addressing the driver in sailor parlance, not very complimentary. After all were rescued alive and unhurt and the driver had meekly borne his share of abuse for his carelessness, we prepared to start again.

Righting up the coach, and being re-seated, we passed the remainder of the journey in laughing and joking over the ridiculous plight to which we had been reduced, the captain declaring he "ran no such risks at sea, where he was much more safe than on terra firma." Upon arriving in Savannah we joined our ship and set sail for New York. At the Brooklyn Navy Yard we found the Frigate *Savannah* fitting out for her first cruise, and bearing the broad pennant of the commodore of the Pacific Squadron. I applied for orders to this vessel, which I received, and reported for duty on board—Captain Andrew Fitzhugh, commanding—October 20, 1843.

As soon as the Frigate *Savannah* was ready for sea we set sail for Rio Janeiro on our way to the Pacific. After a remarkably pleasant voyage we anchored off Rio on the 18th of December. The geographies truly say that the peerless bay of Rio, upon which the city is situated, is scarcely rivaled in beauty by the far-famed Bay of Naples. On nearing the coast the first object that presents itself to the mariner is "Sugar Loaf Mountain." This mountain is about nine hundred feet above the sea. There are many

RECOLLECTIONS OF A NAVAL LIFE   15

other mountains, among them the "Organ," so called from the resemblance it bears to the pipes of a huge organ; also "Table Mountain," whose summit is flat. I believe it is this mountain that is called by the Portuguese "Square Topsail," as it quite resembles that article of rigging to a practiced eye. Of course the climate of Brazil is warm, and subject to the dread usurper of such climates, yellow fever; but it is very much tempered by the breezes that come from the sea. The city of Rio has a great deal in it to enjoy. We midshipmen went on shore at the first opportunity, and being somewhat tired of ship fare found our way to a restaurant and ordered a supper. When the bill was presented it was up in the millions in their currency (with which we were not then familiar) and was truly startling. We became very much alarmed and thought we were a lot of "busted individuals," but managed upon a financial explanation to settle the bill. Previous to this supper we had "taken in" the town, visiting, among other places, the beautiful Cathedral. Upon entering this building we handed a very officious and self-important guide some small change to show us around. After showing us through the Cathedral proper he invited us into a feast-room, where he told us the priests the night before had held a banquet. Judging from the empty ale bottles it must have been quite a banquet! He kindly offered us some of the ale (of which we partook), this being my first and last experience of ale drinking in a church.

After taking in water and provisioning ship, we continued our voyage around the Horn, encountering rough weather, heavy gales, boisterous seas, and a very low degree of temperature, being nearly frozen for three weeks off the pitch of the Cape. The violence of the gales forced us down to latitude 62 degrees south. After rounding the Cape we shaped our course northward in the broad Pacific, and welcomed the more temperate clime of the lower latitudes.

RECOLLECTIONS OF A NAVAL LIFE

On the 17th of February, 1844, we came to anchor in the Bay of Callao, the seaport of Lima, the ancient Capital of Peru. The Bay of Callao is formed from a peninsula on which formerly stood the old city of Callao, submerged more than a hundred years ago by a terrible earthquake, the chimneys still showing above ground. An English company were proposing at that time to excavate for the buried treasure of that once wealthy city. It is related that during this terrific earthquake a Spanish frigate was carried by the incoming sea several miles in the interior and left there by the receding waters.

The island of San Lorenzo forms the western barrier or sea front to the bay, thus forming a very snug anchorage. Callao was built after the style of old Spanish towns—subject to earthquakes—of adobe, with one story only, and tile roofing. Lima, about six miles from Callao, is famous for its old cathedrals of great wealth and magnificence, dating back to the days of Pizarro. In one of these we were shown by the priest a body embalmed and claimed to be that of Pizarro himself. A beautiful stream passes through the city, and along its banks are shaded walks, where the Spanish maidens and duennas are seen in their peculiar dress, with a mantilla over the head having an opening for but one eye. This eye, often of brilliant appearance, united to a graceful, queenly carriage and walk, leaves great scope for imagined beauty. Across the stream is a famous amphitheatre, where the renowned bullfights took place at that time, a great attraction for the city and country around—doubloons and bouquets being eagerly thrown to the successful matadors. It was of course our privilege to witness one of these scenes of wild excitement and great brutality. Often fine steeds were gored and the matador himself fatally injured, and finally the poor bull would succumb to the torture no longer endurable. Then would be brought in a truck pulled by four magnificent horses richly caparisoned, the carcass thrown upon it, and amidst the shouts of the multitude carried out, when

RECOLLECTIONS OF A NAVAL LIFE

another animal would be brought in to go through the same ordeal. Lima was famous for her bullfights, the cruel sport of a semi-barbarous age and time. At Callao I was transferred to the Schooner *Shark*, under the command of Lieutenant Neil M. Howison. Mr. Howison came out as flag lieutenant with Commodore Dallas, ordered to command the Pacific Squadron. The commodore's flag was hoisted on the Frigate *Savannah*, but he did not live to take a cruise. He was taken sick and died on shore at Callao. The Schooner *Shark* was given to his flag lieutenant as a select command, and it was a privilege to serve on board. I, being only a midshipman, was placed in charge of a watch. My first experience was an amusing one. The *Shark* was ordered to take some of our officers leaving the squadron to Panama on their way home. While on this voyage we passed quite near the Lobas group of islands, or really a group of rocks, where seals and sea lions reared their young in great numbers. We were running with a free wind with our square sails set, and the course given me took us quite near the rocks. Upon the near approach of the schooner the seals set up a great roaring as they rolled into the water from their rocky beds and frolicked around in the water in our wake. It happened to be just at dinner time, and the officers taking passage were at table with the captain. I put my head down the hatchway and called to the captain to "come and see the seals playing around the vessel." He replied: "Will be up as soon as I finish dinner," but one of the officers came up at once. Calling out, he said: "Howison, come on deck!" As the captain came up he was surprised to see our nearness to the rocks; still I was keeping the course given me, but there was evidently a current setting us on toward them. The captain at a glance took in the situation. He directed me to "put the helm down and haul on the wind and give good distance in passing the rocks, remarking, by way of pleasantry, "Mr. Kell, you must think you are in a coach and four, driving round a

18 RECOLLECTIONS OF A NAVAL LIFE

street corner." I was strictly carrying out my orders, but was wanting in experience as a watch officer. For a long time after that I heard a great deal of "those seals and my coach and four." •

We reached Panama after a pleasant voyage, and took leave of our officers, who crossed the Isthmus on their way home. We anchored off the island of Toboga, which was then in its primitive state, and occupied by the native Indians, with the exception of an old Irish woman, who had married one of the head men of their tribe. She did the washing for the officers, using as a smoothing iron the conchs picked up on the seashore. This was truly a lovely spot in its primeval growth and beauty. Its limpid streams ran down from the hills above into grottoes, making beautiful natural bathing houses, which we enjoyed to the fullest extent. From our refreshing baths we would stroll up into the pineapple fields and gather the fruit ripe from the plant, and only those who have eaten it in this way know its exquisite perfection. After getting on board sufficient water for our voyage, with what fruit, vegetables, and poultry we could gather from the natives, and our supply of clean linen from our Irish washerwoman, beautifully clean, but conch ironed and minus buttons, we took our departure from lovely Toboga, one of the natural garden spots of God's great universe.

Returning along the coast of South America, with pleasant breezes and smooth seas, we stopped in the port of Payta, where a limited trade is carried on with coasting vessels and whalers. We also ran into the small port of Huanchaco. There, in company with the captain and one or two other officers, I left the schooner for a day's ride in the country to visit the ruins of one of the cities of the Incas, who occupied that country when Pizarro passed along on his conquering march to the city of Lima. We could distinctly trace out the streets and the foundations of some of the buildings. In our ride through these ruins

RECOLLECTIONS OF A NAVAL LIFE

we frightened up a fox from his lair, and had a wild chase over the old town, which was royal fun for a lot of sailors.

On our return to the village of Huanchaco we were entertained at the house of one of the priests of the village, where we enjoyed a most delightful drink made from a species of the passion flower, or May-pop, called there the "granadelia." It is quite as acid and has a more pleasant taste than the common lime. We returned at sunset on board ship and next morning early got under way and stood down the coast for Callao, stopping at convenient points for hunting and fishing, for little health runs on shore, and other amusements of various kinds.

Chapter III

In the very early part of this cruise I find from old letters (one of which I will insert) that I was very much impressed with San Domingo and the surroundings, and must have picked up some traditions from the islanders.

Latitude 18° 43' N., Long. 75° 23' W.
May 6.

My Dear Mother: We have in sight St. Domingo and the small island of Navaza, the latter noted for being the place where some of Columbus' men landed in crossing from Jamaica to St. Domingo in canoes, having lost their vessel on the former island. There were but two among his crew that would volunteer to cross, so after working on and improving the canoe to enable it better to stand the sea they started, taking Indians to paddle them. Before arriving at this island one of them died famishing for water, and after landing on the barren rock they found pools of water. The poor natives insisted upon drinking their fill, and would not listen to the precautions of the Spaniards, and several others died. Had these daring adventurers missed this island they would certainly have perished before reaching St. Domingo, and Columbus no doubt would never have been heard from, but left to die by the hand of the savages. Soon after this adventure the natives stopped bringing him provisions, and it was with the greatest difficulty he could procure subsistence for his men. I was struck with the stratagem he used for inducing the natives to furnish him with provisions. He ascertained that within three days there would be a total eclipse of the moon in the early part of the night. He therefore sent to the principal caciques, or head men, of each tribe, and summoned them to a conference, appointing for it the day of the eclipse. When they arrived he spoke to them sharply for having prevented their people from furnishing him with food. After haranguing them for some time he told them he and his followers worshiped a God who lived in the skies, who favored all that were good, but punished transgressors; that this great God was angry with the Indians who had refused to furnish his faithful followers with food, and intended to chasten them with famine and pestilence. Should they disbelieve his warning, a signal would be

RECOLLECTIONS OF A NAVAL LIFE

given that night that the moon would change its color as a token of the punishment that awaited them. Many scoffed at him, but waited most anxiously the coming of the night. The moon rose majestically and all eyes were fixed upon her. At the time Columbus told them, the moon grew darker and darker, and abject terror seized upon them. Hurrying to Columbus they implored him to intercede with his Deity, and they would hereafter bring him everything he required. Columbus left them, promising to intercede. When the eclipse was nearly over he returned, saying his God had deigned to listen, and would pardon them on condition that they kept their promise, and that the darkness would now be withdrawn. When the moon emerged in her brightness they were overwhelmed with joy, and furnished Columbus ever afterwards abundantly.

The island of Navaza is also remarkable for a fountain of fresh water gushing up near it in the sea, which sweetens the surface for some distance. Should we be favored with fair winds to-night I think we may be at anchor off Aux Cayes to-morrow evening, as we are distant some sixty miles.

After this digression I will proceed to Callao, where we arrived and safely put into our old anchorage, March 6, 1845. We found there at anchor the Store Ship *Relief*, the English Line of Battle Ship *Collingwood*, the English Steamer *Cormorant*, and the French Sloop of War *Triumphante*. This made it very gay. Every evening we were off watch or duty we fell into our old habit of going on shore for a horseback ride or some other pastime. In looking back at those days when, as the poet beautifully expresses it, "Life was in its spring," it took very little to awaken our mirth, and less with health and freedom from care to make us happy.

On the 2d of April we set sail for Valparaiso, taking on board Captain Armstrong, returning home. After a very boisterous passage we arrived in Valparaiso on the 20th of April, and on the 25th experienced a very heavy gale from the northwest, which made our little vessel toss and pitch terrifically, with seas breaking entirely over us. One or two ships went aground. The next morning the shore presented an appearance of wreck and disaster. We were glad to leave this insecure bay, and on the 29th sailed on

RECOLLECTIONS OF A NAVAL LIFE

our return to Callao, having landed Captain Armstrong at Valparaiso.

This city is the principal port of Chile, and while the bay upon which it is situated is capable of sheltering a large fleet or squadron, it is open to the north, and when winds prevail from this quarter it is scarcely a safe anchorage. Its name being interpreted means "Vale of Paradise," which it must have acquired from the delightful climate and picturesque scenery. It is quite a seat of commerce and is in the direct route of vessels proceeding to the countries bordering on the Pacific.

My service on the Schooner *Shark* ended here and I was transferred to my old ship, the Frigate *Savannah*, bearing the broad pennant of Commodore John D. Sloat.

While the service on board the little Schooner *Shark* was very much enjoyed, it was a pleasure to get back to the strict man-of-war discipline and etiquette of the frigate. We had a fine band of music on board, and were constantly receiving and exchanging visits with the officers of the foreign ships in port, principally English and French. After weeks of this life we were rejoiced to hear "all hands up anchor," bound for the Sandwich Islands. This voyage took us across the broad Pacific, and after falling into the trade winds we sailed for days without changing the course of the ship or trimming the yards. The entire voyage— so calm was the sea and so moderate the wind—might have been made in an open boat. ᠈We came to anchor in Byron's Bay, Island of Hawaii, a beautiful land-locked bay, with the tropical growth coming down to the water's edge, while high up in the mountains could be seen streams rushing down precipices to mingle with the waters of the bay in silver spray. No sooner was the ship brought to anchor than we were surrounded by canoes with outriggers to steady them from capsizing, loaded with tropical fruits of all varieties. The natives, instead of passing from one boat to another to reach the side of the ship, would pass the fruit and disappear overboard, coming up along-

RECOLLECTIONS OF A NAVAL LIFE

side the ship. As they were unencumbered by dress, this diving was easy to accomplish, and they appeared quite as much at home in the water as out of it. The deck of the ship was soon spread out liberally with all the beautiful fruits, thereby rejoicing the eyes that love the beautiful in Nature, and giving pleasure to officers and crew with the feast in anticipation, grown in this Paradise of the tropics. The natives then were a simple and confiding people, influenced for good by a missionary's family who lived among them. The dress of the females consisted of a loose flowing gown made from the bark of a tree. The males wore a coarser fibrous material of the same sort. The chief luxury in life seemed to consist in bathing. On the outskirts of the village was a beautiful pool of fresh water, formed by a stream coming down the mountain side, and they could be seen at all hours of the day going in and coming out, as merry as dolphins at play. Little children, just able to scramble up the rocks, would reach an elevated position and spring over into the pool with the exquisite grace of nymphs. Upon this island is the famous volcano of Mauna Loa, which has several times poured its streams of lava down the mountain side into the sea, destroying the fish for miles along the coast. The day after our arrival several of us got permission to visit this volcano, and secured a sufficient number of natives to carry our change of clothing in a "Sandwich Island trunk," which was really two immense gourds fitted into each other, the larger half over the smaller, thus making it air and water-tight. The mode of carrying was also novel, one on each side of a pole over a man's shoulder, being evenly balanced; the sticks so smooth and glossy that they did not even bruise the bare shoulders of the carrier. We at once began to climb the mountain, through beautiful groves of guava, a fruit peculiar for its water properties of slaking thirst, and which we enjoyed freely when no spring or stream was by. In many places we passed over beds of lava, like molten glass of greenish hue. After a tiresome

24 RECOLLECTIONS OF A NAVAL LIFE

day's jaunt we came to the "half-way house," utterly broken down. We were glad to rest on the clean mats furnished us, and enjoyed still more the relief afforded by their process of lomi-lomi, or, as it would now be called, "massage treatment." This was a gentle pounding of every muscle of the body and limbs with the fists. Before retiring, however, to this refreshing treatment we took the precaution to order our supper. They suggested a nice dog, but we said we preferred chickens and vegetables. They cook delightfully, in holes lined with smooth rocks in which they build fires. When the rocks become thoroughly heated to the highest degree they put in the poultry cut up in pieces of convenient size, wrapped in large plantain leaves so as to retain all the juices; then they cover these carefully prepared packages with hot rocks, over which they bank earth, leaving a vent hole for the steam to escape. This process of cooking retained all the flavor of meats and vegetables, and was delightful. I suppose it is akin to the process of barbecuing still practiced in portions of the world, especially our own South. We arose in an hour or two and enjoyed this royal feast, "fit for the gods," then indulged in a cigar or two, and after a little merrymaking sought our luxurious couches of mats and slept soundly until the sun awoke us the next morning. Awaking with renewed energy we had the remnants of our feast of the evening before, with the addition of a nice cup of coffee, and proceeded up the mountain, arriving at the crater of the volcano about noon. The view was strikingly grand and wonderful to eyes that had never before beheld such workings of Nature. At the bottom of this extinct crater, about seven miles in circumference and several hundred feet deep, was a burning lake of lava some three miles in circumference and boiling like a pot of hominy. Our guides proposed our going down to the burning lake, to which we assented, and with long staffs furnished us we began our perilous descent. This feat we accomplished without accident, walking upon the

RECOLLECTIONS OF A NAVAL LIFE

congealed lava to the very edge of the burning lake. Our guides were very careful to approach on the windward side, as it would have been instant death to have the wind blow on us across the molten lake. We however approached it in safety and near enough to put our staffs into the burning lake. After accomplishing this feat we gladly retraced our steps, and were a little hurried in doing so when told "that a shift of wind would destroy us."

Now came the "tug of war" in the ascent of the precipitous sides of the cavern, often stopping at convenient points to view the depths below. We reached the surface above just at sunset, and surveyed with amazement the wonderful fissures in the earth through which came sulphurous fumes and steam. Along the margin of these fissures were beautifully crystallized formations of sulphur. As night approached we seated ourselves to view the magnificent pyrotechnics of Nature. The boiling caldron below presented a lake of fire spurting up the boiling lava in every conceivable and beautiful shape. This wonderful sight banished slumber from our eyes till the "wee sma' hours," when we could no longer resist "tired Nature's sweet restorer, balmy sleep." Early the next morning, after partaking of a light breakfast and a cup of refreshing coffee, we retraced our steps down the mountain, delighted with the specimens of lava we had obtained and put in our Sandwich Island trunks. We arrived at the village by the sea just in time to take passage in the sunset boat for our ship. The enjoyment of this visit to the crater of Mauna Loa lingers with me still, and is one of the unforgotten pleasures of my life.

Chapter IV

In a few days we took leave of this charming island and its beautiful scenery and made sail for Honolulu, Oahu Island, reaching that port in two days. This port, even at that day, was the most important among the group of Sandwich Islands. Here the whalers gather to transfer their cargoes of oil and do their trading. Drunkenness and debauch was even at this early day showing itself among the poor natives from their contact with (so-called) civilization. Different, indeed, from Byron's Bay, where innocence and purity were presented in its primeval state. Our first visit to the shore was an official one, that of the commodore and his staff (of which I was a member) to call upon King Kamiamaha the third, then reigning monarch. Upon entering his palace each one, from the commodore to the least important of the party, was requested to place his signature in a book presented by one of the king's officials. The reception room was nicely furnished, but presented no feature of European royalty. In a few minutes the king entered the room dressed in a full uniform in European costume liberally covered with gold lace. He seemed very ill at ease, but was a fine specimen of the Kanaka, or Sandwich Island type. After exchanging the compliments usual on such occasions we took our leave. When out of the palace the missionary who accompanied us remarked, "The king will soon get out of his trapping and don his tappa-robe and go to the beach and his bath, where he spends most of the time." The surf bathing practiced by these natives is of a most exhilarating character. Taking a little float of reeds, called a balsa, they work their way outside the heavy rollers, then watch their opportunity and get their balsa pointed in towards the

RECOLLECTIONS OF A NAVAL LIFE 27

shore, and on top of the largest billow would come rushing in at tremendous speed to the beach, where the receding billow would leave them stranded. Shouldering their balsa they would go through the same sport time and again, till wearied of the healthful exercise and pastime. The natives generally were a fine-looking class of people; olive-colored, with black eyes, and long black hair, and of dignified mien. At that day there were very few foreigners on the island—only a few missionaries and their families. The women were fine equestriennes and always presented a picturesque appearance. There is a famous ride there through what is called the "valley of death." The legend that gives it this name is this: During one of their tribal wars the victorious tribe drove their flying foe up this valley, which terminated in an abrupt precipice of 1000 feet or more, violently precipitating them into the sea, and, like Pharaoh's hosts of old, "the waters covered them up" and they were seen no more!

After making quite a stay at Honolulu we sailed for Mazatlan to gain some information from the United States of the rumored threatened war with Mexico. Mazatlan lies on the west coast of Mexico. Here we remained from November 18, 1845, till June 1, 1846. Six months we passed waiting anxiously for the treaties between the United States and Mexico, which all seemed tending to war. During our long stay at this port we sometimes amused ourselves hunting. The game was fine and abundant. Upon one occasion, going some distance back in the country to shoot pheasants, a party of us called at a good-looking cottage on a ranch and asked for buttermilk. We were invited in, and found a number of nice-looking women and a few very surly looking Mexicans. We were served with delightful milk, and left. After we got out of hearing we remarked to each other upon the cut-throat, brigandish looks of the men, and decided to be on our guard and within hearing of each other in our hunt. We were not mistaken in our suspicions. A short way

28 RECOLLECTIONS OF A NAVAL LIFE

from the ranch we noticed the fellows tracking us, guns in hand. Catching sight of them before they did of us, we changed our course, taking a direct line to the coast. They evidently intended to shoot us from the thicket. Notwithstanding this damper to our enthusiasm as sportsmen, we got up a fine flock of pheasants, and water fowl from the lake near the sea, returning on board with a nice lot of game and no disasters.

On the 1st of June, 1846, learning that war had been declared with Mexico, we set sail for Monterey, where we arrived in safety and found at anchor the Sloops of War *Cyane* and *Levant*. On the 7th day of July we landed with a strong force and took formal possession of California, and hoisted the American colors. The name "California" is said to have been first used in an old book in Spain, and to mean "Island of Gold." While the legend is incorrect as to California being an island it may correctly be termed a country of gold, possessing as it does the richest gold mines yet discovered in the world. California at the date of which I write was almost an unknown country. A Jesuit mission was founded there in 1776, and through the rich valleys were missions, walled to resist the depredations of the natives. In the grounds surrounding these missions they cultivated the fruits and vegetables of Europe, which grew so luxuriantly as to surpass anything ever seen in their native country. The vines, too, grew to great perfection and the pears were splendid. The grape had become so popular when we were there that the people of the country would bring pitchers of home-made wine— a most palatable and delightful beverage—to refresh us when we went among them. The women were kind and polite when we had occasion to stop and ask questions, but the country homes were conspicuous for the absence of the male members of the family. These were forming in squads or being organized to resist the invasion of the country. We left on shore a sufficient number of soldiers

RECOLLECTIONS OF A NAVAL LIFE 29

and seamen to hold possession of Monterey, it being at that time the Capital of California. There was no demonstration by the natives against our holding peaceable possession of the town.

After properly appointing the city authorities the squadron sailed for San Francisco to take possession of that point. There landing a force we immediately proceeded to build a blockhouse to guard against any attack from a large force. At that time the town of San Francisco consisted of only about half a dozen frame houses. Leaving a sufficient force at this place we sailed for the bay of San Pedro, where we arrived October 7th. On entering the harbor we passed the American Merchant Ship *Vandalia*, with a large body of men on board. She was at anchor. She saluted us with two guns, and gave three cheers, which we returned. Captain Gillespie, of the Marine Corps, came on board and reported that he had evacuated the Puebla de Los Angelos on account of the overpowering force of the enemy. He retired on board the *Vandalia* after having spiked his guns. He also reported that all lower California had risen in arms against our authorities, headed by Flores, a captain in the Mexican Army.

We made preparations for landing at daylight the next morning, when we landed 299 men. A few of the enemy, twenty or thirty men, were in sight on the Angelos road, a few more showing themselves and drawn up as if inclined to give battle. At 8 A. M. the entire force, under command of Captain Mervine, took up the line of march for the purpose of retaking the Puebla de Los Angelos, the enemy retreating on the advance of our forces. A whaleboat arrived from San Diego bringing news that Captain Merritt, a volunteer, had been forced to retire on the American Ship *Stonington*, the enemy cutting off all provisions from them and collecting in great numbers. About 10 o'clock several discharges of artillery were heard distinctly in the direction of the Angelos road. About

30   RECOLLECTIONS OF A NAVAL LIFE

11.30 we discovered our forces returning toward the landing. At 2 P. M. the expedition arrived at the landing, having encountered the enemy with a field piece, which they moved from point to point, with their horses attached. Our men made three gallant charges, chasing them each time about half a mile, but they being on fine horses would keep out of musket range, when they would wheel and fire on our men, killing several. Finding it impossible to capture the gun the retreat was sounded. Upon arriving at the landing a council of war was held. It was decided that without horses for hauling a field piece rapidly it would be useless to make the effort to capture the enemy, and the forces embarked.

Dispatches being received from San Diego, stating that Captain Merritt with forty men had taken possession of the town, Lieutenant George Minor, with Midshipmen Morgan and Duvall and a force of fifty men, were sent on board the Whale Ship *Magnolia* to take passage to San Diego to reinforce Captain Merritt. One week after I was dispatched in the second cutter to ascertain the condition of affairs at San Diego, a distance of sixty miles by sea, which I accomplished successfully, making the trip and returning in four days, and reported everything in favorable condition. We now got under way and sailed for San Francisco, where we found the enemy operating in the valley of Santa Clara. An expedition was at once ordered to be fitted out, and knowing from our sad experience at San Pedro the want of cavalry, I was ordered in our launch to transport from the north to the south side of the bay a number of horses. It was a difficult feat, but I accomplished it. My last load of horses, six in number, got very restless and could not be managed. I expected every moment to see them stamp holes in the bottom of the launch, when all hands would be lost. I determined therefore to jump them overboard. It was truly wonderful to see the instinct of the animals. They struck out for the

RECOLLECTIONS OF A NAVAL LIFE

shore, though a mile or two distant. To my great surprise we found them all the next morning safely on shore near where they landed. We now landed from the ship a force of blue jackets and marines, with a field piece, accompanied by the cavalry, and started in pursuit of the enemy.

Chapter V

From sources apparently reliable we learned that the enemy were in force in the neighborhood of Santa Clara Mission. We made easy marches, coming to camp about sunset, always sending some cavalry ahead to select a camping ground and butcher beeves in readiness for our arrival. After the fatiguing march of the day we would arrive at camp thoroughly prepared in appetite to enjoy the California beef. The cattle grazing on the rich grasses and wild oats of the fertile valleys were superbly fine. "Jack Tar," with his brother marines, would sit round the camp fires and roast his rib of beef with as much zest and pleasure as though he were native to the plains.

The second morning after leaving the ship the courier came in and reported the enemy in camp in a piece of redwoods up in the hills. As it was a rough road ascending the hills, the artillery piece and the infantry were ordered to keep in the plains, while the cavalry were detailed to reconnoitre and ascertain the exact locality and force of the enemy. Being mounted myself, I obtained permission to accompany the cavalry. We were armed with carbines and revolvers. At early dawn we started on the march. A thick fog enveloped the hillsides, and here occurred one of those strange phenomena—an optical illusion. Three of us were riding abreast, somewhat in advance of the column. Simultaneously each of us cocked and raised our carbines to our shoulders to fire upon what seemed to be a few cavalrymen of the enemy coming toward us down the hill. The next instant the fog cleared and instead of the cavalry we found only a clump of bushes! We proceeded up the hill, using great caution, and in silence. Upon reaching the summit we discovered

RECOLLECTIONS OF A NAVAL LIFE

the camp of the enemy, just abandoned. We followed their trail down into the plains again, and soon rifle shots were heard and our scouts came in and reported the enemy just ahead of us, in large force, mounted. We had by this time joined our infantry and field piece. We advanced upon them, they firing indiscriminately from their horses, and retreating as we advanced. They evidently meant to draw us on to the open prairie beyond, where they could maneuver their cavalry to greater advantage. As we emerged from the timber land the enemy surrounded us, and dismounting from their horses, were completely hid by the tall prairie grass and commenced a rapid fire upon our body of men. We returned the fire, aiming only at the smoke from the discharge of their guns, for neither men nor horses could be seen. I now worked the field piece to great advantage, loading with grape and canister, and trained the gun on the point from which came the greatest discharge of the foe. The grape and canister tearing through the high grass would flush the fellows from their cover like a covey of partridges before a fowling piece, when they would mount their horses and ride to a more respectful distance. In this way we carried on a running fight till we neared the old Mission of Santa Clara. The occupants, who had crossed the mountains and taken refuge in the old mission, came out joyfully to join us in the fight. Very soon the Californians were routed and dispersed in all directions. We were received with great joy by our countrymen from the East who had crossed the plains and the mountains. Early the next morning a courier came in from the enemy to treat for peace. The offer was accepted, on condition that they deliver up all arms and horses that had been unjustly taken from the people and that they retire to their homes and become peaceful citizens. These terms were accepted, as that distant territory of Mexico had little in sympathy with the government. The large drove of horses captured were driven into a corral and we saw for the first time the dex-

3

34   RECOLLECTIONS OF A NAVAL LIFE

terity with which they used the lasso. Citizens coming in and claiming their horses, such animals were immediately lassoed and turned over to the owners. It is said that the California boy, as soon as he can run around the yard, uses his lariat in catching chickens, dogs, ˙cats, and all the domestic animals for their infantile sport, as the American boy would play marbles. The guns were all stacked up in piles, and presented a motley appearance of ancient fowling pieces that would have done credit to Falstaff's ragged regiment, and were calculated to do more harm to the persons using them than to those against whom they were directed. This no doubt accounted for the fact that only one of our men was wounded in the engagement of the previous day. We remained at the Mission of Santa Clara several days, till all hostilities were quieted, amusing ourselves hunting wild geese that covered the plains around Santa Clara in such numbers that when they rose for flight they almost obscured the sun like a cloud. We found them excellent food, and took numbers of them on board the ship. A courier was dispatched to the commodore reporting the treaty made with the Californians and their quiet retirement to their homes. Boats were then sent to the head of the bay, where we embarked our artillery piece and infantry forces, and returned to our ships, the cavalry returning by land to San Francisco. Thus ended our military operations against this peaceful people, who cared more for tending their flocks and herds and sitting "in the shadow of their own vine and fig tree" than they did for warfare. General Fremont had reached the Pacific Coast, crossing the plains and the Rocky Mountains with a forcé of cavalry woodsmen from the Western country, and his presence there had a most beneficial effect in suppressing any disturbances through the interior while the Navy garrisoned the seaports.

We sailed from San Francisco for the harbor of Monterey, and on the 18th of March, 1847, the joyful call of the boatswain and his mates, "all hands up anchor for home,"

RECOLLECTIONS OF A NAVAL LIFE

resounded through our ship. A salute of thirteen guns was fired in passing the Frigate *Independence*, the flagship of Commodore Stockton, who had assumed command of the Pacific Squadron. We manned the rigging and gave three hearty cheers, and stood to sea.

After a long and very monotonous voyage we came to anchor in the harbor of Valparaiso, with several cases of scurvy showing itself among our crew, the result of living without vegetables. On the 24th day of May we hoisted the English flag at the fore and the American at the main and mizzen in honor of the birthday of Victoria, Queen of England. On the 28th of May Lieutenant Commanding Neil M. Howison left the ship to return to the United States by the way of the Isthmus of Panama as bearer of dispatches from Commodore J. Biddle to the Government at Washington. On the 31st of May we stood to sea on our homeward passage. Off Cape Horn we encountered heavy gales, as usual off that stormy. coast, and welcomed the more moderate temperature and pleasant sailing when we reached the South Atlantic.

Standing to the northward on the 21st of July we exchanged numbers with the U. S. Frigate *Columbia* at anchor in the harbor of Rio Janeiro. We saluted the broad pennant of Commodore L. Rousseau with thirteen guns, which was returned with the same number. We anchored in this beautiful harbor, and here got the news of the surrender of Vera Cruz to our Army and Navy; also of the battle of Buena Vista, where General Taylor, with 5000 men, had been victorious over Santa Anna with 20,000. On the 27th His Excellency Henry A. Wise, U. S. Minister to Brazil, visited the ship. We manned the yards and saluted him with seventeen guns. On the 28th of July we hove up anchor and made sail for the harbor of New York, at which port we arrived about the middle of September, rejoiced to reach our native shores after a long, arduous and eventful cruise, with successful duty and service in the Mexican War.

Chapter VI

The joy of the home coming of a sailor after years of absence is something that can scarcely be imagined by one who has never known long absences from friends or found "a home on the ocean wave." In the course of a week we were all detached from our ship, where we had passed over four years, and while happy in the thought of reaching our homes, there was pain in parting from those with whom we had been associated as one family for so long a time. Of course we might hope to meet again, but things, places, persons, surroundings would "never be as they had been;" and change, the universal change that is written on all human affairs, brought over our hearts and spirits a sadness known only to parting friends. Mine was perhaps the most distant home to reach. Now began my fears as a sailor of the mode of land travel by railroad. I was possessed with the idea that I might be killed before I could reach the seaboard of Georgia, and not until I reached home did I draw a long and comfortable breath! Sailors are universally believed to be very superstitious creatures, and I dare say as a boy I had my visions of "flying Dutchmen," ghosts, dreams, etc., but maturer years have shattered these follies as the baseless fabric of dreams and I have learned to look through Nature in all her grandeur and beauty up to Nature's God! I could only spend a few weeks in the home of my childhood, as my class were all assembled at Annapolis (the Naval Academy) studying hard for the coming examination in the spring. On my arrival in Annapolis I was placed in the room with some of my friends and companions of the Pacific Squadron who had preceded me and were applying themselves with all diligence to their books. The earnestness with which they

RECOLLECTIONS OF A NAVAL LIFE

went to work in the evenings after lamps were lit gave me serious alarm lest I should never be able to school myself to such close application. These roommates, who have proved the friends of my life, Robert D. Minor, of the grand old Commonwealth of Virginia; Robert C. Duvall, of the old North State, and Abercrombie, of Maryland, making the quartette of our room. Let me introduce my roommates more clearly as they stand reflected pictures, as it were, on the walls of the sacred halls of memory! Duvall, or as we called him, "Duvy," was the eldest, and stood 6 feet 3 inches in height, as noble and generous in every impulse of his true warm heart as he was grand in stature as a man. He applied himself with so much zeal and closeness to his studies that he was stricken down with fever. His restless nights were made miserable by his endeavor to work the difficult problems of his geometry lessons even in his delirium or sleep. He would wake unrefreshed in the morning, declaring "if he could only solve those problems, he thought he might get well." Finally the problems were all solved and he did grow strong and well again. Abercrombie, always mild and pleasant, I see him in my mind's eye rubbing his head (already a little bald), vowing vengeance against old Chauvenet, our professor in mathematics, for giving us such long and difficult lessons to try our souls. Bob Minor—our youngest, jolliest, happiest boy! Quick to learn and master his lessons, as quick to laugh at those who had not been so fortunate; always first to close his book, with a most triumphant smile, and exclaim, "Ready for bed!"

Our room, unfortunately, was located at the head of the stairs on the second floor of the building known as "Rowdy Row." It was often the pleasure of those for whom it was named to make night hideous with their frolics. One favorite amusement of theirs was to get a number of 32-pound balls from the battery near by and, taking them up the flight of stairs to the end of the long piazza, roll them

38 RECOLLECTIONS OF A NAVAL LIFE

in quick succession the length of the piazza, where they would go thumping down the steps with the noise of thunder, rousing the sleeping inmates of the building. There was no use trying to hunt up the perpetrators of this mischievous performance—they were always "soundly sleeping." Similar annoyances were carried on throughout by those who were not caring for the approaching examination. I am glad to state, though, that we had in that day none of those disgraceful, cruel hazings that are now practiced and are so criminal.

Upon the approach of Christmas I received a box from home—and herein I must relate a hard joke on myself. Among other things came an enormous fruit cake. Of course I had "to make merry with my friends" and give a Christmas entertainment. After smuggling in a few bottles of wine—for what would the cake be without the accompanying refreshment?—I found I had forgotten the all-important corkscrew (though I had furnished a few wine glasses). What was to be done? We resorted to the only means to get at the wine. Snapping the necks of the bottles with a quick stroke of a knife (which was accomplished dexterously), our feast began. We enjoyed both cake and wine "hugely," as our English cousins would say, but oh, the consequences! Next morning there was a tale to be told. I—the host—was ill, very ill. I at once dispatched a messenger for the surgeon, fearing I could not survive till he came. I freely unbosomed to him my violation of all school discipline, and he, like a true medical adviser, did not betray the confidence of his patient. I heard nothing of my secret and impromptu entertainment, and was much relieved in mind and body by the good doctor's visit, he assuring me that violent and acute dyspepsia, and not broken glass, which I supposed I had swallowed, was the root of the trouble! Since that fateful night I have never had a weakness for fruit cake— no matter how black or rich—but I regret to say I have always had a tendency to dyspepsia, a reminder of youth-

RECOLLECTIONS OF A NAVAL LIFE

ful folly! After the Christmas holidays I applied myself most earnestly to my books, and passed a fairly creditable examination—that is, in a class of 200 I passed number 27. This class was a celebrated one and passed some remarkable men—men who are now the head of the Federal Navy; but many of the most gifted gave up their positions and stood by and were true to their Southern homes. Among these W. H. Parker, who took the first honor in the class, shared with Catesby Jones of glorious memory!

From the Naval School I was ordered to join the Sloop of War *Albany* at Norfolk. Norfolk is a famous old seaport town, renowned for pretty girls; and being one of the principal Stations, or Navy Yards, had always an abundance of young Navy Officers on hand. Our accomplished classmate Wm. H. Parker here found his bride, one of the belles and beauties of Norfolk. After a lapse of many years I was very happy in meeting them both at the unveiling of the statue to General R. E. Lee in Richmond, Virginia, both well preserved and happy. Norfolk in those old times was very gay, and we, being much elevated at the insignia of passed midshipmen on our uniforms, were prepared to add to the gaiety.

We were some months in fitting out the ship, and by early fall sailed for the West Indies, a delightful cruise through the Windward Islands. This cruise, however, was destined to be of short duration. While we were anchored at Fort du France—the memorable home of Josephine in the Island of Martinique—there was a want of harmony between the lieutenants and the passed midshipmen which resulted in an order that we should perform strictly the duties of midshipmen, such as "calling the watch, and lighting the candle of the lieutenant who had to go on duty." It so happened that the first order was given to me. I declined to obey it, stating that the duty had been previously performed by the quartermasters, I considered it a menial service, and would not do it. The lieutenant of the watch urged me strongly to do it, or he "would

40   RECOLLECTIONS OF A NAVAL LIFE

have to report me for disobedience of orders." I replied that "I had made up my mind fully to perform no menial duty and that he was at liberty to report me," which he did. I was then summoned into the presence of a very irate gentleman, Captain Victor M. Randolph, of Virginia. He stormed at me violently; said he "would have me court martialed and dismissed from the service." I very quietly told him "I would not obey the order."

Thereupon he directed the lieutenant to "suspend me from duty and report the case to the first lieutenant of the ship in the morning." The three other passed midshipmen in like manner refused to obey the order and were also suspended, making a very strong case of "mutinous insubordination." We continued our cruise along the south side of San Domingo and Cuba, stopping in at various ports, which we, however, under suspension, were never allowed to visit. This continued for three months, when the confinement so affected our health that the kind old surgeon, Dr. Spotswood, reported that the "passed midshipmen must be permitted to visit the shore for exercise," which requirement was granted and our health improved. From Cuba we ran down to Vera Cruz, where we met the flagship of the squadron, and charges were preferred against us without delay. The commodore ordered our ship immediately to the Pensacola Navy Yard, the rendezvous of the Gulf Squadron, he following soon after. On arriving at Pensacola a court martial was ordered for our trial. Here at Pensacola I made the acquaintance of Lieutenant Raphael Semmes, who had just been admitted to the bar of Alabama. He had shortly before this obtained a leave of absence from the Navy Department for the purpose of studying law. He little dreamed then the important part this knowledge of international law would bear on his future life, so thoroughly fitting him for his work in after years while in command of the world-renowned Confederate States Steamer *Alabama*.

RECOLLECTIONS OF A NAVAL LIFE

But to return to the court martial. He very generously tendered his services as counsel in our case. His distinguished ability, however, was not sufficient to overcome the precedent which custom had made a law. The result of the trial was our "dismissal from the service for wilful disobedience of orders." To show that the sentiment of our brother officers was with us, and that they approved our appreciation of our position as officers in objecting to doing menial duty, after the sentence of the court one of its members, who resided in Pensacola, gave us a very handsome reception, inviting all friends to meet us before we departed for our homes.

I found my way into upper Georgia, where my mother's family were spending the summer in the little town of Roswell. After a rest, a friend, Daniel Stuart Elliott, and I took a buggy and made a tour of upper Georgia, stopping each nightfall at country houses, where we enjoyed some rare fun and experiences with our entertainers—I being always introduced as a "traveled officer who had seen service in California and seen a great deal of the outside world." My narrations about the gold regions may have upset some quiet country homes and sent some squatters out to the "diggins" across the rockies. One old man in particular became so enthused he exclaimed, delightedly, "I am just going to hitch up my team an' take my ole 'oman and that boy and gal [his children] and start across the plains"—as though he thought it a day's jaunt or a May-day picnic!

We passed through the little town of Dahlonega, then occupied by a rough set digging for gold, reported to be abundant in rich deposits, and where a mint had been established. This town is the seat of a branch college of the State University, under military discipline, and an honor to Georgia. From there we went to Tallulah Falls, enjoying the wild and beautiful scenery. We also took in on our trip the villages of Clarksville and Gainesville. One night, in the depths of the country, we came

RECOLLECTIONS OF A NAVAL LIFE

upon an old and humble hut, but it boasted an independent proprietor. He refused us shelter, said he "had nobody to feed our horse," etc.; whereupon we told him we preferred attending to our animal ourselves. He then remarked, in a surly way, "Thar's the corn-crib, go feed." We obeyed, and after doing so went into the cabin. He was very sulky, but we determined to win him over, or talk him into a good humor. After spinning him a few sea yarns he begged us to stay with him some days, and really turned out to be a pattern of hospitality! His house had lately been visited and made headquarters for the wares of a clock peddler. I think there were at least twenty-five or thirty clocks of the old-fashioned striking kind—no soft cathedral bell tones of the present-day clock! All these were wound up, ticking loud, and no two striking at the same time. If they did not make night hideous, they certainly made it noisy. The good wife proceeded to get supper for us, and after enjoying a cup of hot coffee—not made after the French style—and a comfortable supper we lit our cigars and drew round the old-fashioned fireplace, and with a fat pine knot to make the evening's light, we entertained our host and hostess with more of my travels, every word of which they drank in with evident delight. We retired at a reasonable hour—but not to sleep. The busy clocks, with their ceaseless ticking and striking, made the night wild and weird. I think I learned in that long, sleepless night to value the blessing of silence!—and we certainly had time drag very heavily on our hands. We made a very early start the next morning and were glad to find ourselves in a few hours at the little village of Roswell, from which we had begun our jaunt, again among family and friends.

Chapter VII

THE pleasant little town of Roswell is situated in Cobb County, and took its name from its founder, Mr. Roswell King, a former resident of McIntosh County, on the seaboard. Its society was made up mostly of low country families of culture and refinement. The sisters of Captain James D. Bulloch, whose name is now famous in history as the agent of the Confederate Navy abroad, were great belles; also Miss Mary Lewis, who afterwards became the wife of one of Georgia's most distinguished physicians, Dr. Wm. Gaston Bulloch, of Savannah. I must here pay a passing tribute to this lady's grace on horseback; she has always been my ideal of an equestrienne, and I recall with pleasure our delightful rides together through the beautiful region of upper Georgia that pleasant summer. Captain Bulloch has made a valuable contribution to history in his able work, entitled "Secret Service of the Confederate Navy Abroad." He further distinguished himself by superintending the construction of the famous War Steamer *Alabama*, and his successful ruse in getting her out of English waters,—but more of that hereafter.

The autumn found us wending our way coastward and homeward. It also found me filled with restless discontent and longing for the service in which I had begun my life and to which I was so much attached. This I think prompted my friends to look forward with hope to having me reinstated (feeling that I had in nowise tarnished my honor as an officer in the United States Navy) to my lost place. My venerable and distinguished relative, Hon. Thos. Spalding, of Sapelo Island, was a life-long friend of Hon. J. McPherson Berrien, Georgia's distinguished lawyer and Senator, though they had in their middle life

44 RECOLLECTIONS OF A NAVAL LIFE

been estranged through political differences. To him my relative generously offered to write, and took the opportunity of referring to their earlier days, in memory of which he desired him to do him the favor of using his influence in having me restored to the Navy. This letter, so well worthy of publication, a copy of which was sent to my mother, I herewith insert.

Hon. J. McPherson Berrien,

Sir: You will no doubt be surprised in the relation we have stood to each other for some years to receive a letter from me,—but at seventy-six years old it is time to sweep from my mind any dust that has been scattered over it. As I owe to politics neither honors nor profits in my long life, it may be but just that I should not be deprived by politics of the good-will of even one gentleman.

John Kell, with three other young gentlemen from different States (passed midshipmen), have all been dismissed from the service for declining to light the lieutenants to or from the ward room.

This was certainly a most extraordinary order, and I was greatly surprised, knowing the character that John Kell in eight years' service had acquired with five different commanders, had not received it smilingly and obeyed it in the same mood, for such an order could only degrade him that gave, not him that obeyed it. This I told John Kell this morning when I gave him promise of this letter, and he assured me "that his refusal to obey originated solely in his respect for what he believed to be his grade in the Navy." With this impression on my mind I ask you to read the evidences given on the court martial of these young gentlemen, and if they have been wronged, and if a remedy is within reach, you will best know after such examination. John Kell has under five commanders been highly spoken of by all, and I understand that the other young men stood well in their several situations. John Kell's letters to his mother and sisters for eight years past have been given me for my perusal. They display great ability as well as correct observation of all around him, and would well have borne publication. But there is one act of his life which will reach the feelings of any father—when he entered the service he applied a part of his pay to the education of his younger brother.

In our many years of intercourse there is one circumstance of my early life I do not remember mentioning to you, the attachment of your mother to my Aunt Hester McIntosh, the grandmother of John Kell. I remember that she communicated to us your mother's death, and that she had watched over her in her last illness; she had received from her

RECOLLECTIONS OF A NAVAL LIFE

some little poems in manuscript. The interest my aunt felt was communicated to my young mind, I being a younger brother to her, and now after sixty-six years there remains upon my memory several lines of your mother's monody, on her brother, that fell with Montgomery at the gates of Quebec. There remains also on my memory two playful lines of hers upon John Hustace whom she had met in Philadelphia when he was the aide of General Lee. Hustace was the wittiest, but the vainest young man (and the most presumptuous) in the Army.

> "Alexis, with grace, can toy a lady's fan—
> Has every art to be a beau, but none to be the man."

The whole life of this young man shows the correct opinion your mother had formed of him. But my letter has grown too long.

Respectfully yours,

THOS. SPALDING.

Fortified by this letter I set out for Washington City, and immediately called upon Senator Berrien, and was received by this grand gentleman with a hearty welcome and courtliness of manner which impressed me with respect and admiration. After reading the letter he expressed the greatest pleasure and satisfaction in being able to accede to the wish of his friend. He said he would review the proceedings of the court martial and do all in his power for my reinstatement. He forthwith took the matter in hand. I remained in Washington city some weeks, but soon after my return home received the official information of my reinstatement, with the other passed midshipmen, to our former rank and position, losing a year's pay, that being the time we were out of the service. I at once applied for orders to sea, and was soon gratified with instructions to proceed at once to Philadelphia to join the United State Frigate *Susquehanna*, there fitting out for a cruise to the East Indies, bearing the broad pennant of Commodore Aulick, with Captain Inman as his flag officer. I left home in the spring of 1851 for another long and very interesting cruise.

Upon passing through the city of Charleston, South Carolina, I learned that the world-renowned songstress,

46 RECOLLECTIONS OF A NAVAL LIFE

"Jenny Lind, the Swedish Nightingale," would sing that night. I remained over for the purpose of hearing her. The memory of her sweet voice has remained with me ever since as one of the greatest musical privileges of my life.

The next morning I took steamer for Wilmington in the face of a heavy northeast gale of wind, and after a boisterous passage reached my destination in safety. Upon reporting to the commodore at Philadelphia he informed me that the Frigate *Susquehanna* had the day before sailed for Norfolk to complete her outfit. He gave me orders to proceed to that point and report for duty to the commander, which I did. On reaching Norfolk I found the officers all quartered on shore and that it would be a month or more before she could get to sea. I enjoyed very much meeting again my old Navy friends and former companions, also my lady friends at Norfolk, from which port we sailed on the memorable cruise in the *Albany*, from which ship I had been court martialed. I took up my lodging at a boarding house on Portsmouth Point, where a number of Navy officers with their families found temporary homes. We enjoyed social life here very much indeed. Among the boarders was a fine old gentleman from the Eastern Shore of Maryland, Major Hall, of the Marine Corps. Passed Midshipman Bennett and I roomed together. Daily as we met at dinner the Major would send his decanter of wine, asking the pleasure of a glass of wine with Bennett and myself. This we highly appreciated, but could not return the compliment, being rather young for the privilege of keeping wine for our use at table in the presence of ladies. We therefore determined to give the Major a wine supper in our room before we sailed. Accordingly, we laid in a basket of champagne and some of the choicest wines the market of Norfolk afforded, accompanied with nuts, raisins, olives, cigars, etc. We also invited a few officers to meet the Major. It is pleasant to recall at this day the memory of that very convivial party that surrounded our table, and the tales told by the genial

RECOLLECTIONS OF A NAVAL LIFE · 47

Major, our honored guest, who was the personification of the old school gentleman, for which the Eastern Shore was so renowned. Toward the "wee sma' hours" we escorted the Major to his room, not without the assistance of his good wife, however, who came for him, his youthful hosts and escorts being about as much disabled by the festivities of the evening, so jovially spent, as was the honored guest himself!

Youth has its joys as well as its follies, and what could matter the headaches that followed such lordly fun—that lightened our purses and our hearts? Soon after this royal entertainment we joined our ship and set sail for the Island of Madeira. We took on board our Minister to Brazil, Mr. Yancey, and his family as guests of the commodore. We had a pleasant voyage to Madeira, and enjoyed the scenery and climate of that delightful island. Madeira is a great health resort for the English invalids. They have added to the picturesque appearance of the south side of the island by building beautiful homes and villas there. This island is world-renowned for the wine made there that bears its name. It is famous for its convent and the lovely lace work done by the nuns, in both of which the officers invested. I laid in several quarter casks of south side Madeira, which was much enhanced in value by its four-years' cruise around the world. Upon my arrival at home I put the wine in glass, and during the Civil War our faithful old carriage driver carefully buried it, and although the old home was often raided by the enemy, the old negro was faithful to his trust and resurrected and returned it after the war. A sale of a portion of this wine came in good time to replenish my empty pocket book at the close of the war. I still retain a few bottles to make merry on state occasions, such as weddings. When I first returned from the China cruise in 1855 a dozen bottles of this wine were used at the wedding of my cousin, the daughter of Commodore James McKay McIntosh, and some months later at my own wedding. Some years ago at the wed-

48 RECOLLECTIONS OF A NAVAL LIFE

ding in my own house of a favorite niece a bottle of the wine was used at forty-five years of age, with a bouquet and flavor unsurpassed. Some years later it was used to drink to the health and happiness of my beloved daughter upon her marriage.

But to return to my cruise and the beautiful Island of Madeira. Horseback riding was a great diversion on the island, a peculiar feature of which was that the hostler from whom you hired the beast enjoyed running alongside of you and occasionally relieved the weariness of his run by swinging on to the tail of the horse. The hostler wore a remarkable cap with a keen pointed end sticking erect from his head, the cap just covering his scalp, which stuck so closely that it must have been kept on by suction. The view to which this really historic ride led was grand in the extreme. It presented the precipitous northern side of the island upon which the waves of the ocean continuously and wildly beat its even monotone, a contrast indeed to the south side, which is a garden of luxurious beauty, where rose geranium and other sweet plants (to us exotics) grow wild and in great profusion, loading the air with perfume, and the grape vine covers every available spot. After enjoying our national holiday, July 4, on this garden spot of Nature, we set sail for Rio Janeiro. We experienced some very rough weather on our passage, and discovered our mainmast sprung, which necessitated hoisting it out and making proper repairs. For this purpose we obtained permission from the Brazilian Government to go into dock, where we were detained a month or two. Captain Inman was here detached from the ship with orders to return home, leaving the command immediately to Commodore Aulick. During our long stay in port we had the opportunity of seeing much of this grand city, built upon a magnificent bay along whose shores are dotted here and there villages of rare beauty, adorned with tropical foliage; in the distance rise the Organ Mountains, remarkable for their tapering peaks and presenting some

RECOLLECTIONS OF A NAVAL LIFE   49

of the grandest views of any harbor in the world. This city is famous for the beauty of its cathedrals and other public buildings. The inhabitants are largely foreign, especially French and Portuguese. The handling of coffee forms the principal part of their trade. One of our greatest pleasures was to ride along the shores of this beautiful bay and visit the Botanical Gardens, a few miles from the city. The walks of these gardens are lined with colossal palms on either side, forming avenues of beauty, and the gardens are filled with every variety of rare plant and shrub of the tropics. Although in latitude $22°$ $56'$ south, the vast quantity of water of the Southern Hemisphere tempers the climate so as to make fires unnecessary, except for culinary purposes, and all the fruits of the tropics grow profusely and Nature wears an aspect of wild luxuriance as though perpetually basking in the sunshine and smile of the Great Creator.

The plumage of the birds in Brazil is gorgeous. The variety, especially of the little humming bird, is very wonderful. Even insect life is rainbow hued, and the beetle is so rich and gemlike as often to be set in gold and worn as jewelry. The nuns in their seclusion work up the brilliant feathers of the birds into flowers, rivaling Nature itself. Among the handsomest of these they imitate the variegated camellia japonica and the superb carnation, both among the fairest of flowers.

Chapter VIII

UNDER the reign of Dom Pedro II. the Empire of Brazil advanced rapidly in civilization and the fine arts. He invited to his empire talent of every kind, and rewarded it with magnanimous liberality. The officers of our ship had the honor of a reception paid us by the emperor and empress upon their visit to the Navy Yard. The emperor seemed indifferent and ill at ease, but the empress was peculiarly graceful and charming in manner, saluting us with smiles of recognition. After completing our repairs we reluctantly bade adieu to this beautiful city and made sail for the Cape of Good Hope on our way to the China Seas, or, as we term it in naval parlance, for the "East India Station." Our run across the South Atlantic had no remarkable features and we arrived at Table Bay after a pleasant and eventless passage. The reception and welcome we met with there from our "English cousins" was warm and refreshing after the contact and intercourse with nations of other tongues. We entertained and in return enjoyed the hospitality of the English families sojourning at the Cape. There were assembled at that time a large number of English people, the soldiers of whose families were engaged in the Kaffir War.

Like all military stations, there was great gaiety and mirth, notwithstanding the nearness to the seat of war. Table Bay is an open roadstead to the northward and westward, and at seasons of northwesterly gales subject to the sea swells of the South Atlantic Ocean. Fortunately, we did not encounter any of these gales. The city of Cape Town is built in crescent shape around this horseshoe harbor, running back to the hills that rise and form the remarkable Table Mountain. Near Cape Town is

RECOLLECTIONS OF A NAVAL LIFE

located the celebrated vineyard where the "Constantia wine" is made. Occasionally we would ride out to enjoy the hospitality of its proprietor and quaff that famous wine, so exquisite, but now little known to the wine markets of the world.

After leaving the city and its suburbs and crossing the point of the cape to Simon Town, where is located the naval station and a more secure anchorage, one passes over deserts of sand over which a wind called the "harmattan" blows with great force and fury, obliging one to veil the face to protect the eyes from the refraction of the sun's rays as well as the sand. A remarkable hostelry on this lonely road attracts attention, famous only for its name, however,—"The Gentle Shepherd of Salisbury Plains,"—and we found a good glass of beer and cheese quite a refreshment and very acceptable after our ride. From Table Bay we made sail around the Cape, still shaping our course eastward. Our next harbor was that of the poetic harbor of Mauritius, said to have been the home of "Paul and Virginia." This tender love story has delighted the youth of many climes and nations. Our first visit after arrival in port was to their graves, where we gathered some flowers from the tomb of this hero and heroine of romance, and returned on board ship quite pleased with our little jaunt. Here also we entertained many visitors on board. One striking beauty among our young lady visitors was a Parsee wearing in her nose a magnificent diamond. Her father, who accompanied her, was a fine-looking man, wearing a spotless turban of white on his close-shaved head, and his entire costume a revelation of neatness. He was said to be worth millions of pounds sterling. The island of Mauritius is remarkable for its rich production of spices, among the most beautiful of which is the nutmeg tree, growing very much in size and shape like an apple tree. The nut is enclosed in a covering similar to the hickory nut, and when ripe cracks open in the same man-

52 RECOLLECTIONS OF A NAVAL LIFE

ner, showing the mace of commerce wrapped around an inner shell which encloses the nutmeg. We procured many specimens in their half-ripe state and brought them home in alcohol as beautiful curios.

Our next port was the very interesting Island of Ceylon. Before reaching the island some amusing incidents occurred on board ship. While far at sea, almost out of sight of land, we were boarded by small boats, conveying merchants of precious stones and gems. Many of these were frauds and cheats no doubt manufactured of glass. The junior officers invested largely, especially my friend Bennett (I will not say how many I purchased), but I was one of the fortunate ones, for among my stones was found a moss agate with an exquisite fossil fern in it, which was beautiful and much admired; but some of the juniors no doubt proved the truth of the old adage, "all is not gold that glitters."

After arriving in port, ready for pleasure of every kind, Bennett and I visited the hotel, which was kept in fine English style, and had to lunch with us an enthusiastic native of pleasant manner and deportment. He suggested a drive out to the cinnamon gardens. We ordered a conveyance and invited him to join us. He proved a very good guide, and pointed out to us the various beauties of the drive. One striking feature was a grove of cocoanut trees through which we drove for more than a mile. Under these trees were built numerous cabins or huts, built of the cocoanut tree. He told us that the native who owned such a grove was considered rich. He at once possessed everything needed for comfort. The tree was his building material; the hull of the nut supplied his cooking and household utensils; the oil was the light for burning; the fruit itself eaten in every stage, and the milk his draught. His chairs or seats were made from the tree and his roof thatched with the leaves. Then what a delicious food the nut. Upon reaching the cinnamon gardens we passed through walks bordered by the fragrant shrub from

RECOLLECTIONS OF A NAVAL LIFE 53

which the cinnamon bark is gathered for commerce. In these beautiful gardens were many rare plants of the tropics, and through memory ran the old strain of the grand missionary hymn of the English Church so frequently sung at home,

> "What though spicy breezes
> Blow soft o'er Ceylon's isle;
> Though every prospect pleases,
> And only man is vile."

We spent here a most delightful afternoon, and only returned to our ship with the setting of the sun. Our new friend, the guide, had evidently taken a fancy to us and cordially invited us to join him in a shooting excursion, stating that English snipe were to be found in great numbers on the marshes of fresh water along the quiet little streams. On an appointed day we met him on shore, fully equipped for a shooting bout. Getting into a comfortable conveyance we drove a little distance into the interior, and upon reaching a beautiful fresh water stream we found prepared for us a "float," being two dugout canoes attached to each other, with a cocoanut thatched roof overhead to protect us from the sun, a platform upon which were placed chairs for us to be seated, a table upon which was a decanter of arack (a native drink), and a bunch of bananas hanging from the roof. A couple of Indian boys on hand paddled our craft while we shot the numerous water fowl as we floated down the stream. This was Oriental pastime in true Oriental style! On reaching the flats for snipe shooting we put our boats to the shore and landed. We found snipe in plenty, had fine sport shooting, and carried a feast to our messmates. This day's hunt proving so successful, it was suggested by our new friend that we take an elephant hunt with him, but the preparation for this, and the distance to be traveled so far, and our time so limited, we could not enjoy so great a diversion, and most reluctantly had to forego the pleasure.

54   RECOLLECTIONS OF A NAVAL LIFE

We witnessed in this port, however, the remarkable use of the elephant as a beast of burden in loading and unloading the shipping, taking the place of our portable steam engine. It was truly wonderful to see the intelligence of these enormous creatures, and very amusing, too. As the bell rung to cease work for dinner each elephant would stop instanter and wait to be led off to his own dinner. Among the curios I picked up at this port were two elephants carved out of ebony.

I never see an elephant without being reminded of an incident of my early boyhood, showing the viciousness of the beast. In those days of "long ago" the "old John Robinson Shows," as they were called, went through the country on foot, taking the public road. We as children went wild with delight. I had a schoolfellow and playmate named James Pepper, a very mischievous youngster. We "took in" the circus together. The keeper allowed us, under his chaperonage, to inspect "Tip," the huge elephant, very closely, for of course with boyish curiosity we were greatly interested in him. We made friends with Tip by giving him apples, peanuts, or anything to please him. But James on the sly gave him an oyster shell, which was not much to his taste! The next day we went again to the circus, and no sooner did Tip spy my friend James than he made at him with a snort of revengeful anger horrible to witness, and but for the timely interference of the keeper would no doubt have killed him on the spot! The keeper in great alarm roared, "Boy, what have you done to Tip?" The culprit had to acknowledge his mischief, and was charged "never to go to another circus to which Tip was attached, for Tip would never forget or forgive him." This little incident has been told my own children, with the moral, "Never to be unkind to dumb creatures," making my playmate's name a household word. I am glad to say when I heard last of James Pepper he was a highly respected deacon in the Presbyterian Church, with all the mischief of his childhood flown with those early days.

CHAPTER IX

FROM Ceylon we set sail, or rather steamed, to the Island of Penang, at the entrance of the Straits of Sumatra. This island, like Ceylon, is under the British flag, and here we met the hearty English welcome.

We remained here only a few days, but long enough for a party of us to accept an invitation from our consul to visit him and spend the night at his bungalow on the hills, several hundred feet above the town. After landing we were first taken in conveyances peculiar to the island, drawn by small but tough little horses, to the foot of the hills, when leaving the conveyances we were comfortably mounted on the backs of similar small horses and ascended a steep and rugged path. Our steeds were as sure-footed as goats, and bore us safely up the ascent. Upon reaching the bungalow we had presented to us a scene of luxury and comfort only to be appreciated in the hot and sultry clime of the East Indies. The house was a low, rambling structure, with spacious halls and verandas, with every conceivable form of easy chair, lounges, etc., made of bamboo and rattan. The grounds surrounding the house were most beautifully laid out by a tasteful landscape gardener, and filled with rare and handsome shrubs and plants. The atmosphere was pure and bracing, entirely different from the sultry breezes below, where our ship lay in port, and from which we had been glad to escape for a few hours. It was a refreshing, restful night of enjoyment. The breakfast next morning was unsurpassed for Eastern luxury. The delicious fresh currie served up hot and steaming in all its perfection, the coffee faultless, and all the fruits of the tropics to feast the eye for beauty and add zest to the appetite. The currie here prepared is a very

56 RECOLLECTIONS OF A NAVAL LIFE

different article, eaten fresh, from the powder we use at home as a condiment for dressing up our stews, and must be eaten in the East Indies to be appreciated. After breakfast our ponies were brought to the door and we left the hospitable bungalow. By noon we were again on board the ship. Remaining in this port but a day or two longer, we proceeded on our course to the port of Singapore, situated at the extreme point of the Peninsula of Malacca. This port is largely occupied by English merchants, who have their residences and grounds beautifully decorated. They were always ready to entertain with lavish hospitality.

On visiting the shore we noticed the stuffed skins of the tiger, famous on this peninsula for their destruction of the natives, and indeed of all persons who venture beyond the thickly-settled towns and villages. He is called the "man-eating tiger," and is a great terror to all. The city of Singapore is one of great importance as the trading place of the islands of the Malay Archipelago. Being a free port, the shipping of all the East center there in large numbers, while the trade of China makes an annual visit, coming down the China Sea with the northeast monsoon, laying up their junks at Singapore during the continuance of that wind, and returning home with the southwest monsoon. The jungles of this peninsula are of dense growth and inhabited by the most ferocious beasts. As a sort of compensation of Nature their birds are very beautiful, with brilliant, gorgeous plumage. I purchased here some rare specimens, ready for the taxidermist's hand. Among the great variety were two grand birds of paradise and the rarer "harp bird." These birds I had mounted and very handsomely set up in glass cases in New York. They adorned my home till in the fortunes of war they fell into vandal hands and were wantonly destroyed. We also procured here some handsome specimens of "Malacca joint," so highly prized as walking canes. Even at the date of which I write the predominance of Chinese trades-

RECOLLECTIONS OF A NAVAL LIFE

men was very marked in this port. The climate of Singapore is very salubrious, the thermometer seldom rising above 85 degrees in summer or lower than 70 degrees in winter. The foliage of course is beautiful, for there Nature wears a garb of evergreen.

From Singapore we sailed for Hong Kong. One remarkable feature of some of these Eastern seas are the schools of snakes through which ships pass. We arrived at Hong Kong, where we met some of our naval vessels, and Commodore Aulick took formal command of the East India Squadron. Here again we greeted the English flag, the emblem of that great power and nation of which it is truly said "the sun never sets on its dominions." We had now sailed over half the circumference of the globe, and after leaving Cape Town every port we entered was a colony of Great Britain. This Island of Hong Kong was ceded to Great Britain by the treaty of Canton in 1841 or 1842, and it was indeed a great acquisition, as it gave to England a foothold on the very coast of China, possessing a fine harbor, and where she has quartered a fine garrison. The climate is very healthy for this latitude, owing to its being a very rocky and barren soil, entirely surrounded by salt water. The body of the water of the Canton River(of which it forms the eastern entrance) passes to the westward along the shores of Macao. This port of Hong Kong was a gay and pleasant place to visit. There many English families belonging to the garrison resided; also some of the families of American merchants located there. These were all very hospitable and entertained us handsomely. My first acquaintance with "pigeon English" was a note of invitation from one of the American ladies to "tiffin," which translated into our language means a sumptuous luncheon. We also attended here a grand military ball given by the officers of the garrison. After the festivities of the evening were over and the dancing thoroughly enjoyed the departing guests were served with a cup of hot beef tea. This was a novelty to us, but the most refreshing beverage

RECOLLECTIONS OF A NAVAL LIFE

after the weariness consequent upon the evening's enjoyment that I ever drank, and I found one did not have to be an invalid to appreciate it.

From Hong Kong we crossed over to Macao. This peninsula was donated to the Portuguese in the sixteenth century for assistance given by that nation to the Chinese against pirates, who infested the seas in that section, and do more or less to the present day. The harbor is an open roadstead for large shipping. The trading, however, was not very much here, for the advantages offered by Hong Kong were greater. The city of Macao is one of the oldest foreign settlements in China, and presents some unique specimens of architecture in residences and public buildings, while the grounds show taste and culture. There is just out of the limits of the city a beautiful grotto where the Poet Camoëns is said to have written his "Lusiad," and the spot is beautiful enough to have inspired a poet's pen. After remaining a week or more in this harbor we went up the Canton River as high as Blenheim Reach, the highest point of anchorage that our ship's draught of water would admit of our going. We passed by the Canton forts, more remarkable for their extent than the strength of their fortifications. During the war between England and China the heaviest of the English ships anchored in Blenheim Reach to operate against the city of Canton, which is about eight miles from this place. On the shores of Blenheim Reach is built up a village of some extent, the houses of which are constructed entirely of bamboo canes. The bamboo grows here in great abundance and to great size. We visited the city of Canton in boats, but were always armed, on account of the river pirates, bold and daring, and often dangerous. Although it is an old and hackneyed story about China, it is nevertheless a true and interesting one in regard to their duck boats. The peculiar fittings or appliances for lowering down the platforms for the ducks to descend into the water for feeding purposes, at which they perform many pranks as they

RECOLLECTIONS OF A NAVAL LIFE

hasten to the shore along the shoal for food. Thus they are kept moving along the river to the most desirable feeding grounds, constantly changing from day to day. These creatures of the feathered tribe are so trained as to know the whistle of their own boat, upon the sound of which they ascend as rapidly as they descended, but with a different motive power influencing them, for the last one that crosses the bridge or platform gets a sound thrashing! The duck is indeed a feature of China. Hatched and bred in great quantities on these boats, having free feeding grounds, they are a great source of revenue to their owners, and are a prominent feature in all the eating shops (which are numerous), baked and hung up to be served out as the purchaser desires.

As we approached the great city of Canton both sides of the river were lined with boats on which large families of people are reared and have been for generations back, who never go on shore except for special purposes, such as marketing, attending worship in their temples, or burying their dead. These boats are of small dimensions and are kept scrupulously clean, and necessarily the scrubbing day comes round very often, when the children are thrown overboard and given a buoy to float upon until the scrubbing is over and the home in order again.

The tea boats present a striking appearance in their gay coloring and gaudy decorations. These boats are anchored off in the center of the stream or at convenient points along the river. To these boats the populace resort in great numbers for quaffing their national beverage, as their more civilized contemporaries would frequent saloons or club-rooms. We landed in that part of the city where are built the residences of European merchants, many of them very comfortable. The men who occupy them supply the world with tea. The best-paid men in this trade are the tea-tasters, who select, classify, and price the teas for the various markets. As we pass these buildings and enter the Chinese part of the city the streets are

RECOLLECTIONS OF A NAVAL LIFE

narrow and paved. The merchants show their goods in the doorways of their shops or on the sidewalks to designate their occupation. The streets are filled with vendors of all conceivable wares. It was by no means rare to see puppies and cats in cages, hung at either end of a pole over the shoulder of the carrier, as unconcernedly as chickens or game would be hawked about the streets of American towns.

The fish shops of China are interesting from the great variety they display. They do not sell oysters fresh (or did not on that day). They kiln-dried them on scaffolds and then packed them away in the dried state for future use, thereby depriving the bivalve and the consumer of its most tempting properties, hence they were not appreciated by oyster-eating Americans.

Chapter X

We visited with a great deal of interest and pleasure the crockery stores, with a view to purchasing some of the beautiful wares. The finest china is, of course, hand-painted, no two pieces alike, having landscapes of their own country, exclusively, in the center (with strange want of perspective), with very handsome borders of birds, insects, butterflies and flowers. It is very rich and showy, their coloring being always intense, and a table set with china of this description is very striking and beautiful. In making a selection there are no regular sets for breakfast, dinner, and tea, but you are at liberty to select what pleases your own fancy, thus making up your own sets. The breakfast set of which I made choice was the very old-fashioned historic willow china in blue, to which is attached a very romantic legend. The legend runs: "A Chinese princess escapes from a window which overhangs the water on whose shores the willows grow and thrive, throwing their graceful shadows on the stream on whose placid waters she floats away from her home with a plebeian lover, with woman's trust and faith, and 'the love that laughs at locksmiths.'" The plates and dishes are double and deep, with a little orifice for pouring in hot water to keep the breakfast delightfully hot while eating it.

I took the opportunity of purchasing a very handsome Chinese punch bowl for my esteemed friend Judge Berrien, which I had the pleasure of sending him on my return home, and received from him a very beautiful letter of thanks and appreciation. I also purchased a very full and handsome set of china—dinner and tea—which is still in use in my family, having been *buried* during the war for safe keeping! When making the selection of the blue

62 RECOLLECTIONS OF A NAVAL LIFE

breakfast china the salesman or merchant surprised me by putting one of the dishes on the floor and jumping with his wooden clogs upon it to prove its strength, presenting a laughable appearance to us who stood by. They proved as strong as he asserted, and half a dozen are still in existence after many years' service. Having made our purchases we sought the hotel in search of a dinner, which was served with a variety of dishes, very Chinese in appearance, being mostly hashes, but very palatable. One in particular had such very small bones that we accused the waiter with serving us up a "rat stew." At this he was very indignant, and angrily protested, "Chinaman no eat rat; none 'cept poor Chinaman, low-down Chinaman." The cat and puppy dishes, however, he did not deny; said they "were good, but no serve Mellican man 'cept he want 'em!"

Had I been served with a "rat stew" it would have been a "righteous retribution" on me for one of the frolics of my early boyhood! Our old carriage driver, "Daddy Jim," my father's body servant, who used to drive him in his gig as he went the rounds of the courts on his circuit, was also a very fancy cook, and loved his own dishes. He was very devoted to his young master and would sometimes save choice morsels for me from his supper the night before. When I went hunting I would bring him in rabbit or squirrel, as my game might chance to be; but one day, in a spirit of mischief and fun, I played a dreadful trick on him. The rats that infested the rice barn and fed on the rice were very large and fat. I shot two or three of them and prepared them invitingly for the pot or saucepan, curtailing their suspicious tails, and they looked for all the world like squirrels. I presented them to "Daddy Jim" for his supper; he was delighted, said "he would cook them nice, and save one for my breakfast." The next morning the old man smacked his lips and told me how good and juicy they were, and he would bring mine to me. I laughed and said, "Daddy Jim, I fooled you; they were

RECOLLECTIONS OF A NAVAL LIFE

barn rats." Such a look of disgust and nausea came over his face, and he shamed me so that I had to run out of his way, but he soon forgave me, with his big and loving heart, and to the day of his death was fond and faithful. Peace to his memory!

The American merchants in China invited us to their houses, and we were pleased at the opportunity offered us of witnessing the mode of classifying the teas by the tea-tasters. They would place a sample of each kind of tea in cups, pour on the boiling water, cover closely, and allow it to draw for a few minutes only, when they would be able to distinguish by their experienced taste the exact quality of the tea and determine the markets to which they should go. My second visit to the city was devoted to the purchase of silks and dress goods, including beautiful Canton crape shawls, rich in color and exquisite in embroidery. There were also in this market lovely dress goods made of the fibre of the pineapple, called "penia cloth." Of this fine fabric handkerchiefs and various things were made, and the embroidery on them was marvelous for its intricate needlework. Our collections, of course, were only meant for gifts upon our return home as mementoes to our families and friends of our sojourn in these distant lands. I must not forget to mention their hand-carved ivory chessmen and sets of backgammon and the unsurpassed lacquer ware in all designs. Upon this lacquer are represented usually their national emblems, the stork and the turtle.

While at anchor in the Blenheim Reach we were visited by an American colporteur, an intelligent man, who appeared earnest in his work of disseminating the Gospel and teachings of religion in the form of tracts translated into their language. Through his representation of the beauty of the country and small villages my friend, Dr. Charles F. Fahs, assistant surgeon of the ship, and myself were induced to accompany him on one of his trips.

64 RECOLLECTIONS OF A NAVAL LIFE

Getting in one of the ship's boats for the trip, we were landed at a point on the river, and taking the embankment which was thrown up as a foot-path through the marsh we passed through little hamlets dotted over this marsh of luxurious growth. After reaching the third hamlet we approached rather a large building with a single hall. This the colporteur pointed out to us as one of their "ancestral halls," where their children were taught. The doors being open and the building unoccupied at the time, we took the liberty of going in, and were remarking on some characters on the wall when a querulous old Chinaman entered and asked our business there. The colporteur, who spoke Chinese, replied that we were admiring their ancient building and the characters on the walls. It was easy to see it was his intention to dispute our right to be there, and his loud talking soon drew other Chinamen, and in a few minutes the hall was filled with an excited crowd. Our acquaintance, the colporteur, had his patience and endurance put to the test. Never losing his patience or temper, he replied to all they said with coolness and decision. The doctor and I being only "lookers on" saw that a serious row was pending, though we did not know exactly what we had done to bring it about. The colporteur suggested (in an aside to us) that we take our departure with all the coolness and indifference we could assume, as any appearance of fear might lead to our being murdered by them, and I verily think it would! We withdrew, leisurely observing the beauty of the streets and the quaintness of the buildings we passed till we reached the outskirts of the village, when the colporteur begged that we accelerate our pace, as he said had one of those infuriated people thrown a stone at us we would not have escaped with our lives; so we made "double-quick" time back to the landing and made signal for our boat, greatly relieved to reach the ship in safety, and unstoned. We could not go with the good man again on his rounds, not being willing to extend his

RECOLLECTIONS OF A NAVAL LIFE 65

good work or even to "take the Kingdom of Heaven by violence," at least the violence of a Chinese heathen mob! We had now remained several weeks in Blenheim Reach, and many of our men were taken down with fever. The weather was intensely hot, especially the nights. All hands were seeking the spar deck, where only the awning kept off the night air, and with a Chinese mat to lie upon, and a bamboo pillow, we passed the nights in search of comfort, regardless of health. The surgeon advised that the ship be taken down to salt water, which was done as a health motive. We steamed down to Hong Kong, our former anchorage, where we greatly enjoyed the sea breezes. Our next move was to Shanghai, higher up the coast some hundred miles, situated on the Woosing River, about fourteen miles from the sea. This city is one of the important *entrepôt* of the commerce between the north and south provinces of China. It also carried on quite an important foreign trade. Many of the foreign missions were established here. The Episcopal Bishop of China, Rev. Dr. Boone, resided here, and I found in his lovely wife a typical Southern woman, a sister of the beloved bishop of my native State, Rt. Rev. Stephen Elliott. I was quite an invalid from the enervating climate, and they kindly invited me to become an inmate of their home till my health should be restored. Bishop Boone had studied medicine to aid him in his missionary work. He advised me to put aside all nauseous drugs and trust to the change to home life. There I enjoyed the nice Southern dishes and everything was done for my comfort. My enjoyment of their true Southern hospitality soon recruited my health. Bishop Boone was an ardent laborer in his chosen work. He established a very successful mission school, and his long study of the Chinese language and character eminently fitted him for his life-work. The mission and foreign residences were situated outside the city, on the banks of a river, in a beautiful grove. The city of Shanghai is a walled city with narrow streets not remarkable for

5

66   RECOLLECTIONS OF A NAVAL LIFE

cleanliness, but in keeping with all other Chinese towns I have ever visited. At this time the city was in possession of the Taiping Wang party, insurgents against the Imperial Government. This party was commanded by a dashing young general, who took a fancy to the officers of our ship. I was one of a large party invited by him to go over the city sight-seeing. Among this party was my old friend Lieutenant George H. Cooper, or, as he was known to his intimates, "Jack Cooper." Jack had with him a favorite little Scotch terrier named "Jerry." Jerry was his master's shadow, and was at his heels on this "sight-seeing" trip. In passing through the narrow streets and seeing, as Jerry no doubt thought, the most outlandish sights and people he had ever seen, he got separated from us (or perhaps he was enticed away, with a view to making a stew of him,—as he was fat and fine,—by some hungry Chinaman). The commander-in-chief offered a large reward for Jerry, but he could not be found at that time. After the return of the squadron to the United States, Lieutenant Cooper was walking in the streets of Norfolk one day, when Jerry came running up to him with expressions of glad recognition and delight. It was ascertained that the Chinese general, true to his promise, had looked up Jerry and put him in the charge of a friend of Lieutenant Cooper, who brought him safely home in the next ship returning to the United States.

While in Shanghai we were invited by the American Consul to a tea-party at his residence, where we were served with several varieties of tea. Among these teas was one of peculiar value, bringing five dollars per pound in that market. Not knowing this, we gave preference to a very ordinary tea, costing there from twenty to thirty cents per pound. This fact perhaps proved that the cheaper tea was the tea to which we were most accustomed in America, and that the finer quality of tea needed to have one's palate cultivated to appreciation of it.

RECOLLECTIONS OF A NAVAL LIFE · 67

The commodore having Mr. McLane, U. S. Minister to China, on board, gathered all the information he could in regard to reaching the city of Nankin, which was then occupied by the Taiping Wang party, and the residence of Taiping Wang himself, with whom Mr. McLane had instructions from our Government to establish a commercial treaty. Having no chart of the river the commodore chartered a light draught, but powerful, river steamer to go ahead of our ship and take soundings as we proceeded up the river. We left Shanghai with the little steamer ahead of us with a good leadsman, and one of our officers in charge, and thus made our way up the Yangtse Kiang, or Yellow River, a bold and navigable stream. We found no difficulty in the depth of water, and went up to the city of Nankin, some ninety miles distant, passing through a rich and fertile valley properly termed the Granary of China. All of this section of the country was then in the possession of the revolutionists, or "Taiping Wang" party. As we approached the city we were boarded by an officer from one of their vessels of war to ascertain our mission and the cause of our presence there. Upon being informed that we had the American Minister on board we were allowed to pass without detention, and came to anchor off the city. Here we were again visited by officials, but Mr. McLane failed to obtain an interview or in any way to effect a treaty with the insurgents in power. Taiping Wang was educated at the mission school in Shanghai, and there obtained sufficient knowledge of the Christian religion to pervert it! He boldly claimed to be the younger brother of Jesus Christ. He was without doubt a man of strength and power in his way, and influenced his people to proclaim him a divine being, and to worship him as such. This fanaticism spread like wildfire over the southern part of the Chinese Empire. He took up his quarters with great wisdom at Nankin, the capital of the old Wing Dynasty, and the center of the Granary of China. His adherents filled the valley of the Yangtse Kiang. One

68   RECOLLECTIONS OF A NAVAL LIFE

of his most binding obligations on his soldiers was that they should absent themselves from their families and live separated till his dynasty was established.

This was the condition of affairs when we visited Nankin, and Mr. McLane failing to obtain an interview or effect a treaty, the officers were allowed to visit the shore. During our stay many of their high officials "dined and wined" with us. They claimed the brotherhood of Christians, and observed strictly the asking of a blessing before meals, and other religious rites. This friendly intercourse was certainly most fortunate for us, as the little episode I will relate will prove.

One beautiful morning Dr. Fahs, Midshipman Hawley, and I, viewing the far-famed Porcelain Tower from a distance, and obtaining permission to leave the ship, armed only with umbrellas, taking with us our Chinese servant boy as interpreter, made the best of our way in the direction of the tower, bent on a visit to it. The tower is outside of the walls and west of the city. We attempted to shorten our walk by entering the gates and passing through the city, but to our surprise and chagrin we were accosted by a Chinese soldier who forbade our doing so! We were determined not to be discouraged by this rebuff, and followed the walls on the outside and made an attempt to enter at the next gate. Failing in this as we did in our first attempt, we decided to walk outside around the city till we reached the tower. Hoisting our umbrellas we started off at a quick pace, knowing the great distance we had to traverse. On the way we would occasionally pass a Chinese hut or cottage, and apparently alarm the occupants, but explaining through our interpreter that we were only harmless tourists desirous of seeing the tower, some would generously offer us a cup of tea, which they always had on the little charcoal fire, and which was used without sugar or milk. These little cups of tea were exceedingly refreshing; drank hot, they no doubt did us

RECOLLECTIONS OF A NAVAL LIFE

more good than a draught of cold water would have done, and acted more beneficially upon our weariness.

After a long morning's walk we approached the object of our desire. We beheld the grand tower looming up high above everything else and situated outside the city walls, but enclosed in a wall of its own, with a village at its base. As we approached the gate we noticed a formidable looking little field piece protruding through a porthole just over the gateway. To our delight there was apparently no sentinel on post, and we boldly entered. We had passed some distance up the street, which was wide and nicely paved, before the inhabitants of the village discovered us. When they did, such surprise, such jabbering and gesticulating as was carried on by these natives is more easily imagined than described! However, we took little notice of them, being bent upon our visit to the tower, the base of which was now plainly visible. After scrambling over rocks and the mutilated parts of this grand structure we entered the defaced portal and witnessed the desecration that had been worked by fire and chisel in the hands of the vandal insurgents, professing to be earnest followers of the younger brother of Our Saviour.

The grand stairway that had led to the summit of this tower had been burned out, leaving only the shell. The sculpture in bas-relief ornamenting the base of the building and representing their gods were special objects of disfavor, the Christians—as they called themselves—claiming it to be idolatrous, had destroyed them effectually. We procured many of the broken fragments as specimens, among which was the remarkable porcelain, highly glazed and green in color, which had resisted the action of atmosphere and weather for centuries, the tower having been built in 1411. It was octagonal, about 260 feet high, nine stories of equal height, each decorated with cornice and covered with roof of green tiling, the roof overhanging, as do all Chinese roofs of temples and public buildings. On the corners of each roof were bells which

70 RECOLLECTIONS OF A NAVAL LIFE

swayed and rang out sweetly with every passing breeze. The pinnacle of the tower was ornamented with a large golden ball. We were told that the interior had contained apartments of great beauty, elaborately gilded and otherwise ornamented, but the fire fiend had done its work before our visit. We could only imagine what its beauty had been, and deplore the fanaticism that could destroy such grandeur. I believe I have not mentioned its peculiar name, which rendered into English means "Recompensing Favor Monastery." Its cost is said to have been $4,000,000.

The staring crowd now began to surround us in such numbers that our Chinese boy told us they were getting very much incensed and excited, and urged our leaving. We told him to ask the most prominent member of the mob if he objected to our taking the broken specimens we had, and we began to throw them down; but he said "it was not that at all, we might take all we wished, but we had no business there." We then said we would leave at once, and began retracing our steps to the broad street and towards the gate through which we had entered. We were followed by an immense crowd, gesticulating violently and wildly jabbering, as only a Chinese rabble can, but we took no notice of it. In a few minutes, to our surprise and annoyance, we saw a company of lancers form themselves across the street to stop our further progress. As we approached, the company dropped their lances in our very faces, and the commanding officer drew his double swords and went through some contortions of the body and cuttings and slashings of swords peculiar only to Chinese warfare. We determined not to be intimidated by this demonstration, and quietly took our umbrellas and shoved the lances one side. This so nonplused the officer that he instantly ordered the gates closed.

We were at our wits' end to know what to do next! We saw them rush to close in upon us, and bringing our poor frightened interpreter to the front we demanded that they

RECOLLECTIONS OF A NAVAL LIFE

"open the gates, as we must be on board our ship at a certain hour; that we were in no way violating their laws, coming ashore only to see their grand tower." The officer replied he had "orders to stop us, but he would take us to the commanding officer of the village." He thereupon escorted us to a formidable structure, where he said that officer "held his court." As we entered through a courtyard we were no little shocked to see the bloody heads of several unfortunate Chinamen hung up in cages or baskets around this court, a glance at which completely demoralized our Chinese boy. His transition was horrible. His hair seemed to stand up on his head, his eyes became suddenly bloodshot, and he presented a most pitiable object of fright and despair.

From this courtyard we were introduced into a large hall in which was an elevated platform with benches around it, upon which we were told to "be seated," to await the coming of the official. The long delay in his coming seemed to be studied to impress us the more with the gravity of the situation. At last he made his appearance, and it was so grotesque as almost to make us laugh outright. He was a large, finely-built Chinaman, with a flowing robe on him of rich blue silk, and upon his head he wore a helmet, and on top of the helmet was a good-sized paper or pasteboard gilded horse. Doubtless this was to designate him as belonging to the cavalry! Before entering into any explanation he required his secretary, who accompanied him, to write in a book describing the personal appearance of each one of us. We were thoroughly worn out with this delay, and growing very impatient. We required our boy to tell him "we were compelled to be on board our ship at sunset." This did not seem to hurry matters at all. His faithful secretary continued industriously "writing us up." After a little we suggested that "he would have to furnish horses for our return." He condescended to reply that "there were no horses at hand," but preserved a very dignified and commanding attitude

72   RECOLLECTIONS OF A NAVAL LIFE

towards us. After his secretary got through he informed
us "that he would send us through the city to be interviewed by the Eastern King," whom we learned afterwards
filled the position of Minister of Foreign Affairs. He said
he would send an officer to conduct us to the king. We
were pleased at this suggestion, as we thought we would
accomplish another wish we had, to see the interior of the
the city. We bowed ourselves out of his presence, left, and
soon after entered the city gates. We were impressed with
the cleanliness of the streets and the superiority of the
buildings to most of the Chinese cities we had seen. We
found that this portion of the city was the residence of royalty during the Wing dynasty and separated from the rest
of the city by a wall. It was now occupied exclusively by
women separated from their husbands by the vows they
had taken before enlisting for the war. The rush of these
creatures to examine the "outside barbarians," and their
scrutiny of our clothes, the quality and quantity and brightness of our buttons, came nearer demoralizing us than the
brandishing swords of the captain of the lancers. The
noisy jabbering of these women was really fearful, and we
dared not show the "white feather," for it is well known
that any show of fear is fatal to one who falls into their
uncivilized hands. Upon having the gates closed upon us
and separating us from these women we drew a long breath
of relief! Under the guidance of our official escort we
wended our way to the residence of the Eastern King.
After walking for some distance through the business part
of the city we were brought to a halt before a building more
pretentious than the surrounding ones. Our escort now
attempted to give us instructions through our interpreter
as to how we must conduct ourselves before "His Royal
Highness, the Eastern King." The prominent feature of
this ceremony was that "we should fall down on our knees
before him and prostrate ourselves." This we protested
against, and positively refused to do. We told him "we
never knelt or prostrated ourselves to any living man; that

RECOLLECTIONS OF A NAVAL LIFE

we only knelt to God; that it was against our religion to do this, and if they were Christians they should not do it either." At this he became very loud in his demands, said we "had to do it; it was a custom and the law of their country." We told him "it was no use to argue the matter, we would not do it." He considered a moment, and then said "he would take us before a high mandarin in another section of the city." We started at once for the residence of the mandarin. As we went we noticed a dense crowd ahead of us, and on nearing them saw the uniforms of some of our brother officers from the ship in like trouble with ourselves, having been arrested as trespassers for entering the city. They, too, had started for the tower, but we being ahead had aroused the Chinese to a more vigilant watch, and it had caused them to be taken in charge much sooner. Among this party was T. T. Hunter, second lieutenant of the ship, a fine specimen of a naval officer. Tall and commanding in person, demonstrative in action, Hunter received us with open arms, verifying and so expressing himself the old adage that "misery loves company."

Minister McLane's secretary and three or four others formed the party. We now joined company for the mandarin's residence, and upon being ushered into his presence recognized the jolly old Chinaman who had dined with us on the ship two days before. He was delighted to see us, and we were most assuredly relieved to see him. He insisted upon our remaining with him till he could order a feast for our entertainment. It was growing dark, and thanking him for his kindness we assured him that we had been detained so long beyond our time it was our imperative duty to return to our ship as soon as possible. He regretted the inconvenience to which we had been subjected (we did not mention our fears of losing our heads), and ordered his lantern-bearer to see to our safe conveyance beyond the city walls, assuring us that the presence of his lantern would be respected by all sentinels on duty. This lantern was a transparency which had painted

74 RECOLLECTIONS OF A NAVAL LIFE

on it his crest, or coat of arms, and rank. We found it absolutely true—the gates flew open on the approach of the lantern-bearer in "open sesame" style. We had now been taken from the opposite side straight through the city, and found ourselves at no great distance from the ship, with an open roadway. We hailed the ship for a boat, which was sent, and about 12 o'clock at night we arrived in safety and reported our fatiguing and harassing day, including our "hair breadth" escape from execution.

CHAPTER XI

THE following day the Chinese Government sent an officer on board bearing an important looking document for the commodore. Said document informed him that "if any more of his outside barbarians attempted to enter the city they would have their heads chopped off." This brought to mind with a shuddering sense of horror the butchered heads in cages we had seen in the executioner's yard through which we had been carried. The commodore, however, did not notice this document. With the little steamer in front of us we now got under way and started up the river. We observed our soundings very carefully, as we were now going up the river further into the interior than any foreign vessel had ever gone. The country presented a vast acreage in cultivation, showing no waste or unused land. Great activity seemed to prevail both on shore and river. Large boats transporting produce and goods were numerous, and the fertile valley of the Yangtse Kiang, as far as the eye could reach, verified the statement of its being the "Granary of China."

We found a bold river, too, carrying a sufficient depth of water to navigate our steam frigate with safety. We took the precaution of anchoring at night, and steaming cautiously in the wake of the little steamer ahead of us, taking soundings as we went. We arrived at quite an ancient city, whose name I have forgotten, but whose old pagoda had been taken quiet possession of by bats innumerable. We came to anchor and were soon surrounded by boats of all kinds filled with produce, and a gaping, wonder-struck people. In one of the large boats we noticed some donkeys. Whether they were meant to be traded to us we never learned, so concluded the visit was one of curiosity

76 RECOLLECTIONS OF A NAVAL LIFE

instead of trade, they being drawn towards us as foreigners; certainly they had never seen a foreign ship or a foreign people before. We gathered from these venders of curios many interesting specimens. The commodore having no special object in continuing his cruise up the river, we weighed anchor and retraced our way, and passing by the Capital, where we had been so rudely rebuffed, we proceeded to our old anchorage at Shanghai. We spent here a week or more, greeted our dear friends at the mission, and then sailed, with Mr. McLane still on board, for Hong Kong. At this point Mr. McLane landed, and the commodore, after a few days of rest, sailed for Manila, the Capital of Luzon, one of the Philippine Islands. On this passage Commodore Aulick was taken desperately ill. The surgeons of the ship pronounced his case a hopeless one. Not so with the commodore himself, however. He had the greatest horror of being buried at sea, or on Spanish soil. On hearing the verdict of the doctors he gave orders that "should he die, his body should be put in a cask of whiskey for preservation and carried to English soil for interment," for he said he "did not wish his last rest to be among the dagos." His will power proved superior to his disease, and to the surprise of surgeons and all on board the ship he rallied and finally recovered.

We entered the port of Manila after a pleasant run across the China Seas, and were delighted to find ourselves out of the reach of China and the "heathen Chinee" with heads on and hearts light. The population of Manila is a race of Mestizas, a mixture of Spanish and the native Indian—the men after the order of the Spanish hidalgo and the women as beautiful as the senoritas of old Spain. The city of Manila was founded in 1571, and has remained one of the most important of the Spanish colonial cities, furnishing to the world the famous Manila cheroot and tobacco, and the Manila cordage; also the finest fabrics made from the pineapple leaf, known as pinea cloth, on which elaborate embroideries are exquisitely done; and here are found

RECOLLECTIONS OF A NAVAL LIFE 77

dainty articles of use and wear and ornament. The trade is immense with England and the United States.

We were very fortunate in making our visit to Manila in carnival time. At this season the whole island is given over to dancing, cockfighting, gaiety and dissipation. Upon visiting the shore we were handsomely entertained by the officers of the Spanish garrison. My friend Bennett and I joined a lieutenant of the garrison in a snipe hunt on the rice fields, and brought in plenty of game. We also had delightful drives in the country. We were struck with the love of the natives for cockfighting. Every countryman we met held under his arm a cock ready for the pit. After our drive we were carried to these pits to witness the gambling excitement over these fights, almost equalling the bullfights of old Spain.

From these cruel sports we went visiting. The inhabitants kept open houses, with music and dancing at the homes of all the most important families in the city. Of course the dancing was a very delightful social pastime to us, the young officers of the ship. To return this attention and hospitality we gave a dance on board the ship. We moved the battery from the quarter deck and decorated the deck with flags and bunting, making chandeliers of bayonets, and covering the deck with an awning we had a complete and beautiful ball-room. Here we entertained the élite of the city of Manila, having the music of our fine band, and a feast worthy of the occasion. It was an evening of great enjoyment to them and to us. The Spanish ladies wore magnificent slippers, many of them set with stones of great value, which glistened brilliantly on their tiny feet. These slippers without heels were kept on the feet by the little toe protruding outside, and in the round dances or the waltz in the back step they would sometimes lose a slipper, to their great annoyance; but of course it was a great amusement to their partner in the dance to see them gracefully return, catch the slipper on the foot, and continue the waltz as if no such accident had

78   RECOLLECTIONS OF A NAVAL LIFE

occurred. This ball was the closing scene of our visit. Our guests departed after midnight, and the next morning, after arranging our decks in man-of-war-style, we set sail for the coast of China.

We arrived at our old anchorage in the hárbor of Hong Kong, and the commodore's health being sufficiently restored, he began making preparation for his return to the United States. Commodore Matthew C. Perry, we learned, was on his way out to take command of the Chinese Squadron. His flagship was the *Mississippi*, under the command of Captain Sidney Smith Lee (brother of our gallant General Robert E. Lee). The *Mississippi*, with several other ships, made a squadron of eight vessels, including those already out there. Commodore Aulick returned by way of Europe. Commodore Perry came out in the same way to join the squadron in Hong Kong, to make there the necessary preparation to visit Japan as Minister Extraordinary.

These ships coming out to join his squadron brought out a miniature locomotive and train of cars, with accompanying rails and all the attachments for running them in a circle of about a mile in circumference, to show those people who were shut up in their own country what was going on in the outside world. They also brought out the telegraph, with batteries and the operators, ready to put it up as soon as permission was obtained to do so. All these wonders to show to a people who for centuries had excluded the foreigner from their shores, also thereby excluding the marvels and progress of the age. In due course of time Commodore Perry arrived, and the various ships of his command. ' All was now active preparation for the expedition to Japan. Here we took on board (he having obtained permission to join us in the capacity of master's mate) the author and poet who has since made his name famous, Mr. Bayard Taylor.

The commodore had secured as interpreter a German, who was quite a fine linguist; speaking English fluently,

RECOLLECTIONS OF A NAVAL LIFE   79

he did good service as a translator. Some of the Japanese officials, being conversant with German, would communicate with him in that language, and he would translate it into English. After completing all arrangements we sailed in squadron for the Lew Chew group of islands, one of the dependencies of Japan. These islands lie south of the Japan group, and are situated off the coast of China. They are inhabited by a race of people mild in their disposition and possessing none of the arts of war in their rude state. These people live after the order of the old patriarchs, and are among the most pleasant people it has ever been my fortune to be thrown among. They are industrious and cleanly in their habits and provide abundantly for their own subsistence.

We were able to procure from them poultry, pigs and vegetables at very moderate prices. The Capital of the great Lew Chew is situated a few miles in the interior, and a body of our troops, marines and sailors marched up to the city, merely to impress them with our strength and power. Our forces were pleasantly received, and reported their public roads in perfect order and their bridges, of arched masonry, artistic and beautiful. Their houses were light structures one story high, covered with tiling, scrupulously clean, with matting covering the floors, and all native visitors were expected to remove their sandals before entering the house, and leave them at the door; this and many of their customs struck us very agreeably. While lying in this port we had the misfortune to lose one of our young engineers. It was a very sad death and cast a gloom over the entire ship. Our poet, Bayard Taylor, commemorated the event by some beautiful lines, which I wish I could remember. They were much admired by us all. Among these quiet, peaceful people he was laid to rest to await the resurrection morning. A stranger in a foreign land, among a strange and unknown people, it touched us all as a sad and lonely fate!

CHAPTER XII

ON THIS beautiful island, the great Lew Chew, where we had been luxuriating for ten days, there was little or nothing to collect in the way of curios or mementos. The people were strictly rural, and plain and simple in their tastes. We were ordered to weigh anchor, and set sail for Japan. In one of my old letters home at that time I find myself airing the sentiments of the day in regard to the contemplated expedition to Japan, and will here insert it:

HONG KONG, *February 22, 1853.*

MY DEAR MOTHER: I must at once give you all the information we have concerning the great expedition to Japan, which is at present of absorbing interest to us. Its merits are largely discussed by all, and the most plausible view we can take of the expedition, since we have the assurance in the President's Message; it is presumed to be entirely of a peaceful nature, taking them presents which will show the improve- ments of the age and through our intercourse with them establish a friendly feeling, and if possible make a commercial treaty. We learn there will be brought out a locomotive with several miles of railroad iron, a telegraph apparatus (and operator), also Daguerrean artist with "cameras," etc., all of which if they will allow to be explained and accept, will no doubt induce them to look upon us in a better light than a set of "barbarians," which term they apply to all foreigners. It is a part of their religion to admit no innovations. Should they refuse, which is most likely, I have yet to learn what right we have to try to force them to have intercourse with us. Others argue that Commodore Perry will not be put off on any pretence whatever; that he will effect his mission peaceably if he can, forcibly if he must; that the United States Government has gone to too much expense in fitting out this expedition to have it return without making some active demonstration; but from what I have heard of the Japanese we will have no just cause to go to war with them. They will no doubt listen quietly to our parley, thank us for our good intentions, promise protection to our mariners who may be thrown on their coasts, and if we insist upon it accept our presents, which will be carefully housed and superstitiously guarded, with a

RECOLLECTIONS OF A NAVAL LIFE

promise to keep them as a lasting memento of our visit, if we but leave and promise to return no more. In that case, what are we to do? Punch has us caricatured landing an army of missionaries under our guns, armed with a Bible in one hand and a revolver in the other; but as a gentleman remarked with whom I was talking, "he could find no place in the Bible where we were told to do evil that good might come." Still, there is no doubt a party in our country—of fanatics—who would have us enter in the cause as defenders of the faith, and convert the Japanese to Christianity, whether or no! Japan cannot be conquered in a day, neither can they be converted in one generation; but as the car of civilization is now coursing the globe, Japan may ere long fall into line and traces! I am a strong advocate for the purpose of the expedition, and believe if properly conducted it will be the beginning of intercourse with that people and lead in time to their civilization; but of course this will take time and cannot be done in a day, as our go-ahead Yankee nation would have it! If Commodore Perry acts prudently,—and as I believe he is instructed to do by our Government,— he will not fire a gun to their annoyance; but after making every exertion of a peaceful nature to induce them to accede to our proposals, if they still hold out and refuse intercourse with us, he will leave their coasts without warlike demonstration. I venture to assert that in a very few years we will be thrown with them again, having just cause for peace or war, for the seas washing their territories is the main thoroughfare of our vessels from China to our Western Coast, which trade is increasing yearly as California becomes more settled. In a year or two we will have steamers sailing in sight of their coast, which has heretofore only been visited by distressed whalers. It is therefore next to an impossibility for her to remain alienated with civilization steaming along her shores. Should our principle of non-intervention, which we claim to hold so dear, be carried out, we may hope to leave Japan this coming fall; otherwise, should we blockade their coasts, we may be detained here longer. We therefore look with much anxiety for the arrival of the *Mississippi*, Commodore Perry's flag-ship. The last mail brought us news of her having sailed from Norfolk on the twenty-fourth of November, so that we may reasonably look for her by the first of April. We also had news of the *Powhatan* breaking some part of her machinery, which may delay her a couple of months longer. I am of opinion that the commodore having left, she will not follow; but it is likely the Department will have instructions awaiting him here, to proceed to Japan with what force he has. The season suiting admirably, we can be there in ten days after leaving this port and be through with our part of the performance by fall. We will no doubt leave a part of the squadron on their coast to carry out some surveys. We have been

82 RECOLLECTIONS OF A NAVAL LIFE

saluting, in company with the other national ships in the harbor, in honor of the day, and to-night our consul gives a large ball. I shall not be able to attend, however, having the mid-watch to keep. Have just heard that we are to leave at daylight for Whampoa. The captain has just received orders from the commodore, who is in Canton on a visit previous to taking his departure for home. His health has so much improved he has determined to go overland. We will only be in Whampoa a week at farthest, but return with the commodore in time for the next mail, he having engaged his berth on board that steamer. I am so glad of all the good news your letter gives me of home, specially that B. is pleased with his work and has Daddy Jim with him. I indulged in a hearty laugh on reading his directions that a pair of "dove-colored pants" be sent the dear old darkey. My letter has grown to great length, so I must close. With a great deal of love to all at home, I am your affectionate son,

JOHN M. KELL.

We first anchored in the beautiful and land-locked harbor of Simodi, which has since been totally destroyed by an earthquake. We here received many of the high officials of Japan. We entertained them with great hospitality and distinction, to impress them favorably with our presence as visitors in Japan. We got permission to land our field pieces and also our marine forces and sailors. They were allowed to drill in their temple grounds and made a very handsome display, and were viewed with great interest by the natives. These people impressed us with their great superiority to the Chinese. They were in every way more congenial in manner and more generous in disposition. The dressing of the hair was the reverse of the Chinese. Instead of wearing the queue, they shaved the crown of the head and brought up the hair to the top to cover it, tying it in a little knot on top. The women paid great attention to the dressing of their hair and succeeded admirably in its adornment.

Before proceeding further in narrations of our visit to Japan I will state what I had forgotten to do before this. We had with us on board ship half a dozen Japanese sailors. They had been picked up floating on a wreck of one of their unseaworthy coasting vessels in the Pacific Ocean

RECOLLECTIONS OF A NAVAL LIFE

and carried to the United States by an American whaleship. The Government took charge of them and placed them on board one of the ships of Commodore Perry's Expedition, to be returned to their own country. This act of the Government was propitiatory, but I very much doubt if it was received in the spirit in which it was meant, for one of their laws for cutting off communication with the outside world, and one strictly enforced, was that any Japanese who left his country under any circumstances was not allowed to return under punishment of death. These poor fellows were no doubt exempted from this law and had their lives saved by being protégés of the United States Government. This law of forty years or more ago must long ago have become obsolete. There was no demonstration made over their return, and we never heard further of their welfare. While on board they gave us a practical demonstration of applying the "moxa." A stalwart Japanese was suffering great pain. He stripped himself to the waist and with face downward on the deck one of his companions applied the "moxa" in little cones and set fire to it at the top, on either side of the spine a few inches apart. It gradually burned out, and either was not very painful or the Japanese had wonderful powers of endurance, as he did not seem to move a muscle. After the operation he got up. apparently much relieved, and quite himself again.

Commodore Perry had taken out with him one of the finest bands of music that ever sailed with a squadron, in fact a perfect band. He gave orders that they should play national airs and martial music to impress the Japanese with that style of melody. They were also taken around the decks and shown the large guns. They looked as little surprised as though they were perfectly familiar with their construction and working of the guns. They were then taken to our engine room, thinking that the beautiful machinery of our magnificent engines would elicit some expression of admiration. They looked at all

84   RECOLLECTIONS OF A NAVAL LIFE

we had to display with interest, but showed no astonishment at anything. In other words, they showed every trait of gentility and culture and impressed us with admiration at their stoicism. After remaining a week or more in the harbor of Simodi the squadron got*under way and we steamed around the Bay of Jeddo. There being no accurate charts of this bay known to the civilized world at that time, we had to keep a boat (one of our cutters) ahead of us, taking soundings as we steamed along, for safe guidance. Finding plenty of water, we made good progress until our boat was discovered, when quite a fleet of native boats loaded with soldiers bearing lances and other weapons were seen to pull immediately across the bow of our boat to stop our progress. The officer in command ordered the men to take up their muskets to defend themselves. The Japanese presented their pikes, but the official or dignitary in command of their fleet of boats waved his fan as a signal for us to come no nearer, and requested an interview to make explanation. He stated that he was sent by his government to stop our further progress up the bay. He begged that this request be made known to our commanding officer, for while we had it in our power to proceed, it would result in his being compelled to commit the "hari-kari," which meant to take his own life by falling on his sword and disemboweling himself! This was a law which had to go into effect for not executing the orders of a superior officer. A cruel law, indeed, of so peaceful and refined a people! Our officer in command at once granted his request. He returned on board ship and reported the same to the commodore. We came to anchor with the squadron and the commodore sent a communication to the Mikado, the official head of the Empire, informing him that he was empowered as Minister Extraordinary to treat with his government, and desired that a day be fixed for presenting his credentials. The officers were much relieved at not having to pass through the painful ordeal of sacrificing themselves, and left with these

RECOLLECTIONS OF A NAVAL LIFE 85

dispatches. At this anchorage we were daily visited by officials from the shore. We received them cordially, and they were usually entertained by Captain Buchanan and Captain Lee, who in true American style would dispense to them during their visit a whiskey toddy. The Japanese would enjoy what they called "Mellican wine," and not knowing its effects would sometimes take more than they could carry comfortably and become very jolly, and a jolly Jap is something worth seeing! The commodore, while he would encourage these visits from the high officials, would never allow himself to be seen. He would have them invited into his cabin, but retire into his stateroom, and there unseen greatly enjoy the interviews between his officers and the Japanese. The conversations were interpreted through the German Secretary. The days now passed with very little satisfaction to the commodore, who was waiting (not very patiently) for the Mikado to appoint a day for his reception. Not receiving such notice as he thought in due time, he sent a communication to inform the authorities "if the time was not appointed within ten days he would land his forces and present his credentials in person at the city of Jeddo." This threat seemed to arouse the tardy Mikado, for he saw our commodore "meant business." The Mikado forthwith ordered the erection of a house in a pleasant location higher up the bay, and within the limited ten days the commodore was notified that an officer of equal rank with himself would receive him at this point. The next day the squadron got under way and steamed up to this anchorage, where we saw the new building. Coming to anchor (as our squadron did) in line of battle, presenting our starboard broadside to the shore, with springs on our cables to cover the landing of our forces, and in case of treachery that our batteries might play upon the enemy, we presented a formidable array. All boats were now lowered and preparation made for landing the forces, the commodore and his staff (of which I had the honor of

86 RECOLLECTIONS OF A NAVAL LIFE

being a member) bringing up the rear. The boats pulled up in column to the shore. As the forces were landed the boats would drop out to the right and left of the landing. The marines forming on the right and the blue jackets on the left, presented an unbroken line from the shore to the building, keeping the Japanese out of that space. The commodore then landed, presenting a fine appearance, being a large and fine-looking man, in new full-dress uniform, accompanied by his staff. Following this a striking feature in this body were three stalwart negroes, neatly dressed in their muster suits, armed cap-a-pie, and carrying in rosewood boxes the credentials of the Minister Extraordinary. This was an imposing spectacle, and the American flag waved for the first time on the soil of Japan in the history of that nation. Each company carried a handsome new flag of the American Union. Thousands of Japanese witnessed this spectacle and observed the strictest order and decorum, while a few of the highest in rank were permitted to approach and witness the ceremonies. The Japanese flags decorated the building and many were carried by the standard-bearers of these officials. As the commodore and his staff drew near to the entrance of the building he was met by the officer of the Japanese Government and his suite, making the salaams of their country, after which we were conducted into the building; the Japanese were seated on one side and the Americans on the other. The interpreter (Japanese) took his position between the two, down on his knees, not daring to look at either party, but merely repeating the communications as an automaton or a machine might have done. Our grand old commodore, with his imposing presence and gigantic stature, delivered with great dignity and solemnity the credentials empowering him to treat with the Japanese nation, doing honor to his country by his impressive bearing, both martial and soldierly. After this formality was gone through with some attempt at pleasant intercourse was passed between the two parties, and this

RECOLLECTIONS OF A NAVAL LIFE

great occasion, which proved the wedge that opened Japan to the civilized world, was brought to a close. The commodore and his staff withdrew from the reception and returned on board ship in the same order with which we had landed. Nothing occurred to mar the very imposing ceremonies in behalf of our country. The fleet got under way and dropped down the bay to our former anchorage, which was better suited for operating our railroad and the telegraph wires brought out by the commodore to display to these secluded people the vast improvements of the age.

In a few days we had in operation the little locomotive and miniature cars. For these we had laid the track in a circle, and it was about a mile in circumference. The Japanese displayed great interest in this steam locomotion on dry land. Some of the more daring ventured to ride on the outside, the cars being too small to admit of their riding inside. What seemed to surprise them more even than this was sending messages by telegraph and receiving answers in reply. They stationed their own officers and interpreters at each end of the line, so had no reason to think we were playing upon their credulity. They greatly enjoyed the display of these inventions, and the purpose we had in view seemed fully accomplished. We felt fully rewarded by their interest and pleasure.

While at this anchorage our chaplain, a man of most inquiring turn of mind, and most persistent in carrying out a purpose, wandered off without the knowledge of the captain, some distance in the interior. The first information received of him on board ship was a communication which described him so accurately both as to person and dress as to be unmistakable, and a request that he be "ordered back to the ship." The bearer, of course, took in return an order, signed by the commanding officer, that he "return at once to the ship." Our poor chaplain came on board quite chagrined. It really was quite contrary to orders for our officers or men to go into the interior (but chaplains have privileges). All officers and men were

88   RECOLLECTIONS OF A NAVAL LIFE

always kindly treated by this courteous, gentle-mannered people. The commodore, having accomplished the object of his visit, departed with a part of his squadron for Hong Kong. Upon our arrival there.we met Captain Ringgold with his surveying and exploring expedition to the North Pacific and the China Seas, of which coast very little was then known, no accurate surveys having been made up to that time. Captain Ringgold's health having failed during this arduous work, Commodore Perry relieved him of his command and sent him home as an invalid. Captain John Rodgers succeeded him to the command. The expedition consisted of five vessels—the Sloop of War *Vincennes*, Steamer *John Hancock*, Brig *Porpoise*, Schooner *J. Fennimore Cooper*, and Store Ship *John P. Kenedy*. After reorganizing this surveying expedition, Commodore Perry began his own preparation for returning home overland, making such transfers of officers as were necessary. His flagship, the *Mississippi*, he ordered to proceed to Japan, and at the same time the surveying and exploring expedition to continue on its survey in that direction. Here I met a young Georgian, Burleigh Baber, a passed midshipman on the Brig *Porpoise*. As he could not hope to reach Georgia as soon as I, at his request I took from him his likeness and letters to bring home to his mother and sisters. His mother was the widow of one of Georgia's most distinguished physicians. I little dreamed in so doing I would bear her the last tidings she would ever have of her son. We sailed out of Hong Kong harbor together, he in the *Porpoise* and I in the *Mississippi*. As we passed out of the.Lymoon passage we encountered a heavy gale of wind. The *Mississippi* had her steampower headed to the northward and eastward (on her way to Japan), from which the heaviest of the gale came, while the *Porpoise* parted from us standing to the southward and eastward in the direction of the island of Formosa. This was the last ever seen of the *Porpoise*. Many were the hopes that lingered long with the friends and families of those on the ill-fated brig. There seemed a bare possibility that some of her crew might have been picked up by the savages in the Pacific islands. But nothing has ever been heard, or ever will be "till the sea gives up her dead." The news of her loss reached the United States before we did, and soon after my arrival at home I delivered in person my charge to his widowed mother, who in sadness and sorrow received them, though not at that time with all hope dead in her heart. I realized what he had been, "the only son of his mother, and she a widow!"

Chapter XIII

AMONG the transfers of officers at Hong Kong I think I have failed to mention that I was made master of the *Mississippi*. After riding out a heavy gale we proceeded on our course to Japan, arriving in the Bay of Jeddo in the month of February. We found there a part of our squadron and the coal ship, from which we supplied ourselves with coals for our long passage across the Pacific Ocean. We met some of our old friends among the natives, and laid in a large supply of fresh stores and provisions. The Bay of Jeddo (or, as there called, Yedo) is a most magnificent one. The precipitous coast of Sagami rises to the left, while far inland are lofty mountains covered with snow, the high peak of Fusi-Yama most conspicuous of all. Pretty little villages and towns stud the margins of the shore, forming a beautiful, restful landscape for the eye of the seaman to dwell upon. The coast of Awa, some ten or twelve miles distant, gave the lovely twilight haze that softens all it rests upon, and gave to Nature even in its wintry aspect a look of cheerful repose. The Japanese were at that time (I do not know what intercourse with the outside world may have done for them) a contented, social people, very dignified in demeanor, never seemed to act impulsively, but always with mildness and decorum. The opening of the spring there seems to inspire the latent poetry of their nature, and it is not unusual, as our interpreters informed us, to hear them greet each other in flowery language, such as this, to express their kindly New Year's greeting: "May your felicity be as broad as the eastern sea and your age as enduring as the southern hills;" "May joys clamber over your blest abode and a thousand lucks pass through your gate." But we must

RECOLLECTIONS OF A NAVAL LIFE

set sail ere long, and after taking leave of our friends and brother officers begin our long and circuitous voyage, "homeward bound."

At the call of the boatswain, "All hands up anchor for home," only the mariner can understand and appreciate the thrill of joy after an absence of years among a strange and foreign people. We were now steering eastward, as we had been since leaving our native shores. Our cruise was to "circumnavigate the globe." All was bright and beautiful as we bade adieu to Japan, the last thing in sight being its snow-capped mountain, which had also been the first point to welcome us as we approached its unknown shores. We had sailed with pleasant weather attending us till the seventh day out, when the skies became overcast and the clouds scudding with a falling barometer gave every indication of an approaching storm. Fortunately for us, our good ship, the *Mississippi*, was lightened by the consumption of seven days' coal when we encountered a most terrific typhoon. This region of the world is subject to such storms, which are circular and progressive. The stanch ship labored heavily, and the seas swept over our decks, tearing away from the davits our metallic lifeboat, which we could see floating away from us like a cork in our wake as far as the eye could reach. Another sea struck us on our bow, tearing away our pivot gun and completely upsetting it. By the prompt action of our daring seamen it was secured and lashed in time to save it from being lost overboard. This state of affairs presented a very alarming sight to one not accustomed to the fury of the winds and waves, but our grand old ship rode out the storm magnificently. Her engines worked so perfectly that there really was no cause for anxiety or alarm, with our hatches battened down to keep the water from going below, and life lines stretched across the decks to which our men could hold and keep themselves from being swept overboard. We rode out the storm in safety with no loss of life. The following day the storm had abated

92 RECOLLECTIONS OF A NAVAL LIFE

and we pursued our way to the Sandwich Islands and the harbor of Hawaii. The changes that had taken place since my last visit to these islands in the Frigate *Savannah*, almost ten years before, were really marvelous. Now in the place of a native village had grown up a town, quite American in aspect, with American inhabitants predominating largely. One could imagine himself in a "down East" town. The *genus homo* of the true "Brother Jonathan" is unmistakable and pronounced wherever he is met with in the world, and the Yankee whaler can never be imitated by other nations without danger of counterfeit, he being entirely original. We remained in port long enough to recuperate and enjoy the delightful fruits and vegetables of this tropical climate. We next set sail for the harbor of San Francisco.

On arriving here there awaited me still greater surprise in the more wonderful changes of this magical city and its surroundings. Ten years had elapsed since my service here in the Mexican War. Then there were but a few wooden structures, where now stood magnificent edifices, fine wharves, beautiful and commodious dwellings with elaborately decorated grounds surrounding them, and gardens filled with luxuriant shrubbery and rare flowers— in fact, a city of magical and wonderful growth. We met here many friends and acquaintances of both naval and civil life. Captain Farragut was here, with no dream of the future honors that awaited him as a successful officer on the winning side in the war between the States a few years later. Richard Cuyler, too, was in "Frisco." They were both much interested in land speculations in that new and growing country. We remained in San Francisco two or three weeks, enjoying great hospitality and pleasant intercourse with congenial friends, and next steamed out of the "Golden Gate" for Valparaiso on our homeward journey. This was quite a long stretch at sea, passing through the temperate and tropic zones without a storm of any kind to cause us anxiety. Arriving at

RECOLLECTIONS OF A NAVAL LIFE

Valparaiso we refreshed our crew with the luxuries of port before starting on the boisterous voyage around Cape Horn. We spent a few days only in Valparaiso, when getting under way we sailed in a southerly direction for Cape Horn. As we approached the Cape Captain Lee determined to go through the Straits of Magellan. The weather was thick and raining violently, so that we were kept anxiously looking for a headland which marks the entrance to the Strait. To our great relief we sighted this desired object, and steered boldly for the shore. Upon entering this rugged passage we suddenly found calm waters, and to the great relief of our entire ship's company we came to anchor that night in a quiet nook and enjoyed for the first time since leaving Valparaiso comfort, rest and sleep.

The next morning at daylight we were under way, steaming through this ice-bound passage with a heavy snowstorm falling. In the midst of the storm we sighted a little canoe pulling off to us. In the canoe was a Patagonian Indian with his squaw, who had her baby lashed to her back without a covering on its head, apparently regardless of the weather. They begged us for something to eat. We loaded them down with "hard tack" and fat meat, which was a fortune to them, and they took leave of us with grateful hearts. We steamed through the Straits the entire day, passing in sight of the penal colony of Chile, and that night anchored again at the eastern entrance of the Straits. The land here presented a flat and low appearance, whereas the western entrance was mountainous and rugged. The following morning we steamed into the broad Atlantic, rejoicing that we were again on the ocean that washed our own shores, and shaped our course northward for the harbor of Rio Janeiro. As we cleared this ice-bound region and approached the tropics we rejoiced in the sunshine, thoroughly airing and ventilating our bedding, wearing apparel, etc. After a pleasant run of about two weeks we entered the famed

94   RECOLLECTIONS OF A NAVAL LIFE

and beautiful harbor of Rio. Familiar scenes greeted us on every side, and we were delighted to find the city healthy and free from the fever scourge, so common a visitant there. Of course we here enjoyed all the fruits and vegetables of this generous soil and climate, and after recuperating we again weighed anchor, for the last time, on our homeward-bound voyage. In the ordinary voyage from Rio to New York, taking the southeast trade winds, we ran to the tropics, and after passing the equator through calms and rain squalls, we entered the region of the brisk northeast trade winds and made a splendid run; reaching the port of New York in April, 1855.

Laying up our good ship alongside the Brooklyn Navy Yard, we bade farewell to friends with whom we had passed through many scenes of pleasure and encountered many trials and dangers, never to be forgotten, in our association for years in foreign lands. Commodore Perry's voluminous and very interesting books upon the Japanese Expedition do not seem to have the historical value they should and do possess, by being found in all public libraries. I regret to say my copy was lost among many other valuables in the fortunes of war. Not only were the note books and journal of the gifted Bayard Taylor, author and poet, made use of by the commodore, but my beloved friend Dr. Charles Frederick Fahs, of the Navy, was a valuable contributor to the same. Being a very scientific man and an enthusiastic botanist, the flora and fauna of those distant lands gave him great delight, and his willing mind was one ever searching for hidden treasure in the wells of knowledge; yet so childlike was his faith (like the great Maury's) that it was beautiful to see how his worshiping soul could look adoringly through Nature up to Nature's God. To the end of his useful and noble life he was never beguiled by the follies of science, but "retained God in his knowledge," and in that knowledge saw the light of revealed truth and the blessed hope of immortality!

Chapter XIV

Early in May, 1855, we turned our faces homeward with a three-months' leave of absence in our pockets. I found family and friends moving from rice plantations to their summer places on the salt water. At this season there is no indulgence of hunting, but boating, fishing, and picnicking was the order of the day for amusement. Among my friends, living about six miles distant, was George Dent, a son of Commodore Dent. He professed to be a rice planter, but thereby was a fine mechanic spoiled (for his genius was in that direction). George had been spending his many leisure hours building a little steamer for use and pleasure on the river inlets and sound in his neighborhood, he living then at Baisden's Bluff. On the completion of the boat he invited me to attend the ceremony of launching it, which occasion was to be a merrymaking to his friends and neighbors. The launch proved quite a success, and she rode the waters gracefully. The gratification of the builder and owner was an enjoyment to his friends as well as himself. The following day Dent proposed taking me to Sapelo Island on a visit, he acting as engineer, with a negro man to assist him, I as helmsman to steer the little craft. We made excellent time, our navigation being all on salt water, and we reached the island before sunset. We anchored in Sapelo Sound, and shortly after my cousin, Randolph Spalding, came pulling out of the mouth of the creek to us in one of his fine race boats. He invited us ashore for the night. We declined, as we were "yachting," and insisted that he should spend the night with us. He vowed that our "craft could not hold him for a longer time than a social call, as he knew Dent's boat was bound to blow up." The next day's ex-

96 RECOLLECTIONS OF A NAVAL LIFE

perience came near proving Randolph's assertion a prophecy. We decided on a trip up to the city of Darien the following day. At first all went well with our little steamer; but as we were passing from the salt water into the fresh the boiler commenced foaming to such a degree as to cause us great alarm. It threw water from every conceivable egress, covering the deck and us. This steam and vapor bath we did not relish much. While we felt courageous enough to die for duty, we did not want to sacrifice our lives simply for pleasure. I changed the course of the steamer for the nearest shore, but before reaching that point the violent ebullition began to subside, and I realized that it was only the change in the water, at which we were greatly relieved, and continued our delightful little cruise, visiting our friends on the sea islands in their summer homes.

In June of this year I made a visit to the city of Macon. On this visit I met for the first time my future wife. Beautiful city of Macon, within your suburbs I found love and happiness in the long years gone by! And now the life within me thrills when I breathe your flower-laden air, and the memories of the past sweep over me with loving benediction!

In October I made a second visit to Macon, and accompanied my relatives, the Reeses, to the village of Roswell to attend the marriage of Miss Rees to Rev. F. R. Golding, a Presbyterian divine, and the author of the "Young Marooners," "The Woodruff Stories," etc., books now known in every land, and translated into several tongues. Returning from this marriage I spent a few very happy days in Macon. "Leaves of absence" will draw to a close, and early in December I received orders to join the Coast Survey Schooner *Arago*, then lying at the Pensacola Navy Yard. Leaving home on these orders, I spent a few hours in Macon, passed through Milledgeville and attended the Governor's reception, my sister, Mrs. Charles Spalding, being there at the time with her husband, Colonel Spald-

RECOLLECTIONS OF A NAVAL LIFE 97

ing being a member of the Legislature. I joined the *Arago* and we proceeded to Galveston, Texas, which port we reached the middle of December, and at once entered on our work, the survey of the coast to the southward of that port. I, with the junior lieutenant, James H. Gillis, (now Commodore Gillis, of the United States Navy), was stationed with a theodolite on shore for angling on the schooner in charge of Captain De Haven and the junior officers, they running lines of soundings. This work was very exacting, being obliged to angle from sunrise to sunset, every eight minutes in the day. This kept Gillis and I quite busy, we being stationed nine miles apart. We were relieved from this hard work, though, by the frequent northers occurring at this season of the year, which would blow the little schooner out of sight for days at a time. Then would come our season of sport and enjoyment in hunting and fishing.

Upon one of these occasions Gillis rode up to the house I was occupying, it being the plantation home of ex-Governor Winston, of Alabama, and to which the family came in summer to enjoy the breezes and bathing in the Gulf. Upon the top of this house I had erected a comfortable observatory, from which I could see for miles across the prairie in the rear. Having noticed this morning a fine buck feeding on the prairie, I suggested to Gillis our trying to secure him for rations, which in the absence of the schooner were becoming short. Gillis gladly seconded this plan, and having a pointer dog for which he had paid forty dollars in Philadelphia, we expected rare sport. Gillis had tried the dog for birds, but at the first fire he made tracks for home. We thought failing to be a bird dog he might prove a deer dog. Taking our sailor man Bloomer, who waited on me, to the observatory and pointing out the deer, I instructed him to tie the dog and carry him around the deer, then setting the dog on and whooping wildly to drive the deer in our direction toward the Gulf. The sailor obeyed implicitly, and the dog per-

7

98 RECOLLECTIONS OF A NAVAL LIFE

formed his work like a well-trained hound, opening a loud
bark at every jump of the deer and bringing him on to us
in fine style. Gillis was armed with a double-barrelled
shotgun, loaded with buckshot. I had a long rifle in
which I put eight buckshot. Knowing that Gillis was
better armed than I, and a good shot, I placed him in
advance in a little clump of bushes and pointed out to him
where the deer would probably run. I charged him not
to fire till the deer reached a certain point, while I took
my stand in his rear. Gillis had never killed a deer and
I really wanted to give him the opportunity, but the noble
animal came on so beautifully that I covered him with my
rifle before he reached the point at which I had directed
Gillis to fire, and to pull my trigger was irresistible. To
my delight, but to Gillis's cruel disappointment, the buck
tumbled over. Gillis was chagrined beyond expression,
and turning to me said in a deplorable way, "Kell, how
could you treat me so?" Of course, I was ashamed, and
my only excuse was that "we were very short of rations,"
and I had such a dead shot on him I had to shoot;
but I do not think Gillis ever quite forgave me. We sent
for Gillis's old horse, and throwing the deer across we
took him to the house, and that day enjoyed fine venison
steaks for dinner, which I hoped would somewhat soothe
the hunter's ire. That was the only opportunity Gillis
and I ever had to shoot a deer while in Texas, and even at
this late day I would be pleased to know if Gillis ever shot
a deer, for he was a most enthusiastic Nimrod, and withal
an excellent shot.

Our little station, the mouth of the Brazos River, which
then had only the summer home of Governor Winston to
distinguish it, has at this writing grown into a city of considerable trade and importance, bearing the name of
Brazos City, this change no doubt having been brought
about by the Eads jetty system in deepening the entrance
to this magnificent stream. Previous to this hunt I had
enjoyed with Mr. Brown, a Georgian, but then a resident

RECOLLECTIONS OF A NAVAL LIFE

of Quintana, Texas, a very exciting chase with his greyhounds, five in number. As the chase of the greyhound is exclusively by sight, the hunt is usually participated in after the burning off of the prairies for the benefit of the stock that feed upon these prairies. Being well mounted, the hounds followed us apparently conscious of the sport that awaited them, and gladly anticipating it. One of the dogs, named "Queen," a graceful, handsome creature, was the favorite of her master, and she seemed to understand his every movement. After a few miles' ride we sighted a noble buck and approached him from the leeward, so as to avoid his scenting us. When within a few hundred yards of the noble animal Mr. Brown beckoned to Queen; she readily obeyed, and coming to his horse's side leaped up on the pommel of his saddle to obtain a distant view, when Mr. Brown pointing in the direction of the deer, she at once took in the object, sprang to the ground and was off like a flash; leading the pack of dogs, she gave chase in the direction of the game. The buck bounded to his feet, making playful leaps as if gamboling for his own amusement. The dogs became very much excited at his appearance and commenced their earnest work of the chase, when their near approach put the buck to his best speed, and off they flew across the prairie. We put spurs to our horses and at first attempted to keep up with them. We soon found, however, that the dogs could outrun us on a long chase, so reining in our horses to enjoy the sport, we watched with intense interest their race until a slight elevation carried them out of sight. The last we saw of the deer the dogs were almost up with him, and we quietly waited to see what the result would be. In about an hour they came back to us, showing evidence of having caught the deer, their jaws reeking with blood. We failed to secure the game, but enjoyed the sport. This was the first time I ever witnessed the sport of "coursing with greyhounds." Their speed was something remarkable. The fishing there was also very successful and abundant.

100 RECOLLECTIONS OF A NAVAL LIFE

We could at any time catch quantities of red fish or snappers, which added to our larder and comfort as well as our sport. Cedar Lake, near which we were stationed, was only a little distance from the village of Quintana, and was in consequence quite a resort for picnics and pleasure parties, and I was often subject to surprises by calls from ladies and gentlemen, horseback riding being a great diversion in those days, and they always insisted on my joining them in their pleasant pastime when not strictly "on duty." Taking it all in all our situation, however, was often lonely and monotonous, the schooner sometimes drifting from us and leaving Gillis and I miles apart, with only a sailor man to wait upon us. After I left my eight-by-ten shanty and moved some thirty miles or more and took up quarters in Governor Winston's unoccupied house I used sometimes to have company. Governor Winston and his brother came to see after the planting of a summer garden and spent a couple of weeks with me. They were very pleasant gentlemen and I did enjoy their company. About this time, or a little later, I had quite a sick turn with chills and fever, and by the doctor's advice went on board the schooner that he might look after my health. I went in the schooner to the city of Galveston, where she was going for supplies. I soon recovered. While in Galveston I made the acquaintance of the Menard family. Mrs. Menard, formerly of the city of Macon (like myself, a Georgian), was a leader in society here and had a charming young daughter, for whose pleasure a large masquerade ball was given, which Dr. Martin (of the ship) and I attended. Not being in time to procure fancy costumes, we had that of monks prepared, and being exactly alike in dress and very similar in size, we had a merry time in confusing our partners in the dance by occasional exchange. I think there are scenes that stand out in relief, as it were, in one's memory,

RECOLLECTIONS OF A NAVAL LIFE

and this evening of merriment I have often looked back upon with pleasure.

Dr. Martin was quite a naturalist in his tastes. He took great interest in collecting insects, birds, reptiles, etc., and he also interested his messmates in this subject and we were pleased to contribute to his collection, especially we who had a good opportunity on shore. One day I caught a rare snake of very brilliant coloring, and knowing what a treasure he would be to the doctor, I pinioned him to the ground till I could go to the house and get a wide-mouthed pickle jar in which to imprison him. When I returned I dexterously induced his snakeship to enter the bottle, where he coiled himself, whereupon I placed the cork very securely, as I thought, leaving a small airhole through which he could breathe. I then placed him in all confidence on my table, quite an ornament in the eyes of a naturalist. The next morning to my dismay the bottle was empty! I supposed, or very naturally hoped, he had made his escape through the door of my cabin, for it was not very agreeable to think he was occupying my quarters with me. I tried to banish the thought of him from my mind, yet I found myself looking for him all the while when not busily engaged otherwise. The next evening I was seated at the table writing when to my amazement and horror I heard a rustling noise in the rafters above my head and the next moment down came the snake on my paper! It took me a very short time (though I was quite nervous) to decapitate him, and that was the last time I attempted to capture a snake for the doctor's valuable collection. Not being very successful with these wily reptiles, in future I assisted the doctor in getting some living creatures less venomous but even more curious. I think our next capture was a couple or more of the horned frogs of Texas.

The constant observations being very injurious to sight, and the advanced summer season, made it necessary for

102   RECOLLECTIONS OF A NAVAL LIFE

us to abandon our survey. My eyes were so affected that they had to be bandaged to avoid the light. Captain De Haven suffered extremely in the same way. On the first day of June we sailed for Philadelphia. After a smooth and delightful voyage we arrived at the Navy Yard and hauled our little schooner alongside the dock. Captain De Haven went to his home in the city. Mr. Gillis's young and charming wife was awaiting him at the hotel, where he joined her. Dr. Martin and Midshipman Livingstone left for their homes, and I remained in the city to bring up the survey with the captain. This work occupied us for three months.

In Philadelphia I met my cousin, James McQueen McIntosh, stationed at the rendezvous there, preparatory to service in the distant West, he being an officer in the United States Army and a graduate of West Point several years previous to this time. His father, Col. James Simmons McIntosh, was a gallant and distinguished officer in the Army and lost his life for his country in the Mexican War. James was very enthusiastic in the profession he had chosen, and loved it by right of inheritance, as it were, and was "every inch a soldier." We had many happy hours together and many delightful drives and rambles in the beautiful Wissahickon Valley and other surroundings of the city of "Brotherly Love," our own hearts drawn to each other by ties of blood and clanship in the distance of the past. James afterward married a Virginia lady, and at the breaking out of the war between the States resigned from the United States Army and tendered his services to the Confederacy. He lost his noble life at the battle of Pea Ridge, having risen to the rank of brigadier-general, and was second in command to General McCullough. They were killed within a few minutes of each other, and surely no more heroic blood was shed as a libation to the sacred "lost cause" her sons so dearly cherish! This was one of the many sad incidents in the late Civil

War in which brother fought against brother, for James's brother, John Baillie McIntosh, was a gallant soldier in the Federal service and lost a leg in the battle of Opequan, Virginia. For his bravery he was promoted to the rank of Major-General, and lived for many years after the war ended to enjoy the honors and distinctions conferred by the winning side of his grateful country.

Chapter XV

In October, 1856, I procured a leave of absence and came to Macon, Georgia, to be married to Miss Julia Blanche Munroe, which happy event took place on the fifteenth day of the month, in Christ's Church, Macon, my relative, Rev. Henry K. Rees, officiating. Having been entitled by previous long-continued sea service to a generous leave of absence, we entered upon a winter of great gaiety and enjoyment. After a few days of pleasure in Macon, made bright by receptions and parties, we visited my home on the seaboard and were entertained by my relatives and friends in the hospitable manner known to that period and section. Elegant dinner parties, dances in the evenings, a regatta given in our honor by Hon. Thomas Forman, of Broughton Island, and a ten days' entertainment of seventy guests at the home of Randolph Spalding on Sapelo Island. Such an entertainment savored of baronial times. The spacious rooms in the grand old Tabby house were occupied by the ladies, while the gentlemen were quartered in tents under the grand old live oak trees which surrounded the house. A beautiful Indian summer, "autumn's carnival," reigned supreme. Amusements of all kinds during the day—driving, riding, with walks on the beach, and deer hunting for the gentlemen who liked the chase. The evenings were given up to dancing, with a fine band of musicians from Savannah to furnish the music. The sumptuous table, supplied with all the good things of land and sea, was set at any and all hours—a perpetual feast.

The regatta to which I alluded was a typical scene of sport entered into by the rice planters of Georgia. The four boats in the race were famous for their speed, and

RECOLLECTIONS OF A NAVAL LIFE

were owned by Mr. James Hamilton Couper, Mr. Forman, Dr. Brailsford Troup, and my relative, Randolph Spalding. There was assembled on this occasion all the élite of the coast—the beautiful daughters of Hon. T. Butler King, the Misses Troup, the Misses Hazelhurst, the charming daughters of Hugh Grant, Esq.—all belles and beauties—and indeed all the families that made the seaboard society so delightful. One peculiar feature attending this boat race gave rise to a very appropriate anecdote which I related upon my first visit after the war to the North in the year 1868 or '69 to a party of gentlemen in New York, in the law office of my cousin, Hon. John E. Ward, and his partners, Mr. Whitehead and Mr. Jones. Mr. Jones was a Georgian, but Mr. Whitehead a Northerner and a leader in the Republican party. One of the gentlemen asked me "how affairs were progressing under reconstruction rule in Georgia?" I replied that "the bottom rail was on top now," and I could illustrate it by telling them an incident of the class that were now prominent in the Legislature of the State. I then told them of the regatta that had taken place a few years before, when the negroes were in the rice fields at work when the race was going on. Upon hearing the loud cheering and hurrahing of Mr. Forman, who always became very much excited during a regatta, one negro remarked to the other, "Dar, now, Massa boat beat, Massa boat beat!" "How you know Massa boat beat?" inquired the second darkey. "Cause," said the first, "don't you heah Massa holler?" "Yes, but don't you know Massa holler beat or no beat?" "That is the element now ahead in Georgia helping to make the laws in my native State."

But I digress, and my thoughts have wandered from the happy time when there was no dream of war or future trouble of any kind; when we thought ourselves living under the happiest government the world had ever seen! In the spring of 1857 I received orders to proceed to Norfolk, Virginia, on board the Receiving Ship *Pennsylvania*,

106 RECOLLECTIONS OF A NAVAL LIFE

which duty was not very arduous, allowing me two days on board ship on duty and two days on shore. This being a famous naval station, I met many old friends, who welcomed me with my bride with true Virginia hospitality. My friends vied with each other in paying us many attentions. Jack Cooper and his estimable wife gave us a charming reception at his house, where the whole Navy society of Norfolk were invited to meet us. The United States Surveying Steamer *Hetzel* came into Norfolk having on board my old friends R. D. Minor, Dr. Fahs and Bayard Hand, of Georgia. They insisted upon giving, in honor of my bride, a party or ball on board the *Hetzel*. This was a very brilliant affair. The decks were cleared for dancing and decorated in true man-of-war style, being enclosed with flags of different nations and brilliantly lighted with chandeliers constructed from bayonets, etc., which was all meant to be a very impressive welcome to a sailor's bride. Here were assembled many of the old Navy families—the Whittles, the Sinclairs, the Carters, the Pegrams, the Spotswoods, and others. Norfolk was for many months a delightful abiding place for us.

In the fall of this year I received orders to the United States Store Ship *Supply*, making in her two trips to Brazil with stores to the South American Squadron. The *Supply* was commanded by Captain Gray, a very nice gentleman, but having a few peculiarities that are common to elderly bachelors, though withal a very genial, pleasant companion. Aaron K. Hughes was first lieutenant; I, second lieutenant, and James H. Gillis, my old companion of the Coast Survey, third lieutenant. Dr. Horwitz, the surgeon, was a very clever gentleman, and to him I became much attached during our intimacy on board ship. The voyage was one quite devoid of interest or incident, carrying salt beef and pork, hard tack, and other rations that make up a sailor's menu, for the Brazil Squadron. Brazil (as I think I have mentioned before) was in that day a fine country, whose emperor had at heart the advancement of

RECOLLECTIONS OF A NAVAL LIFE

his empire and the good of his people. Both Dom Pedro and his Empress Amalia were beloved sovereigns. Upon arriving at Rio we found the yellow fever rife. The squadron had gone down to the river La Platte. When we entered the port the health officer, an old physician whom most of us had met before, boarded our ship, and after saluting us, cordially remarked: "Gentlemen, you should board me, instead of my asking after the health of your ship. Yellow fever is decimating the ship's crews in this harbor, and if you remain a week in port you will not have enough men left to weigh anchor." At the same time he pointed out a number of ships that he said "had only watchmen on board, the crews having all died, or the few that remained been removed to hospitals on shore." This was a very depressing state of affairs. It was very perceptible, even on the face of Nature. There was a heavy cloud overhanging the city, and the absence of the brisk sea breeze enlivening the bay with the sail crafts moving back and forth was very noticeable. Our orders, however, were peremptory to proceed to Rio and land stores, and our captain did not hesitate to carry out his instructions, so we continued to our anchorage off the plague-stricken city. We were soon visited by a messenger from the consulate bringing us dispatches from the commodore saying "the squadron had left for Montevideo and to follow without delay." This was a great relief to us, and early the next morning we took advantage of the nauseous land breeze and left for a healthier atmosphere. Although our stay was very short (one night only) in the infected port, yellow fever showed itself among our crew as soon as we reached the pure air of the broad Atlantic, which is a characteristic of this disease, developing itself more rapidly when the victim is removed to purer air. We had no fatal cases, however, and were soon in usual health.

Montevideo is the Capital of Uruguay and is situated on the north shore of the river La Platte, at the mouth of the river, which at this point is seventy miles wide. The

108   RECOLLECTIONS OF A NAVAL LIFE

city is built on an elevated peninsula forming an anchorage in the shape of a horseshoe opening to the westward and subject to violent storms called "pamparos," which blow across the prairies. The first breezes show the violence of the coming storm by the cobwebs caught in the rigging, which indication warns the prudent mariner to send down all his yards and house topmast, and depend solely on his ground tackle for the safety of his ship. The experience of one of these blows during our stay made a hero of our junior lieutenant, James H. Gillis. Gillis was on shore when the storm came up, as were a number of other officers of the ship, together with boats and their crews from ships in the harbor, which could not pretend to pull against the violence of the storm to reach their vessels. At this juncture the cry of alarm spread through the city that a schooner had sunk on the sea-face of the city and the crew were clinging to the masthead for their lives, in momentary danger of being swept away, as the sea was breaking over them. The entire populace rushed to the scene of danger. Gillis in his enthusiastic ardor conceived the idea of saving them, and returning to the mole, or landing place of the boats, called out for "volunteers to go with him to rescue those drowning men!" At once a dozen or more stalwart seamen stepped to the front. From them he selected six, manned the whaleboat, and taking the steering oar in his hand shoved bravely off, facing the storm. All eyes were now riveted upon Gillis and his bold boat's crew, who were risking their lives to save their fellow-beings. To the great joy of his brother officers Gillis managed his boat beautifully, keeping her head always to the sea, and gradually pulling around the point of the peninsula till he got in position to drop down with the bows still facing the storm, till he fell to leeward of the schooner's mast, when one by one he rescued the men from their perilous position. He laid them down in the bottom of the boat, apparently more dead than alive. The stalwart seamen began their difficult

RECOLLECTIONS OF A NAVAL LIFE 109

task of pulling again to windward in order to round the point of the peninsula and secure their landing at the mole. When the last man was taken down the cheers of the multitude on shore were very encouraging to the life-savers, and when the boat landed Gillis was lifted upon the shoulders of some of the most prominent citizens and carried in triumph to the hotel amid the cries of "Make way for the brave American!" in Spanish. Our purser, a bluff old fellow who had recently passed through the bloody border warfare in Kansas, threw a damper on all this wild scene of enthusiasm by exclaiming, "Why, what is all this about? What has Gillis done?" but this did not detract from the daring and bravery of his action. Gillis was presented with a very handsome gold-bound album, with the names and thanks of all the prominent citizens of Montevideo, and the grateful thanks by letter of the government to which the schooner belonged. This gift I doubt not is, as it should be, an heirloom and treasure to his wife and children.

It was on this cruise that I remember witnessing for the last time a time-honored custom, then even almost obsolete. It was the visit of Neptune and his suite to a ship about crossing the equatorial line. It is ostensibly for the purpose of "christening all young sailors who are for the first time passing from one hemisphere to the other, after which initiation they are ever thereafter entitled to roam old ocean as one of Neptune's own." On board of our vessels of war, if permission was granted by the captain, the crew would get up a very fair and creditable performance. Neptune on this occasion was personated by one of the oldest sailors, a veritable "Jack Tar" of the olden time, with a great curling wig and an immense beard of rope yarn, bearing in his hand his trident, and drawn aft upon the deck in his car of state, fitted out of a gun-carriage. He was accompanied by eight or ten of the stoutest seamen as attendants to execute his will. After saluting the officer of the deck he asked "permission to examine

110 RECOLLECTIONS OF A NAVAL LIFE

the crew that he might learn if there were any on board that ship to be christened." Of course his attendants knew all who had never before crossed the line and began immediate search for the victims. They were brought up by force into the presence of "His Majesty" and a few questions of form put to them. "His Majesty" then ordered them to be first shaved, next christened. The attendant who acted as Neptune's barber then lathered the face and beard most thoroughly with tar, and with a huge wooden razor scraped the face vigorously. He was then plunged in a boat filled with salt water, and rising from this presented a most forlorn and deplorable picture, and all hands saluted him as an old tar, the son of the great Neptune, to the merry enjoyment of his brother sailors.

It is a privilege to the mariner, especially to one who is fond of astronomy, to visit the southern latitudes and view the starlit heavens. The "Southern Cross" is one of the most beautiful of the constellations here. Only those who "follow the sea in ships" can realize the wonders and grandeur of the deep, and surely nothing can more deeply impress the thinking mind with belief in the Great Creator, "who holds it all as in the hollow of His hand, whose voice the winds and the sea obey."

One day while it was blowing quite a gale and we were perhaps a hundred miles or more from land a swarm of butterflies swept over our deck. They were too sprightly to be caught, but as the wind was blowing favorably for their resistless voyage they no doubt found their way safely to shore.

Upon first arriving at Montevideo, having been one hundred and five days on ship with but a two hours' visit to the shore at Porta Praya, we determined—Dr. Horwitz, Lieutenant Gillis and I—upon a walk. We trigged off in our best citizens' clothes, got in a boat and pulled for the shore, a mile distant. We were pleased to find here a nicely constructed iron wharf, the building of which, we afterward learned with regret, had caused the failure of

RECOLLECTIONS OF A NAVAL LIFE 111

the enterprising Englishman who ventured its construction. He had every reason to believe that so favored a city would rapidly increase in trade, and visions of immense profits rose before him; but "Dame Fortune" often disappoints the most sanguine of her votaries, and very soon after the poor Englishman finished his wharf a revolution broke out which lasted for years, trade ceased, and his investment paid little or nothing. The custom house there was quite an imposing structure. The immense cathedral which so impressed us with its grandeur from a distance was disappointing on a nearer approach. The constant revolutions had prevented its completion and the outside walls were rough and unfinished. The interior, however, was in better condition, presenting a wide aisle with immense columns on either side, and a beautiful rotunda. The walls were hung with rich paintings of the Virgin Mary and our Saviour, and wax figures of the different saints. One of the fine paintings was said to be a very rare production of art, and was a gift to the church from Louis XIII. of France. We chanced to be in Montevideo during the "Holy Season" or "Passion Week," and as in all other Roman Catholic countries it was most sacredly observed. On Good Friday every good churchman and woman habited themselves in deepest mourning and spent the day in going from church to church and from service to service. This is kept up till the following Sunday, when the mourning is turned into joy and upon the Ascension of the Risen Saviour all is gladness. In the aisles and upon the altar, and indeed throughout the immense cathedral, were huge silver candlesticks and candelabra with lighted candles, giving an effect of great beauty, and the thronging masses of heart-filled worshipers—some kneeling before the Holy Mother, some kissing the golden girdle on the image of her more Holy Son—was truly a grand and impressive sight, even to those outside the pale of Rome's communion.

112   RECOLLECTIONS OF A NAVAL LIFE

There was one pleasure we enjoyed at Montevideo, and that was the privilege of the reading room, always open to us. Strolling into this sanctum one day I took a lounge, and seating myself comfortably with the leading papers of Europe and America before me, whiled away some leisure hours. There was much news of interest, giving the progress of the wars in India and China; the murderous attempt by a lot of Italian assassins on the life of the Emperor Napoleon; the launching of the *Leviathan*, the immense sea steamer built by England, six hundred feet in length, the successful navigation of which was expected to revolutionize the commercial world. The English papers were filled with particulars of the festivities to take place upon the approaching marriage of the Princess Royal Victoria of England to Prince Frederick William of Prussia. In looking back upon these items of news, then filling the papers, one is startlingly reminded of the changes time can make, of the mutations, and, after all, the vanity and briefness of human life.

Chapter XVI

Learning that the fever had abated in Brazil, it was now our great pleasure to leave for Rio, as upon the delivery of our stores depended our speedy return to the United States and our homes and families. We reached Rio safely, and instead of the death pall that was shrouding it in our few hours' detention on our way out, the city seemed restored to the vigor of health. Trade was brisk, and air and breezes delightful.

Brazil is the country for diamonds, and I took the opportunity to select one. Captain Grey was a connoisseur in gems, and offered to accompany me, which offer I gladly accepted. We found our way to the largest dealer in stones. He proved to be an officer in the Brazilian Army, who took the opportunity while stationed at the diamond mines to make some very choice selections. We were ushered into his rooms, where we were fairly dazzled with the wealth and brilliancy that surrounded us. Diamonds were grouped in parcels on tables or stands all around the room. Upon discussing and admiring the beauty of the gems, the officer asked "if we had ever seen a black diamond?" He said "they were very rare, but not to be compared to the others, and if we would excuse him, he would go into his wife's room, as she had a fine black diamond he would like us to see." He deliberately walked out, leaving us two strangers to himself surrounded by diamonds! The captain turned to me and remarked, "Kell, that is a very trusting man, or he has a detective with his eye on us, and our situation is not a pleasant one." The merchant soon returned with his wife's rare gem, holding it up for our admiration. It did not equal in beauty the ones we had been examining, as we admitted. The cap-

114   RECOLLECTIONS OF A NAVAL LIFE

tain remarked to the merchant that "he was surprised at his leaving us two strangers to him with his valuable possessions surrounding us." He smiled complacently and said, "Ah, gentlemen, I know whom to trust." I made a selection and he had it set for me.

Brazil is also famous for the beautiful work done in feathers. From the natural feathers, so exquisitely and highly colored, the nuns make flowers—the camellia japonica and carnations being among the handsomest. The birds of this latitude are very gorgeous and beautiful. The charming little humming bird is a marvel from its great variety, there being several very distinct kinds. I procured a handsome bunch of the flowers, and a few of the little stuffed birds to poise upon them to make the bouquet complete. The butterflies and beetles here are simply gorgeous. Insect life is here seen in its most beautiful aspect, and it seems to me one must acquire in Brazil the tastes of a naturalist if their eyes and hearts are open to take in the beautiful handiwork of Nature's God.

Our officers were invited by the French Minister to attend the "Te Deums" to be offered for the preservation of the lives of the Emperor and Empress of the French in the late attempted assassination. I did not leave the ship, it being my day's duty on board, but it was, I learned, a grand occasion, all officers from all the ships in the harbor appearing in full dress uniforms to do full justice to this occasion for thankfulness.

Even the beauties and diversions of a foreign country became wearisome to hearts growing anxious for a sight of their native land and reunion with families and friends, and it was with great rejoicing that we found our stores all landed and the orders given to set sail "homeward bound." Our voyage home was quite eventless, except that our patience was often sorely tried by the calms we encountered; but the month of July found us safely landed in New York harbor, from which port we had sailed eight months before. Home and happiness! Oh, dwellers on

RECOLLECTIONS OF A NAVAL LIFE

the land, can you imagine, or, far more, can you appreciate, the joy of a sailor's welcome home? But this joy was to be of short duration—only three short weeks. I found I could not be detached from the Store Ship *Supply* and have it count as a two years' cruise to me unless I made the second trip in her. Late in September I returned to the Brooklyn Navy Yard, and the 9th of October found us again "outward bound." The last link of communication was broken as the Highlands of Navesink disappeared below the western horizon. We had a glorious breeze directly aft and ran at the rate of eight or nine knots an hour. Several little sparrows took refuge on board, having been blown off by the fresh northwest wind. I endeavored to revive them by giving them bread crumbs and fresh water, and these little passengers of the feathered tribe staid with us some hours. When not on watch or duty I amused myself reading "Pickwick Papers," then a new and popular book, or if tired of that light pastime, varied my reading with the "Chemistry of Common Life." Our lovely weather was not of long duration. About the middle of the month found us with head winds and a rough sea tossing and pitching most uncomfortably, and two ships in sight almost in company with us. One of these was a large clipper ship, and she presented a beautiful sight as she passed near us under a perfect cloud of canvas, like a great bird with outstretched wings seeking a place of safety from the coming storm. We had now to prepare ourselves for a gale, or a succession of gales, from southeast, northeast and northwest points of the compass; the last, rising to its height at noon, was certainly grand and magnificent. The "pen of a ready writer" or the brush of a skilful artist might convey a faint picture to the imagination, but one must be an eye-witness to appreciate the grandeur of such a storm at sea. Picture to yourself a wild horse of the prairie with nostrils distended, mane flying to the breeze, eyes flashing madness as he exerts every muscle in speed to

116   RECOLLECTIONS OF A NAVAL LIFE

escape the consuming fire as it roars in flames and rapidly encroaches upon his fated heels! Such a comparison presented itself to me as on my watch I stood by the helmsman and watched his careful steering as* our ship sped before the gale under close reef sail at the rate of thirteen knots an hour, huge billows bursting in an ocean of foam close upon our wake, often washing our feet as we stood upon the upper deck, so madly did the waves dash on us; then would our good ship strain every cord, as it were, to escape the fast-following sea, as towering high above the billows would break close upon our feet. Indeed, the sea was not like itself. It resembled more a desert of floating sand driven by the tempest. The sun shone bright in the clear sky above and the wind howled as it lashed the combing sea, driving the spoondrift like mist through the air and covering the vast ocean in a sea of foam—a scene grand and magnificent to behold! How constantly are those reminded who travel on the great deep of the wonderful works and goodness of the Great Creator! One day tossed and driven by the raging tempest, the next evening, perhaps, sailing pleasantly along under quiet skies with a full moon beaming upon a stilled and tranquil ocean.

Having only three lieutenants on board, our watch seemed to come round very fast and keep us very busy. Some sport we sometimes had. Our men thought to enliven our quiet by doing some fishing. From a school of "trigger fish" they caught quite a number, which we had for dinner, and were surprised to find them quite palatable. It is a small fish, about the size of a fresh-water perch, with a skin in roughness resembling the shark, and teeth like a sheepshead; but the name is given to it from a peculiar fin on the back which can be set like the trigger of a gun, and by touching a spring the fin will fall. We also caught a beautiful dolphin. and our cook excelling in preparing chowder, we had fish chowder and dolphin steaks; but the dolphin's hues really seemed too gay and

RECOLLECTIONS OF A NAVAL LIFE

beautiful to make him a dish for food. It was like utilizing the rainbow! We had not been long enough at sea to need a replenished larder, and even in that day we had many canned goods and French preparations, soups, etc., that kept up a creditable table for us in mid-ocean. There are few fish that a ship's cook or caterer will not try his hand upon by way of experiment and variety.

Our sailing was now becoming slow and monotonous, as we were nearing the belt where storms and gales scarce ever intruded. We sometimes, however, had heavy rains. During a pouring downfall orders were given by the caterer to turn out the ducks that they might enjoy several inches of fresh water swashing our decks. They enjoyed it to the full, as their lively quacks testified. Then the pigs were marshalled out with orders to be scrubbed! Such squealing was perhaps never before heard on a well-organized ship, but it was a very amusing scene to officers and crew. Our voyage was necessarily a very slow one, being heavily laden with stores. We were peculiarly unfortunate in having to contend with light head winds. It was at this time my pleasure and privilege to read for the first time a book, then new, Captain Maury's "Physical Geography of the Sea." He mentioned rare instances of similar weather to that we had been having, and accounted for it in a scientific way, explaining that the heat of the African deserts cause there a vacuum, which the trade winds rushing to fill leave latitudes of the ocean subject to irregular winds and squalls, and the fine winds and weather we should have had were doubtless refreshing some wild Africans in their distant desert homes. I know it is very bad taste ever to differ with science, but I was almost persuaded to add to my science a little of a sailor's superstition and to lay our ill luck in bad weather and detention of voyage to the death or suicide of a favorite black pet cat on board. Some of the men in their kindness of heart overfed the poor beast with raw beef, whereupon its deranged digestion caused violent fits, and in one of these

118 RECOLLECTIONS OF A NAVAL LIFE

attacks overboard it went! But I would not like to acknowledge to my friends that I belonged or adhered too closely to my sailor brotherhood in their superstitions of "Flying Dutchmen," "black cats," "sailing from ports on Friday," etc. Bad weather, like many other ills, cannot last always, and before very long we were again sailing on smiling summer seas. I recall with delight, even at this distance of time, many of my beautiful watch hours on board the Store Ship *Supply*. Sometimes the morning watch, with the sea as smooth as glass, a pleasant breeze and our good ship under all sail traveling at the rate of six or seven knots an hour, the stars brilliant in the blue vault above, the eastern horizon softly lighting up for the coming day, after which the glad sun in all his glorious majesty rose behind a well-defined cloud whose edges fringed with the brightest golden tint gave glory to God and peaceful gratitude to the heart of man. In these lonely watches a man's heart is filled with the haunting memories of home and loved ones, and one becomes transported there and holds sweet communion with home's inmates on winged winds of thought! I remember reading at this time a book that interested me very much, McIlvaine's "Evidences of Christianity." It is scarcely less charming than a book of more recent date, Sir Henry Drummond's "Natural Laws in the Spiritual World."

We arrived in the city of Montevideo December 5, 1858. Soon after our arrival we were boarded by a boat from the Flag Ship *St. Laurence*, the officer of which informed us that we were the first vessel of the Paraguay expedition out from the United States. We had hoped to find the Frigate *Sabine* there with late news and letters from home. Of course the papers were filled with the prospect of war with Paraguay on account of indignities offered to the American Consul and our flag. Upon inquiry we found it was the current belief and the opinion we had formed ourselves, that President Lopez would readily apologize and treat upon equitable terms sooner than fight. He

RECOLLECTIONS OF A NAVAL LIFE 119

was said to be more willing to do this than to pay damages for the loss of American property. The English had lately called him to account for disrespect offered their minister. Lopez made amends, and it was the general opinion that it only required the arrival of our forces in full to have our troubles amicably adjusted. We soon had at anchor the Frigate *St. Laurence,* the Sloop *Falmouth,* the Brigs *Perry* and *Bainbridge,* and the day after we arrived the Steamer *Fulton* made her appearance, and shortly after the *Water Witch* followed. We took advantage of the first fair breeze and got under way for Buenos Ayres on the morning of the 8th. We had only gone about forty miles above Montevideo when the wind hauled ahead and we were obliged to anchor. The view here from deck was very singular. Although the water was only about twenty-five feet deep, there was no land in sight, and but for the freshness of the water and its clay or mud color we might have imagined ourselves on the broad ocean. It took us about two days to make the trip to the city of Buenos Ayres. But our nearest approach to the town was about eight miles distant, on account of the shallow water. A few years previous to this even small boats could not approach nearer than several hundred yards, when horses and vehicles would drive out to take passengers to terra firma. At the time of which I write, however, affairs had wonderfully improved in the completion of a long wharf, alongside of which the boats landed in comfort and convenience. There was another great achievement in the enterprise of the people, adding to the comfort of seafarers, in the running of a little steamer several times a day from the city to the shipping. It was both convenient and pleasant for us to take steamer and go to the city in the morning, spend the day sight-seeing or visiting and return to our quarters on board ship at night.

The city of Buenos Ayres is one of the finest of the South American cities. It is the Capital of the State of its name, and also the Capital of the Argentine Republic

120 RECOLLECTIONS OF A NAVAL LIFE

or Confederation. It is on the western side of the La Plata estuary, which is about thirty or forty miles wide, and about one hundred and fifty miles from the sea. It has the very great disadvantage of trade in the difficult navigation of the La Plata and the want of a commodious harbor. It is also subject to the pamparos which sweep across the pampas from the Andes with relentless fury, and which I have before described as witnessing at Montevideo. There are some very handsome public buildings, notably the cathedral, which covers half a square, its walls being adorned with some of the finest pictures (from the old masters) known to Spanish art. The name, signifying fine or "pure air," would seem very indicative of good health, but the water, a most essential factor for good health, is not good. The numerous wells have a brackish taste, and the only really fine water is the cistern water gathered from the roofs of the houses of the rich, and apparently for their use alone. Living there must be very cheap, for the finest beef in the market only brought two or three cents a pound, and to see the fine animals in their slaughter pens that were to be sacrificed for their hides and tallow alone was both a surprise and regret to North American spectators. From these South American ports we saw shipped, every few days, shiploads of horses, some very fine ones purchased here for a mere song, from ten to twenty dollars each, and carried to Calcutta or other ports in India for the use of cavalry in the India wars. Of course, it is easy to account for their cheapness, for it costs little or nothing to rear them, as the rich, luxuriant grasses on the pastures afford inexhaustible food for herds of horses and cattle. As a variety for our table, the caterer purchased some ostrich eggs, and we had omelette for breakfast, one egg taking the place of a dozen fowl eggs. I cannot say that our mess relished the omelettes much, they being very coarse in flavor, wanting the delicacy that is always found in the poultry-yard luxury.

RECOLLECTIONS OF A NAVAL LIFE

While on this cruise our men harpooned a porpoise, from which our cook gave us steaks, fried liver, and forcemeat balls—quite a variety of dishes, but alas, they all savored of porpoise! Half-famished mariners have compared the meat to fresh pork, which comparison may hold good in the anatomical structure of the animal—also its habit of rooting in the mud and sand for food, from which it gets the name of "sea hog;" but the meat I should call something between tough beef and pork, with a decided flavor of fish oil, and since the caterer showed an economical desire to save stores, our mess decided "we would have no more porpoise harpooned for this voyage."

Of course we had a great amount of "war talk" each day on board ship, and always heard "current opinion" when officers went ashore. Lopez was not thought to be a coward, by any means, but he had great wealth, and had with his acquisitions cultivated a miserly love of "filthy lucre." It was thought by some that sooner than pay large damages he would fight the trouble out, while others thought he would wisely pay a reasonable amount and apologize. While we had not enough of the good old-fashioned "John Bull" in us to be "spoiling for a fight," I think most of the squadron, officers and men, held themselves in readiness to resent the insult to the "Stars and Stripes" and hold themselves a defense for American Consuls, citizens, or seamen wherever found on foreign soil!

Chapter XVII

CHRISTMAS at sea, or Christmas in a foreign land! How different from the dear and happy season in one's own land and home. But I must not complain of that far-from-home Christmas in "the backward distance of the past." The outcoming vessels of the Paraguay Expedition brought out many near and dear friends of mine—Robert D. Minor, roommate, classmate, friend of my boyhood; Charles F. Fahs, Robert Carter (of the kingly Carters of Shirley), Captain Pegram, and many old and valued friends. Many of those friends that made bright that long-past Christmas in South America have gone before me to a home that is eternal! I often think wonderingly if it be possible that any class of naval officers have ever formed so brotherly an attachment for each other as did the Class of 1841.

Between Christmas and New Year we had fitted out with armament and stores the Steamer *Fulton*, which with Commodore Schubrick and suite, and our commissioner, Mr. Bowlin, was to proceed up the river, to be followed by the other vessels as fast as we could arm and store them. We learn that the Emperor of Brazil had dispatched a special minister to President Lopez to advise him to "pay all demands and avoid a collision with the United States, and should he be in want of funds Brazil would advance the required amount." This, of course, we were glad to hear, and gave some credence to, for we were very anxious to learn the prospect of the return of the squadron to the United States with a peaceable treaty with Paraguay.

There is on shore at this place a very fine hospital, and attached to it a beautiful little chapel, to which several of us repaired, in one of our walks, seeing that great crowds

RECOLLECTIONS OF A NAVAL LIFE

were tending in that direction. We learned that five fair young ladies were to "take the veil," or become nuns. The chapel was lighted with two hundred or more large wax candles, reflecting a beautiful light upon the rich hangings of the altar and walls of the chapel and the gorgeous robes of the priests, of whom there were quite a number officiating. The services were very long and at times tiresome and monotonous, from being conducted in Latin, and the pantomime of the priests quite unintelligible to us, but the music throughout was very beautiful and solemn. The young ladies came in robed in purest white with wreaths of orange blossoms on their heads. After many prayers and much chanting by the priests they were led up one by one to the officiating high priest, and kneeling before him received his blessing. After this he clipped from the heads of each three tresses of hair, one from each side and one from the top of the head. As a spectator I supposed this was to be done more thoroughly afterwards, and the young maidens would in being shorn of what St. Paul calls "a glory to woman" show their desire or. willingness to give up the vanities of the world and the show and pride of life. After this ceremony followed more chanting, during which the maidens were led into the vestry-room, leaving the kneeling multitude a silent throng. In a few moments they returned, the wreaths of orange blossoms gone, or replaced with plain long white veils, and on the shoulder each one carried a black wooden cross, three or four feet in length. This scene was very impressive indeed. To me it was a very sad one. This resignation in those so young of the greatest joys of life and the truest mission of woman! Even the blessed privilege of being saints of holy firesides and happy homes, leading the hearts therein through her sweet influence and example to happiness and Heaven!

Among the last of the vessels coming out to the Paraguay Expedition was the *Preble*, commanded by Captain Thornton A. Jenkins. The three lieutenants—Lowry,

124 RECOLLECTIONS OF A NAVAL LIFE

Breeze and Minor—were old friends and classmates of mine, and I began to think strongly of volunteering on board this ship, that I might take my part in battle if such duty were necessary. The two frigates and the store ship were to remain at Montevideo, as they drew too much water to ascend the river to the rendezvous, Corrientes. I think there is nothing a young man hates so much as inactivity and monotony. The weary weeks of waiting after all the ships were fitted out and filled with stores seemed something to be dreaded. In the event of war all that could be spared from the frigates, the *Falmouth* and the store ships would, of course, be sent up, but they must wait for further news. I determined not to wait. The Province of Corrientes is eight hundred miles up the river, and the rendezvous appointed was at the confluence of the rivers La Plata and Parana. I was very much pleased that permission was granted me to leave the *Supply* temporarily, and Captain Jenkins accepted my services. I took up my quarters on the *Preble*, sharing the comforts of my friend Minor. The wind and tide not being very favorable, we did not leave Montevideo for a day or two. One afternoon Minor and I thought we would enjoy a stroll together through the beautiful public garden, "Margat's," which is several miles from the city, a fashionable drive for ladies, and a very pleasant horseback ride for us. Having always been a lover of flowers, and wishing to make some return for the attention of the guide and gardener, I ordered a bouquet. He gathered, it seemed to me, from everything rare and beautiful, and a great quantity, till Bob begged me to stop him, whispering that my "bouquet might cost me five or ten dollars;" but I let him follow his own taste and discretion. Minor turned aside, still enjoying the garden, and I asked my indebtedness, and was amazed to find it about fifty cents. Of course I did not tell it, but had Bob's sympathy in consequence, he believing it to have been very costly. Now both he and I were married men, but our friend Breeze was visiting

RECOLLECTIONS OF A NAVAL LIFE

and enjoying as a young bachelor calls on the beautiful Spanish senoritas on shore, in love with half a dozen; so we determined, at Minor's suggestion, that our bouquet should give a great amount of pleasure, as he thought it had cost a considerable sum. Attaching a card, with name of fair one and compliments, we had the bouquet placed in Breeze's room as soon as we reached the ship. Breeze, being on shore in another direction, never found out the joke we played on him, and we never had the satisfaction of hearing his exclamations of delight over his beautiful bouquet. Minor was one of those large-hearted men with life and face all brimming over with the sunshine of his happy heart. A very "Nathaniel in whom there was no guile." I felt that I gained a great deal by my transfer to the *Preble* temporarily in the opportunity afforded me of taking the trip of six or eight hundred miles in the interior of South America. The *Supply*, after delivering eight heavy guns and a quantity of stores, was so very much lightened that it began to be hoped that she might be able to cross the bar and join the expedition. Much good was hoped to accrue from the display of a strong force to sustain our commissioner and the proof of easy access of our squadron hundreds of miles into the very heart of the country. Before we were able to leave Montevideo, on account of head winds and unfavorable weather, we heard of the arrival of our commodore and commissioner at Corrientes, the port where the whole squadron was ordered to rendezvous. Our passage up the river was very slow. On account of danger of the water shoaling we had sometimes to anchor and send the little Surveying Steamer *Argentina* ahead of us for soundings; and the Steamer *Southern Star* ordered to tow us not having much power, we were obliged to be very much governed by the winds. We arrived at Colonia, a little town almost opposite Buenos Ayres, about the 20th of January. Here we had the encouraging news or report that "President Urquisa, of the Argentine Republic, was acting as

126   RECOLLECTIONS OF A NAVAL LIFE

political adviser to President Lopez, of Paraguay, and was insisting upon amicable terms and an immediate treaty of peace." This made the prospect of war grow quite dim before our eyes and encouraged the hope that not a hostile gun would be fired. With the Empire of Brazil and the Argentine Confederation on our side we were safe.

Sunday on board a ship depends very much upon the temperament of the person if it be a day of enjoyment. Of course there is the usual routine—muster, inspection of quarters, reading the Articles of War, etc. If there is no chaplain, the captain, if he is a religious man or desires it, usually reads the service, the crew attend if they wish and the officers almost without exception do; but the men without work or duty find light reading, or gather in groups and spin yarns for the general amusement of their fellow-sailors. I have often thought how beautiful it would be to see an entire ship's company influenced by religious principles, every man performing his duty with cheerfulness and alacrity. The efficiency of such a ship's crew would arrive at the height of human attainment. It is said of General Havelock, who has left a name memorable in history for deeds of gallantry and daring in the wars of India, that in selecting recruits for his command he was governed principally by the religious education and morals of the men, trusting to their making the best soldiers. He gathered around him such a body of men that when deeds of valor were required, when any "forlorn hope" was to be carried, "Havelock's Saints"—as they were termed in the army—were always called upon. Thus will it ever be—true religion and heroism go hand in hand. In our late Civil War who were the heroes?—Stonewall Jackson and Robert E. Lee, Christian gentlemen, Christian warriors, God's faithful soldiers and servants till their life's end!

In going up the Parana River we stopped at the town of Rosario, about a hundred and eighty miles from Buenos Ayres. Breeze and I went on shore for a walk. We

RECOLLECTIONS OF A NAVAL LIFE 127

found it a town of considerable commerce and between fifteen and twenty thousand inhabitants. Upon first landing we found a species of crimson verbena, apparently wild, and we imagined the flora of the country must be very bright and beautiful. The shrubs about the residences were handsome and luxuriant and the vegetable gardens looked inviting and tempting, but upon leaving the outskirts of the town the country presented itself in one broad expansive view, a flat prairie with close-browsed grass dotted over with herds of cattle, horses, hogs, dogs and gulls. Such a landscape can be seen through this extensive country for hundreds of miles, with little variation. There are immense slaughter houses, too, for the only articles of export are hides, tallow, horns and bones. The dogs and gulls so numerous were leading bandit lives, feeding upon the offal of the slaughter pens. Flowers were rare, and excepting the accident of brightness and beauty in the little red verbena that welcomed us at the landing place, we saw none.

A day or two after leaving Rosario we learned from a passenger steamer that passed us with news from Asuncion, the Capital of Paraguay, that the commodore and suite and our minister, Mr. Bowlin, had reached Asuncion and been graciously received by President Lopez, who evinced every disposition to have an amicable settlement of our difficulty, and to establish with us a new treaty. There seemed nothing now in our way unless the bombastic Spaniard, always conceiving it undignified to move or act with promptness, assumed a procrastinating slowness, for which he is noted. We arrived at Parana early in February, and our first news was "peace is concluded." Happy intelligence! At four o'clock in the afternoon of the 6th day of February the captain invited five officers (myself among the number) to accompany him in fulldress uniform to call upon our minister, Mr. Yancey, and his family. His first salutation after greeting us was congratulations that a treaty had been concluded between Commissioner Bowlin and President Lopez, of Paraguay.

128 RECOLLECTIONS OF A NAVAL LIFE

After a pleasant visit to Mr. Yancey we accompanied him to be presented to President Urquiza. We found him an agreeable and accomplished gentleman. He had been the principal adviser of Lopez and had just*returned with the pleasing news of amity. He visited our ship the next day at the early hour of six in the morning, with Mr. Yancey. We had a grand turn-out in full dress, manned the yards and saluted. The ladies visited the ship at 10 o'clock, and in the afternoon we made ready for sailing to meet the returning commodore and commissioner. We had not long to wait. We met the Steamer *Fulton* with the party on the 18th of February, and were ordered to "turn about" and follow the *Fulton* to Rosario, the rendezvous, after which all would proceed to Montevideo, preparatory to fitting out for home. Arriving at Rosario on the 22d of February, we found the entire Paraguay Expedition anchored, "returning home from the war." It being Washington's Birthday, the ships were gaily dressed with flags, and at meridian a salute was fired by all the vessels of the squadron. In the afternoon I was detached and transferred back to the Store Ship *Supply* with the men I had taken with me. I was joyfully welcomed by my messmates, one claiming the old hat of Lopez, another his epaulettes, etc., all of which I had promised to capture in warfare and present as trophies on my return. Peace having been proclaimed I claimed exemption from the fulfilment of my promises so rashly made in view of war. I had a picture of Lopez, however, which caused a great deal of amusement, and which now adorns an old scrap-book. It is said not to be a caricature, either, though I really hoped it was, for it had no claim to beauty and very little to intelligence. The forehead is narrow and the lower jaw immense, showing more the look of a *bon vivant* than the leader and ruler of men and a republic—rather a despot at that! We did not linger long at Montevideo, glad of our orders "homeward bound," and arrived in the city of New York early in May, 1859.

Chapter XVIII

A few short weeks of happiness at home, and the fourth of July found me under orders to "proceed without delay to the Pensacola Navy Yard and report for duty to Commodore James McKay McIntosh." While I should like to have had a longer leave, these orders pleased me, for they meant two years or more on shore, and it was the first shore-station duty I had ever been ordered to since I entered the Navy. The position on receiving ship at Norfolk could scarcely count for shore duty, since I was on positive duty and not able to leave the ship at least one half or more of the time. The Yard at this time was one of the most beautiful and attractive in the United States. It was handsomely laid out, with a very wide, well-paved center walk, which led from the wharf to the commodore's residence; half way up this walk was an archway formed by the building in which the stores were kept. The commodore's was the center house, with six handsome residences on each side, which were occupied by officers according to rank. Surrounding these houses were beautiful grounds, filled with tropical plants, lading the air with perfume of jasmine, heliotrope and violet at most seasons of the year. A wide brick pavement ran the entire front length of the thirteen houses in row, giving great comfort and convenience, and well-kept parks or grass plats delighted the eye in front. In the center of these parks were two octagon buildings, one containing the offices and the other the chapel of the Navy Yard.

In the ship yards on the right of the landing were being built or nearing completion the fine Sloops of War *Pensacola* and *Seminole*, which were launched during that summer. To the left of the landing were the residences of the

130 RECOLLECTIONS OF A NAVAL LIFE

junior officers and quarters of the men. Outside the Yard gate on one side was the little village of Warrington, built up for the convenience of trade, and through which we passed to the naval hospital, and beyond the hospital was old Fort Barancas, famous for having been built by the Spaniards. The United States Army officers and their families sojourned at Barancas, and were within pleasant visiting distance of the Yard, and many were the social civilities exchanged. General Winder was in command of the Fort. Lieutenants Gilmore and Slemmer were the officers next in command, both of whom took active part and rose to high rank in the Civil War on the Federal side. At the time of which I write the thought of war scarcely showed itself, even as a speck on the mental horizon of the wise and far-thinking men of national reputation. Few, I think, would have allowed themselves to believe that our differences could not be settled, if brought to issue, on the floors or in the halls of Congress. Our commander at the Navy Yard was E. Farrand. He was of Northern extraction, but his heart was in the land and State of his adoption, and his loyalty and bravery in time of need was very earnestly given to the State of Florida and the Southern cause. Next in rank was the first lieutenant, Chas. W. Hayes, of Alabama. I filled the place of second, or junior, lieutenant. Dr. Bishop was surgeon. Purser Warrington (a son of the commodore of that name) was paymaster. He was a clever gentleman. Rev. Chas. W. Thomas, our faithful and efficient chaplain, was very much respected and beloved by officers and men. The master of the Yard was Captain Pearson, and Mr. Porter was the naval constructor. To his inventive brain some believe we are indebted for the original idea of the ironclad, brought into service some years later. Porter was a very modest man, of few words, and not being on the "side of the strongest artillery," or the winning side, of the Civil War, he died shortly after its close almost penniless. Mr. Abert, a very cultivated, pleasant gentle-

RECOLLECTIONS OF A NAVAL LIFE

man, was civil engineer, with Mr. Alexander as assistant. Mr. Gonzales was the storekeeper. The commodore's secretary and nephew, Lachlan H. McIntosh, resided in his household. These dozen or more families, combined with hospital and fort families, being within visiting distance of the city of Pensacola, made up a very delightful society, and the incoming ships for repairs or rendezvous added gaiety and pleasure of every kind. The commodore's receptions were as grand events of their kind as the entertainments of the exclusive "four hundred," so paternally watched over by the late Ward McAllister, and etiquette was strictly observed upon every occasion by him. Of course we kept open houses, to which our brother officers coming in from sea were warmly welcomed at any time, and where they were glad to spend their evenings, if only to be reminded of distant homes and as happy firesides!

This Navy Yard, being the only one south of Norfolk, was kept very busy, and did a great deal of work for the Gulf Squadron, the work always being very ably done. Although cut off in a great measure from the rest of the world and in a port of limited commerce, we lived in great comfort and luxury. The waters afforded us the finest fish and oysters in the world, and the surrounding country furnished us abundance of game, such as wild turkey and venison, and we had very fine poultry of every description. Gophers were abundant, we buying them by the barrel, and sea turtle were a luxury sometimes brought in by the ships. The country people kept us supplied with fine fruit in the season, and the little coasting schooners made the tropical fruits a daily enjoyment, especially pineapples and oranges. The flowers in this congenial climate make a wonderful growth. I began a little conservatory, through the kindness of Mrs. Farrand, a great botanist and lover of flowers, and my next-door neighbor, and by the time I could bring my family to the Navy Yard, the first of November, the plants had grown not inches but

132   RECOLLECTIONS OF A NAVAL LIFE

feet in height. Jessamines, geraniums, heliotropes, and many lovely plants looked as though my little greenhouse had been "a thing of beauty" for several years.

There were several very pleasant and notable families residing in Pensacola at this time who were on sociable terms at the Yard, among them Senator Mallory (he was afterwards Secretary of the Confederate States Navy), Major Chase, an Army officer, and the charming widow of Commodore Dallas. This lady was the sister of Madame Murat, the widow of Achillé Murat, whose father the first Napoleon had made a king. When Napoleon III. came to the exalted position his uncle had occupied he did not forget the past, and Madame Murat was invited to his Court, and made a visit there during the reign of the beautiful Eugenie. While we were residents at the Navy Yard a very brilliant social event occurred in the city of Pensacola—the marriage of Senator Mallory's charming daughter Maggie to a gentleman of Bridgeport, Connecticut. The Roman Catholic Bishop of Florida performed the ceremony, which was very impressive. He specially wished the young couple and the assembled multitude to know (or to remember) that in the Roman Catholic Church there was no such thing known or allowed as divorce! That literally and most solemnly the vows they were taking upon themselves were holy, and that the ties indissoluble; that those whom God and His Holy Church had joined together, no man, or laws of man, "could put asunder."

Social life at the Navy Yard and Fort was really the ideal life perfected—so many warm and brotherly attachments as then existed between the officers making the interest in their families deep and abiding with its undercurrent of sincerity and affection. It is so pleasant to look back and see in memory my loved friend Minor, the gallant Maffitt, dear Willie Whittle, Eggleston, true as steel, Gillis, and so many that shared those early days, sitting in comfort on my wide verandas, tossing my little sons

RECOLLECTIONS OF A NAVAL LIFE

about, or walking with them in their arms, or listening to their sweet prattle with keen relish and delight, some with homesick longing, no doubt, for their own "lares and penates." Maffitt was a widower at this time; with a true sailor's appreciation and admiration for the female sex it was no wonder that he was a great favorite everywhere. But the summer was wearing away, and the latter part of it found the shadow of death hovering over the beautiful Navy Yard in the declining health of the commandant, my relative, Commodore McIntosh; also the angry clouds of war were gathering ominously to burst upon us and our beloved Southland in a few short months! Ah, little did we surmise then that the next spring, as Nature was crowning herself with verdure, there would open for us four years of desolating war through which nothing could have sustained us but the holy fire of patriotism that burned on the altar of our hearts, sacred to love and home! War to a disappointed end, with nothing to comfort or uphold the spirit in defeat but the consciousness of duty eagerly and nobly done in the cause that we deemed just, and true, and right! But I anticipate.

We were still living happy lives in quiet homes when illness came, and then death, to claim as his own the noble spirit of Commodore James McKay McIntosh. He died on the 4th of September, 1860. For nearly fifty years he served his country, and literally "died in harness." A man of Southern birth and parentage, a compeer of the gallant Tatnall, Buchanan, and many other noble officers of his date and age, one can conceive the pain he would have borne in severing (as they did) the ties and duties of fifty years' service under a flag he loved and honored. But death spared him any sacrifice of feeling, and in the sunset glory of his days, honored and respected in his profession, and by his fellow-men, we laid him in a temporary tomb, till Georgia, his native State, claimed what remained of

134 RECOLLECTIONS OF A NAVAL LIFE

her noble son, and early in March, 1861, he was buried
with his ancestors at old Midway Churchyard, Liberty
County, Georgia.

> "Close his eyes, his work well done.
> What to him is friend or foeman,
> Rise of moon, or set of sun,
> Hand of man, or smile of woman!
>
> "As man may, he fought his fight,
> Proved his truth by his endeavor.
> Let him sleep in solemn night,
> Sleep forever and forever!
>
> "Fold him in his country's stars,
> Roll the drum and fire the volley,—
> What to him are all our wars,
> What but death bemocking folly?
>
> "Leave him to God's watching eye,
> Trust him to the hand that made him.
> Mortal love weeps idly by—
> God alone held power to aid him!"

In the latter part of December I obtained a month's
leave of absence and repaired to Macon, Georgia, where
my wife and children were in her father's home, and here
I was when the State of Georgia held her convention. I
went to Milledgeville and was present when the ordinance
of secession was passed. I at once forwarded my resignation to the Government I had served from early boyhood,
and espoused the cause of my State, deeming it my sacred
and honorable duty to take this step. I did not question
my heart as to the pain involved. I knew it would be the
severance of many pleasant ties and manly friendships.
From this time my life seemed divided into two parts, and
so I will divide this history of my life.

At the beginning of the Civil War I seemed to leave
my youth and the service of the country I had faithfully
served for almost twenty years, far behind me in the past;

RECOLLECTIONS OF A NAVAL LIFE

and life began anew for me, stern and sacred duties, to which I gave myself with the best ability at my command.

I wish in the second part of this my narrative to give to history and posterity the truth of the cruises of the Confederate Ships *Sumter* and *Alabama*, and the part it was my privilege to take and share as executive officer of both in their glorious and successful work.

PART SECOND

Chapter I

*"A long remaining glory
Of things that now are old!"*

Captain Marryat in one of his very entertaining books tells his hero to "give his memory leave [or opportunity] to take a stroll." This advice I often take to myself, having arrived at the age when one loves to dwell upon the past, especially its brightest scenes, and people the halls of memory with friends and pictures that seem more dear and bright than the panorama that is daily passing before our eyes, for pictures graven on the heart need no camera to revive them or make them live again. The year 1860 (and some months of the year before) passed at the Pensacola Navy Yard are very dear to memory. There with the sharer of my destiny we presided over the first home we called our own. We had many little experiences that were very amusing to us, and frittered away a great deal of money on pineapple jam, brandy peaches, elegant preserves, jellies and pickles, which, adorning our store-room shelves, were the next winter to find their way into the Confederate soldiers' hands at the surrender of the Yard. My wife still rejoices that they fell into their hands instead of the enemy's, and hopes they enjoyed them! We often talk of the back country that fed the Pensacola Navy Yard as a veritable "Land of Goshen," and its remembered luxuries seem as did the "flesh pots of Egypt" to a famishing, exiled people. We there rejoiced in all the dainties and good living of land and sea. Our fish car never became empty; the oyster

138   RECOLLECTIONS OF A NAVAL LIFE

boats were daily replenishers; the country people brought in wild turkeys and venison occasionally, domestic fowls of every kind, with splendid fruit in season; and the little schooners brought the West India fruits•to our wharves. We kept "open house" and hospitality knew no limit, for with the best old negro cook that Georgia could produce our housekeeping was an endless pleasure. The cook was very ambitious that her young mistress should equal, if not surpass, the oldest housekeepers in the Yard, and she was the youngest! Her energy was untiring and her zeal wonderful. She listened patiently to the reading of "Soyer," and if she could not understand his French dishes, she at least tried to rival them, and soon learned to make the Spanish omelettes, filled with the sweet bell peppers chopped into mincemeat, to perfection. We found we had something to be proud of in our cook and our housekeeping.

Bob Minor, Jack Cooper, John N. Maffitt, Willie Whittle, "Youngster" Eggleston, and many others, dear friends of the past, were daily with us, and unless Bob made our baby boys sick with too much candy or his favorite "gum drops," we had nothing to disturb the brightness of our home. Occasionally we "showed off" in a grand dinner in honor of some of my senior officers.

But these pleasures were doomed to be shortlived, as the cloud of war was rising above the horizon and we were nearing conflict that we little dreamed would plunge us into the dreadful war of four long, bitter years; when the South would fight the world, with no hand stretched out in friendly sympathy to aid, and at last give up, unconquered, from sheer exhaustion and despair!

The 20th of December, 1860, found me on my way to Macon, Georgia, where my family had preceded me to spend the coming holiday season at home. The 19th, as I was journeying, news came over the wires that the State of South Carolina had upon that day seceded from the Union. To some it seemed appalling. To others, burn-

RECOLLECTIONS OF A NAVAL LIFE

ing with patriotic zeal, the step seemed none too hasty for resenting our sectional grievances, and in all there seemed a desire to do one's duty by one's own home and State. Mississippi soon followed the example of her plucky sister State, withdrawing on the 9th of January, 1861. Alabama two days later passed her ordinance of secession, and upon the same day—January 11—Florida withdrew from the Union. At this news I returned to the Pensacola Navy Yard for the gathering up of my household effects, for we had left our home with the pictures hanging on the walls, everything as we had occupied it, and our faithful old cook, Maria, in charge of the establishment— she and Poll, the parrot, having a very lonely time. I found great changes. Our house, being untenanted, was made headquarters for the Confederate officers, for the Yard had surrendered in my short absence. Commodore Armstrong had retired and Commodore Victor M. Randolph had taken command. Our neighbor, Mrs. Farrand, had gone into our house and, with motherly care, removed the pictures and bric-a-brac, taking all to her own home, including our silver and valuables. The Confederate officers were very civil and polite to me. I got permission to remove all that was mine from the house, but much had to be left and sacrificed for want of transportation. The uncertainty of the future movements of those still in the Yard made purchasers scarce, though I did sell the good cow, that had been a great comfort to us, for a twenty-dollar gold piece. I bade adieu to this beautiful home, its frames and verandas covered with evening glories in fullest bloom, and the conservatory filled with rare exotics, with a feeling of lingering regret. We had been so happy there, and the future, with its lowering clouds of war and turmoil, promised no compensation (though fortunately we could not foresee its disasters and woes!) for our vanishing happiness.

On the 19th of January, 1861, I attended the State Convention of Georgia, witnessed her withdrawal from the

140 RECOLLECTIONS OF A NAVAL LIFE

Union, went to the hotel and wrote my resignation (within an hour from her secession) to the Government of the United States, waited its acceptance, and then offered my services to Governor Joseph E. Brown. If not the very first, I was among the first to take this step. Commodore Tatnall was in command at Sackett's Harbor. He being the senior naval officer in the State of Georgia was of course later, on his return, put in command of her naval forces; but just now there was no Navy.

Governor Brown accepted my services, and commissioned me to proceed to Savannah, purchase a steamer, take command of her, and hold myself in readiness for harbor and coast defense. The secession movement of Georgia drew her sons to her soil, and soon all were within her borders. The gallant Tatnall, Charles Morris, my intimate friend and senior; the young Armstrong brothers, Wilbourn Hall, Graves, Stone, all came home to abide by the decision of their State and to share her fortune for good or ill!

Through old letters of daily correspondence at this time (February, 1861), I find this item: "The *Everglade* returned to Savannah to-day. She has her papers correct, so that the purchase will probably be closed to-morrow, when I will take command. She is to be called the *Savannah*. I have twenty-five men shipped, and hope to make up the fifty men required before I leave."

On the 28th of February I write: "I took command of the Steamer *Savannah* this afternoon, with officers and men numbering forty-five. I have only three watch officers—Midshipmen Armstrong, Hooper and Merriwether —but I hope to have Lieutenant Armstrong before we sail. I am making every exertion to leave here by Monday or Tuesday next, but find so many repairs and outfits to be made that it will be as much as I can possibly do to be ready by that time. I am occupied every moment of time, but hope in a few days to get things regulated."

My first duty was to go to Fernandina, and with permis-

RECOLLECTIONS OF A NAVAL LIFE 141

sion of Governor Perry, of Florida, to take two guns from that point to Fort Pulaski. On March 22d I write: "I have just arrived in Savannah and find that Commodore Tatnall is here. I shall report to him in the morning. Charles Morris's steamer, the *Huntress*, has arrived. He will probably get off for duty in a week or ten days." March 25th: "The commodore visits this steamer to-morrow, and will take a trip down to Fort Pulaski." Early in April I find this item: "While at Brunswick to-day, received orders from Commodore Tatnall to 'proceed to Savannah without delay.'" The Monday previous to this date I record: "A very black and threatening cloud making its appearance in the western sky late in the afternoon, and rapidly covering the heavens, by 8 o'clock it became so very dark I had to anchor under the north point of Sapelo Island. Finding it bright and clear the next morning I got under way, and at 3 o'clock in the afternoon I anchored off old 'Sunbury,' the home of my childhood. The terror-stricken inhabitants were sure the 'Yankees were upon them.'" One man took to the woods, and not until I went on shore and made myself known would they believe themselves safe. I was then welcomed heartily, and a Mr. Anderson, whom I found living in our old house, kindly offered his vehicle and proffered to drive me to Captain Abiel Winn's (whose wife was my relative). I spent a very pleasant evening with the family and the venerable Colonel Maxwell, much beloved in that county. Upon my return to Savannah I received orders from Commodore Tatnall "to go at once to St. Simon's Island and take the Jackson Artillery from that point to Savannah." This company were from Macon, commanded by Captain Theodore Parker, First Lieutenant Charles Nisbet. Officers and men were the flower of chivalry of Georgia's central city. In these later years I have heard many amusing anecdotes related of the members of this interesting company. To meet Dr. Mataner, then its efficient young surgeon, and Judge James T. Nisbet, an honored member

142   RECOLLECTIONS OF A NAVAL LIFE

of the company, and hear them "spin yarns," as I am told they do in memory of those patriotic days, must be a genial social treat. The handsome Lucius M. Lamar, one or both of the' Blooms, and many others of Macon's favorite sons belonged to this company and were "illustrating Georgia" at this time. I landed them with guns, equipments, and baggage in safety in Savannah. Captain Parker received orders to leave the guns, and his company were granted one week's leave of absence. The following day I received orders to proceed to Sunbury, taking on board my little steamer to that point the remains of Commodore James McKay McIntosh, which had been brought from Pensacola (where they had been temporarily interred) by his nephew, Lachlan H. McIntosh, and which, through the interest of his native State and by Act of the Legislature, were to find a final resting place in the burial ground of his ancestors in old Midway Churchyard, Liberty County. His relatives, Major William McIntosh, Lachlan H. McIntosh, Judge McQueen McIntosh, of Florida, his nephew, John McQueen McIntosh, of Darien, and myself were privileged to accompany these remains as escort. In honor of this event the Savannah *Morning News* correspondent, of date of April 18th, says:

The remains of the late Commodore McIntosh arrived in Sunbury, Liberty County, the place of his nativity, on Tuesday, the 16th inst., for final interment in his native county. The body was conveyed from Pensacola by railroad to Savannah, in charge of his nephew, Lachlan H. McIntosh, and thence in Steamer *Everglade* (or *Savannah*), Captain Kell, commander, to Sunbury, accompanied by the relatives of the deceased. It was here received by the Liberty Independent Troop, with appropriate remarks by Mr. W. C. Stevens, a member of the corps, and briefly responded to by Captain Kell. After the ceremony of reception was over it was escorted by the L. I. Troop to the cemetery at Midway, nine miles distant, its final resting place.

An impressive and appropriate prayer was offered at the grave by Rev. C. C. Jones, D.D., and after interment a wreath of roses and olive branches, entwined by the hands of Mrs. Jones, suspended from the headstone of the grave. I herewith transmit copies of the addresses,

RECOLLECTIONS OF A NAVAL LIFE 143

a publication of which in your columns would no doubt be gratifying to the friends of the lamented dead.

ADDRESS OF MR. STEVENS.

Captain Kell: Permit me as the organ of the Liberty Independent Troop to express to you their just appreciation of the service which brings you to these shores, and their heartfelt co-operation in the funeral obsequies of the occasion. In the social relations of life, loved and esteemed by his friends for his kindness of heart and manly qualities, Commodore McIntosh was to most of us personally unknown, but history has recorded his public career and his grateful countrymen are ready to award that meed of praise which is the just tribute to merit. By reference to an excerpt of his life we find that he entered the naval service of the United States, September, 1811, and for a period of forty-nine years continued in the active exercise of different vocations, passing through the various grades of service—midshipman, passed midshipman, master, lieutenant and commander—as rapidly as the service would admit. Although never engaged in actual hostilities (if we except the first period of initiation into service) we find him during a reign of national prosperity in offices of important trusts and great responsibility, requiring the exercise of sound judgment and a character distinguished for fearlessness of danger. In 1821 he was attached to an expedition under Captain Kearney for the extermination of pirates on the West India coast. In 1851, after receiving his commission with the rank of captain, he was ordered to the command of the U. S. Frigate *Congress*, attached to the Brazil Squadron under the command of Commodore McKeever. Soon after this he was removed to the command of the Naval Station at Sackett's Harbor, where he remained till 1857, when by order of the President of the United States he became flag officer of the Home Squadron. This command was conferred at a time when British fleets in Southern waters became exceedingly troublesome by attempting to board and search American vessels, but by prudence, judgment, a dignified courtesy, and firm determination, he vindicated and maintained the position his country had ever taken against the right of search, and received for his conduct his country's unqualified approbation. Subsequent to this period Commodore McIntosh was placed in command of the Navy Yard at Pensacola, in which station he expired on the first of September, 1860. Here closed his earthly career, almost up to the point of the dissolution of the Government which he had always served with fidelity and honor, and upon the eve of a great and momentous revolution. Had Commodore McIntosh survived to see this day it is not difficult to surmise what would have been his position in the recent inauguration of political events. Had he lived

144 RECOLLECTIONS OF A NAVAL LIFE

to behold the Confederate flag of these Southern States thrown proudly and defiantly to the breeze, his ardent and true Southern heart would too surely have reflected the sentiment of its emblematic colors—valor, purity, and truth. But, sir, while we may regret the necessity that sunders the bonds of earthly existence and view with sorrow from life's circle its gems drop away, we must bend to an inexorable fate and bow with submission to the Will of Providence! "The boast of heraldry, the pomp of power, all that beauty, all that wealth e'er gave, await alike the inevitable hour. The path of glory leads but to the grave." And now, sir, with hearts alive to the duties of the occasion we bid you welcome here, and thrice welcome the mortal remains of the gallant Commodore James McKay McIntosh to a final interment in the soil of his native State, and the county of his birth!

To this I replied:

Gentlemen of the Liberty Independent Troop and Citizens of Liberty County: In behalf of the widow and children and the relatives of the deceased I tender you their warm and heartfelt acknowledgments of the consideration and respect thus shown to his memory. It would have been a satisfaction (melancholy, it is true) to his old comrade-in-arms, and brother friend, the gallant Tatnall, to have responded to the kind words that have been spoken. It was his intention and earnest desire to accompany the remains of his deceased friend to their last resting place, but danger threatens our people and he stands at his post ready to meet it. His duty to his State alone prevents his being here, and I know that the noble spirit of his late comrade looks down from Aloft with responsive sympathy and approval. Again do I thank you in behalf of the family and friends of the gallant departed, and beg to present as one of his relatives my own warm appreciation of your sympathy and consideration.

My command in the service of my State was destined to be a very short one. I had two or three more trips southward, including a very pleasant Sunday, when we anchored off Cumberland Island, and I spent a few hours with my friend Mr. Nightengale and family. On returning to Savannah, headquarters for reporting my movements, the last week in April, I received "confidential orders" from the Confederate Government at Montgomery to "report to Captain R. Semmes, at New Orleans, without delay."

Chapter II

THE first day of May I parted from my family at Macon, Georgia, as I thought for a few short months, but as it proved in the Providence of God, and in the line of my duty, for three years and four months of the most eventful period of my life. Fort Sumter had surrendered and the times were assuming a warlike aspect, foreshadowing our years of deadly strife. Of this great war I do not propose to write a history. Abler pens than mine have undertaken this work, some satisfactorily. The book written by my great commander and senior, Admiral Semmes,—worthy an honored place in the library of every cultivated American,—discussed the questions of national and political significance of those troublous times. I only wish to give to posterity and to history in these recollections of my life the part it was my duty and my privilege to act in the great drama of the Civil War between the States. I trust I have in some measure outlived the animosities of those "times that tried men's souls," at least sufficiently so to hold the impartial pen of truth, without which history (no matter how sensationally or attractively adorned or bedecked) must be utterly valueless!

Arriving in New Orleans on the third day of May I reported for duty to Captain Semmes, who had preceded me by a week or ten days. During a long talk with him I found that a steamer had been purchased by the Confederate Government, which he was to command, and that at his request I had been ordered to this vessel as executive officer. I found her a neat, fast passenger steamer that could be converted into a vessel of war, but many alterations were required for this purpose. The captain had immediately upon arrival commenced this work of re-

146 RECOLLECTIONS OF A NAVAL LIFE

modelling. I found her at Algiers, the shipyard across the river, and as many workmen as could be employed were cutting away the light passenger cabins, strengthening decks for supporting the battery, and shaping her for her destined work. This was no easy task to perform with the appliances at our command. Our pivot gun, whose unique carriage and circles was constructed of railroad iron,—the ingenuity of whose construction was due to the inventive genius of Mr. Roy,—proving the truth of the trite old adage, "necessity is the mother of invention." Our 32-pounders (four in number, as broadside guns) were furnished us from the Norfolk Navy Yard, but the gun carriages had to be improvised, and were very creditably gotten up by our mechanics at the shipyard.

In a few days all our officers reported for duty and were detailed for superintending work in the different departments. With the great disadvantages under which we labored our work progressed slowly, and consumed much more time than we anticipated. During this detention in fitting our ship for sea the enemy had secured a blockade of the mouths of the Mississippi River, quite effectually making the hope of our escaping lessen day by day, but the delay was unavoidable. About this time we had a sad accident, resulting in the loss by drowning of one of our young officers, Midshipman John F. Holden, of Tennessee. While performing the difficult task of taking out an anchor for the *Sumter*, as she lay in the swift current of the Mississippi, his boat capsized, and before assistance could be rendered three of the crew, with himself, were drowned.

On the third of June work had progressed sufficiently for us to put the *Sumter* in commission. Our colors were presented by some fair ladies of New Orleans. After completing our outfit we invited on board a number of prominent citizens of New Orleans, together with the ladies who had presented our flag, to accompany us on a trial trip up the river, when we tested the speed of the ship and the quality of our battery, both of which proved

RECOLLECTIONS OF A NAVAL LIFE

quite satisfactory. On the 18th of June we steamed down to the barracks below the city to take in our powder, and that night, with a beautiful moon shining, we continued our passage down the river and by daylight next morning came to anchor off Fort Jackson. Here we remained several days, exercising our crew with the battery.

Although our crew were most of them fine sailors, they were not "men-of-war's men," and had to be drilled at the guns. Our crew at this time consisted of 92 men, 20 of whom were marines. Our officers were as follows:

Commander, Raphael Semmes; First Lieutenant, John M. Kell; Lieutenants, Robert T. Chapman, John M. Stribling, William E. Evans; Surgeon, Francis L. Galt; Paymaster, Henry Myers; Captain's Clerk, W. B. Smith; Lieutenant of Marines, B. Howell; Midshipmen, Richard F. Armstrong, William A. Hicks, Albert G. Hudgins, Joseph D. Wilson; Engineers, Miles J. Freeman, William P. Brooks, Mathew O'Brien, Simeon W. Cummings; Boatswain, B. P. Macasky; Gunner, Thomas C. Cuddy; Sailmaker, W. P. Beaufort; Carpenter, William Robinson.

On the 21st of June we hoisted anchor and dropped down to the head of the passes for the purpose of taking advantage of the movements of the blockading fleet. The Frigate *Brooklyn* was at Pass à la Loutre and the *Powhatan* was at Southwest Pass. To our great annoyance we had some difficulty in getting a pilot. Captain Semmes dispatched an officer to the pilot's station with a written demand that a pilot be sent immediately on board the *Sumter*. They furnished a very inefficient one, who, when the opportunity offered, declared that he knew nothing of Pass à la Loutre. Captain Semmes, realizing that the opportunity could not be allowed to pass, sternly ordered him to "take us out, and if he ran us ashore or put us in the hands of the enemy he would swing him to the yardarm as a traitor." This threat convinced the pilot that Captain Semmes "meant business" and could not be trifled with, and alarmed him very much, but at the same time

148   RECOLLECTIONS OF A NAVAL LIFE

we hoisted a pilot signal. This opportunity was given us by the *Brooklyn* giving chase to a vessel off the harbor. All hands were called to "up anchor," and the engineer ordered to get up steam. This was eagerly obeyed.

Our crew had been so tormented with the heat and mosquitoes in the river below New Orleans that they begged to go to sea and fight the enemy, rather than endure such torture, with consequent loss of sleep and rest. We were soon on our way. As we approached the pilot station we saw a small boat shove out from the shore, and in less time than it can be told the boat was alongside of us and a line thrown out to pull it to our gangway without stopping our headway, and the next moment a stalwart young fellow jumped over our side and took his position at our pilot stand, saying, "give her all the steam she can carry." During this time at the pilot station handkerchiefs were waving and all eyes turned in that direction saw the pilot's young wife and sister were waving him and us God-speed and success! This was the last we were to see of the South and our native shores for long months and years!

As we approached the bar there was a vessel ashore with hawsers across the stream to haul her off, which by signal of the pilot were slackened up to allow us to pass. As we rounded this point of the bar the pilot said: "Captain, she's all free; give her hell and let her go." Ordering his little boat to haul alongside, the next moment he and the old pilot (now supremely happy) jumped in, cast off their lines, and pulled for the shore. The *Brooklyn* was now approaching, us (having given up her chase) under full steam and sail. We shaped our course to the east, hugging the wind as close as our yards could brace, and putting on all the steam we could carry. We had the advantage of the *Brooklyn* in laying closer to the wind and thus eating to windward of her. With a smooth sea we held our own, and after a chase of forty miles she fired a gun, which fell short, and putting up her helm and clewing

RECOLLECTIONS OF A NAVAL LIFE

up all sails she gave up the chase and steamed quietly back to her anchorage at the mouth of the passes.

Seeing our advantage, and being greatly relieved, we manned our yards and gave "three cheers for the Southern Confederacy!" All hands were ordered down to "splice the main brace," in other words, to take a drink to the success of our cause. The next order was to secure our guns and anchors for sea, always keeping a bright lookout for sails, as of course we were now in the track of the enemy's cruisers. We made a pleasant run that night, and the next morning, the second day of July, was a lovely day. We shaped our course to pass to the south side of Cuba, not sighting any sail, for which we were thankful, as we wished to pass out of the land-locked waters of the Gulf.

On our third day out a sail was reported from the masthead standing to westward. As she approached her lines and sails satisfied us that she was the enemy's ship. We rapidly neared her and fired a gun and hove her to. Captain Semmes sent a boat on board, with which the captain returned, bringing his papers. She hailed from Maine, "way down East," and was named the *Golden Rocket*. She was in ballast on her way to Havana for orders. The captain upon being told that his ship would be burned expressed great sorrow, which touched our hearts. He stated "that he had lost one ship, and now to have this one destroyed he would be a ruined man, and could never hope to have another command." He was told to return to his ship, gather up the goods and chattels of his own and the crew, and the officer in charge of the boat directed to set fire to the ship. Seeing his ship in flames he shed tears, and we were so sympathetic we at once made up a purse for him. It was a sad sight to sailors' eyes, the burning of a fine ship. We had not then grown accustomed to the sight with hardened hearts. Some weeks afterwards we read through the Northern papers his account of the capture, in which he denounced us as pirates, etc. This proved a

150   RECOLLECTIONS OF A NAVAL LIFE

check to our unappreciated generosity and closed our sympathetic hearts to future expressions of woe on the part of our enemies.

The following day, continuing our course eastward, we descried two sails, apparently brigantines. We fired blank cartridges to heave them to. They proved to be American, loaded with sugar for English ports, one named the *Cuba* and the other the *Machias*. We placed a prize crew on one and took the other in tow. We could not burn them, as their cargo was neutral, so we determined to take them to Cienfuegos and place them in the hands of a prize master till their capture should be proved legal. Our midshipman, the prize master in charge of the *Cuba*, inadvertently went aloft to look out for land, and a portion of his crew proving treacherous, he was shot and wounded and had to surrender. The other brig we had to cast off (and put in the hands of a prize master) to accelerate our movements to make other captures. The same afternoon we took the *Adams*, of Massachusetts, and the *Ben Dunning*, of Maine. We put prize crews on board and directed them to hold on to the light-house at Cienfuegos till daylight. At that time, as we anticipated, several other sails came out with the land breeze. We allowed them to pass beyond the marine league, which is the limit of neutrality by international law. By 10 o'clock A. M. we had captured three more ships, two barks, named, respectively, *West Wind*, of Rhode Island, and *Louisa Kilham*, of Massachusetts; also the Brigantine *Naiad*, of New York. When we set sail we had quite a little fleet proceeding to Cienfuegos. On passing the fort the commanding officer fired over our heads two ball cartridges from muskets and directed us to come to anchor, our prizes going on. We dispatched an officer to the fort to demand an explanation of this conduct. The officer replied that "our flag was a strange one among the nations of the earth, and having never been seen in these waters before he could not let it pass." In a short time the commandant at the fort

RECOLLECTIONS OF A NAVAL LIFE

called upon Captain Semmes, with permission from the Governor of Cienfuegos to proceed to the town. We ordered one hundred tons of coal to be brought to us in launches, and in thirty-six hours we were ready for sea. The captain visited the shore to take observations to test his chronometers, taking with him the junior lieutenant. Upon their return on board we made ready for sea, leaving about midnight.

Our course was now shaped for the Island of Barbadoes, from there for Cape St. Roque, where we hoped to intercept the northern trade for the Pacific and the East Indies. The trade winds, however, were so strong against us, as well as the current, that after seven days out, finding our coal nearly exhausted, we had to resort to sail, and hoisting our propeller we sailed with the wind a point free for the Island of Curacoa, which lay to leeward of us. We encountered some very rough weather on this passage, but on the 17th day of July got up steam and reduced sail to enter the port. We made signal for a pilot, who came off to us late in the evening, but after ascertaining our nationality he informed us "that it was too late to get up to St. Anne (the little town), but he would come the first thing in the morning to carry us in." Upon his return to shore and advising the American Consul of our nationality, the consul entered a protest against our being allowed to come into port, regarding our war as a rebellion. Captain Semmes, feeling justly incensed, wrote a letter to the Governor of the Island asking that he give a written statement that Holland had closed her ports against the Confederacy. If such were the case he wished to report the same to his Government. Lieutenant Chapman delivered this letter in person. A parley of all the Island officials was held, and in two hours Chapman returned, with the news that we could enter port. We steamed in, passing through a small entrance, almost like a canal, with hotel and stores on either side, opening into a little lake. We rounded to, let go our anchor, hoisted our boats and spread awnings,

152 RECOLLECTIONS OF A NAVAL LIFE

and a few minutes after were surrounded by bumboats ready to supply us with fruits, vegetables, and everything pertaining to the tropics. Our purser was dispatched to purchase, and we at once set to work, wlth lighters alongside, to coal ship. The water here is so beautifully clear and transparent that one of the amusements of our men was to throw silver coin of the smallest size in the water and see the little boys—the street "gamin" of the town—dive for them and bring them up from water fathoms deep before they reached the bottom.

The American Consul gave us some trouble here, tampering with our men and trying to induce them to "desert from the piratical craft." After coaling, watering ship, and laying in fresh stores, we left this little land-locked harbor, trying our course to the eastward, against the strong trade wind and equatorial current. We stood over to the Spanish Main to intercept the trade with that coast. Early on the morning of the following day "sail ho!" was cried from aloft, and by half-past six o'clock we had captured the schooner *Abby Bradford*, loaded with flour and provisions, bound for Puerto Cabello. There was no mistaking the "cut of her jib"—she was a "down Easter." We took her in tow and proceeded to port. In the evening we cast off the *Bradford*, with orders for her to hold on to the light, as we did. There being light land breezes and no current, we easily held our position all night. The next morning Captain Semmes communicated with the governor in regard to leaving the prize in the port till properly disposed of. The governor objected most decidedly to this, whereupon the captain concluded to run the risk of sending her in to the Confederacy with her cargo of provisions, placing on her an intelligent quartermaster, who had some knowledge of navigation. He was to take her in by the western passes to New Orleans. In making this attempt, approaching too near the passes, she fell into the hands of the enemy, and our prize crew were taken prisoners, but were not long in being released or ex-

RECOLLECTIONS OF A NAVAL LIFE

changed. We got clear of the harbor, and it was not long before we discovered a sail in sight. We chased her seven or eight miles and finally captured her. She was a bark bound for Puerto Cabello, a part of her cargo belonging to a Venezuelan merchant of that city, and was named *Joseph Maxwell.* Captain Semmes hoped to induce the governor to allow the vessel to remain as a prize till lawfully adjudicated, he giving up the neutral portion of the cargo. The governor, being influenced by the American Consul, disputed the capture as within the marine league. This being so foreign to the truth or facts, Captain Semmes decided to place a prize crew on board, with Midshipman Hicks in charge, to take her to a Cuban port to be placed in the hands of our agent there, then with his crew to make the best of his way to the Confederacy.

We now put out under steam to continue our voyage eastward, and to avoid the current setting westward we hugged the coast of Venezuela with its high mountains running up from the sea. By this track we avoided the trade winds and partook of some of the influence of the land breeze. In making this trip we encountered heavy rain with violent thunder storms and vivid lightning. In these waters we passed over the coral reefs surrounding the islands called the "Friars," from their resemblance to monks' heads. Looking down in the pellucid waters one sees exquisite landscapes and fish of every brilliant hue. I am sure that Jules Verne could never have visited these enchanted waters, or we should long ago have been treated to a description of them from his marvelous pen. The next land we sighted was the "Dragon's Mouth," three islands so called from their peculiar shape. Through these we passed and entered the port of Spain on the Island of Trinidad. On this island is that wonderful freak of Nature, a lake of pure asphalt, a liquid almost as black as jet, which since that day commerce has made wonderfully useful.

154 RECOLLECTIONS OF A NAVAL LIFE

Upon my visit to the shore with a brother officer, walking in the principal street of the town, what was my surprise to be greeted by name. A former resident of Savannah, Georgia, whom I knew in my early youth, had become a resident of this island. Mr. Cunningham was very cordial in his greeting and invited us to his house to tea. There we had the pleasure of meeting his sister, who was making a home for him on the distant Island of Trinidad. Their comfortable house was literally embowered with vines, and sat enthroned in the most beautiful and luxuriant tropical foliage. We enjoyed the evening with them very much, and they no doubt enjoyed the talk of old friends and their loved former home in Savannah, for I was able to give them late news, having had my headquarters in that city when in command of the little steamer *Savannah*, I being on duty there when ordered to the *Sumter*. We were allowed to coal here, which delayed us only a day or two, after which we continued our course to the eastward, passing through what is called the "Mona Passage" from the Caribbean Sea into the broad Atlantic.

The coast of Trinidad is very picturesque and mountainous—one might almost say precipitous—and Nature there seems evergreen, so bountiful and beautiful is the foliage of shrubs and trees. As is usual in such countries and climates, bird life is very abundant and the plumage gorgeous and beautiful. Water fowls, pelicans, etc., and in the interior parrots and paroquets and the brilliant little humming birds fill the air. We were told that there was a small species of deer on the island, but we had no time in our busy cruise to devote to the pleasures of hunting, and the chase to which we were to devote ourselves was the chase of ships, and not of the harmless denizens of the forest!

We pursued our course, contending with wind and current (which were both against us and increased daily), with a clear sky overhead. Thus we ran on for some days, when it became evident (our coal running short) that we

RECOLLECTIONS OF A NAVAL LIFE 155

would have to seek a port to leeward. Captain Semmes ordered the fires banked and sail to be made, shaping our course to Cayenne, in French Guiana. There we hoped to re-coal, and from there continue our course to our desired cruising ground for intercepting the trade which passes around Cape St. Roque from the Pacific and East Indies—in other words, all the trade south of the equator bound to Northern ports. As we approached Cayenne, the Capital of French Guiana (also a penal settlement of France at that time), we found a pilot-boat waiting to take us to a suitable anchorage. Shortly after we arrived we heard salutes being fired, and upon inquiry found it was in honor of the birthday of the French Emperor, Louis Napoleon, it being the 15th day of August. We found Cayenne and its people rather inhospitable, and we could make no purchase of coal, so we proceeded down the coast in the direction of Dutch Guiana. The water on this coast is very shallow, averaging from three to five fathoms. We passed some beautiful islands. On the crown of one of the islands were some guns mounted, and a fine looking building, which we learned was a French hospital or sanitarium for sick soldiers and sailors.

On Sunday, the 18th of August, we approached the mouth of the Surinam River, when the lookout reported a steamer standing towards us. We at once got up steam and beat to quarters, to be ready for a fight if necessary. All the indications were that she was about our size and battery; but our anxiety was somewhat relieved by her coming to anchor about nightfall. We now came to anchor and the crew were allowed to leave their quarters and turn in for a rest, not knowing "what a night might bring forth." The next morning we got under way at daylight. We exchanged colors with the steamer. It proved to be a Frenchman, bound up the river for Paramaribo, as we were. They got a pilot from the light-boat and we followed close in their wake. We steamed up the river, the scenery of which resembling that of

158   RECOLLECTIONS OF A NAVAL LIFE

Southern rivers, with sugar plantations on either side, but far more tropical, even, than our Southern waters.

Paramaribo is the capital city of Dutch Guiana, and what strikes one most about the city is the growth of the tamarind tree, of which there are beautiful avenues on every side. It somewhat resembles the live oak tree, though it does not grow to such size or spread its branches to the extent of that grand tree. While at Paramaribo we had a ball given in our honor by the "merchant princes" of all classes, without even the distinction of color. Indeed, the coal merchant who favored us most was a quadroon, and quite a gentleman, having been thoroughly educated and cultivated in Holland. The daughters of this man were among the prominent belles and beauties at this ball, bedecked with diamonds and attired in handsome Parisian gowns, and were very graceful in the dance as they were led through its mazy intricacies by our brass-buttoned, lace-bedecked young officers. "When one is in Rome one should do as Rome does," etc. One striking feature of the ball, as the evening and exercise grew warm, was the waving of perfume holders, which was very refreshing. At a late hour we repaired on board ship, feeling that we had enjoyed rather a novel experience at the hands of our hospitable entertainers. But "variety is said to be the spice of life," and life has many phases.

Chapter III

Having completed our coaling, we made sail the following day, coasting prudently along to avoid the currents as well as the coral reefs, that are so dangerous on that coast, taking advantage of the winds as much as possible to save our coal. We felt our way to the southward and eastward, making for the port of Maranham in Brazil. We rounded Cape Garupi, off which we found very uneven soundings, causing us to draw out as the soundings shoaled, and came to anchor that night in the open sea. The next morning, upon heaving up our anchor, we found it broken from the pitching of the ship and the surging of the windlass. Not seeing any pilot-boat, we continued our course under constant use of the lead and line, drawing off as we shoaled the water. Suddenly we ran upon a reef, which gave a shock to all on board. The engine was stopped and reversed, when the influence of the tide in this reversed condition swung us clear. Some fishermen about half a mile from us made attempts to warn us of our danger, whereupon we at once came to anchor and sent a boat for one of them to come and pilot us. To our great relief he did so, and with this aid we hove up anchor and stood in for the town of Maranham. There we arrived safely, through an almost miraculous escape from wreckage on the coral reefs. Our little ship showed no evidence of injury.

We arrived in Maranham on the 7th of September, a gala day to Brazil,—as the 4th of July is to America,—the day of Brazilian independence and establishment of an empire. The customary official visits were paid, and here Captain Semmes took a little needed rest in a refreshing visit to the shore, while we coaled, provisioned, refitted

158   RECOLLECTIONS OF A NAVAL LIFE

and repainted ship. The men were given "liberty days," and the officers enjoyed their strolls ashore, where they were hospitably received and entertained at the various city clubs, and met many pleasant people. The middle of September found us ready for sea, and getting a pilot on board we left the harbor under favorable auspices, and with pleasant recollections. The following day found us out of sight of the coast of Brazil, and in a favorable position to intercept the trade, which had been the object of our cruise for some months past.

We now let the steam go down and uncoupled the propeller and cruised under sail. After some days sailing we encountered some most remarkable phenomena in tidal waves and currents, which would occur at certain hours of the day. Like a wall of water, roaring and foaming in its approach like a cataract, it would toss the little ship about like a plaything, making it difficult to keep one's footing. As often as I had crossed the equatorial line I had never before witnessed these tide-rips. As they rolled to the northward and westward all would become calm again. After remaining in this latitude and longitude for a few days, one morning the cry of "sail ho!" was reported from the masthead—a very welcome cry, for the quiet of the calm belt was growing very monotonous. Hoisting the "Stars and Stripes" from our peak they were replied to by the same flag. As the brigantine approached near enough to hail we hauled down the United States flag and hoisted our own, requiring him to "heave to." We found the vessel the *Joseph Parke*, of Boston. We kept the *Parke* for awhile, putting Lieutenant Evans and a prize crew on board, to be used as a scout. To our astonishment we found the ocean almost devoid of the enemy's flag, and after keeping the *Parke* a day or two longer we concluded to make use of her as a target before burning her, which was her final fate. It was a great disappointment to us to find this highway of trade almost deserted by the Federal vessels, for we had long looked

RECOLLECTIONS OF A NAVAL LIFE

forward to reach this cruising ground, with hope of great success. The neutral ships were abundant, but the enemy had grown wary. One little English Brigantine, *The Spartan*, resembled the Yankee so closely that we gave her a long, stern chase. We made her "heave to" with the American flag at our peak. Upon boarding her we found her a Nova Scotian, with clean hull and long, tapering mast. The captain (no doubt out of patience with the chase we had given him and not in the best of humor), upon being asked the latest news, told us "we [he supposed we were Yankees] had been whipped like the devil at Manassas;" and he did not seem at all sorry for it! Our boarding officer remarked upon his apparent "want of sympathy," when like a true Briton he replied, "I like pluck, and never like to see a bully try to whip a little fellow." Of course we enjoyed the joke, and so did he. We continued in this latitude some days and encountered more of the tide-rips, and some very tempestuous weather as we were nearing the northeast trade winds. We passed through a curious phenomenon of Nature in a cloud of yellow dust, being precipitated apparently from the skies on our decks.

On Sunday, the 27th of October, while enjoying a fine morning and a smooth sea, "sail ho!" was cried from the masthead, reporting a gaff topsail schooner, with taut mast and white sails, showing her Yankee build. As soon as we could get up steam we began chase. We found her very fast and the chase was a long one. When near enough we fired a blank cartridge across her bow, which brought her to with the "Stars and Stripes" flying at her masthead. Upon boarding her she proved to be the *Daniel Trowbridge*, from Connecticut, with a cargo of provisions for the Spanish Main. This capture gave us a full supply of the nicest provisions, of which we were much in need,—beef, pork, all the canned vegetables and fruits from the Northern markets, with crackers and breadstuffs of the finest quality, and a deck load of live stock, such as

160   RECOLLECTIONS OF A NAVAL LIFE

pigs, sheep, and geese. The transfer consumed a day or two, but was very welcome work to Jack, and gave us several weeks' provisions.

We now steered for Martinique, and soon after entered the harbor of Fort de France. After coming to anchor an officer was dispatched to pay the official call on the commanding officer of the port, the French Admiral Condé, governor of the island. He received our officer very courteously, and showed a kindly disposition to the Confederacy and our struggling cause. The next day Captain Semmes called upon him and obtained permission to land prisoners and get a supply of coal. This being a military port we had to go to St. Pierre to purchase from the market, having sent our purser ahead to secure the same on reasonable terms. We weighed anchor and stood for St. Pierre, where we came to, close in shore, with our anchor in deep water and a hawser securing our stern to the shore, where we lay comfortably to coal and have some necessary repairs done to our machinery. After coaling ship and waiting for repairs we heard from recent newspapers of the capture of Messrs Mason and Slidell, forcibly taken from the English Steamer *Trent* by Captain Wilkes, of the United States Steamer *San Jacinto*. Such a high-handed measure on the part of the United States Government elated us with the belief that war with England would ensue, not supposing for a moment that Seward (the shrewd statesman) would apologize or give up his prisoners after the approval and commendation of the people of the Federal States and Congress, and by the Honorable Secretary himself, of this action! This act was too flagrant a violation of the laws of nations to pass. Earl Russell was very positive in his instructions to Lord Lyons to "demand an apology to be made within seven days, or return with his legation and papers to London." This act of course would mean a declaration of war, and England would have been sustained by the European powers, but the Secretary of War humbled himself and

RECOLLECTIONS OF A NAVAL LIFE

the Nation and he made the apology demanded. The Confederate ministers and their secretaries were given up and the South lost the opportunity of recognition and an ally, much to our disgust.

But to proceed with our cruise. I leave history to record the facts that led to the immediate restitution of the Confederate ministers, Messrs. Mason and Slidell.

CHAPTER IV

MARTINIQUE is one of the Windward group of islands, is of volcanic formation, running from north to south, and is in a higher state of cultivation than the islands that surround it of that group. Its harbors are indentures in the land formed on the west side, and protected entirely from the trade winds. St. Pierre, its mercantile port, runs from the top of the mountains down to the sea, and the streets being paved so as to leave a gutter in the center of the street, shower of rain washes them clean. In the rear of the city are fine botanical gardens, filled with tropical plants. The grounds are beautifully laid out, with inviting springs here and there, charming grottoes, and everything to please the eye and taste. Twenty-four hours after we arrived at St. Pierre the Federal steam Sloop of War *Iroquois* came in, evidently in search of us. She came near enough for us to see the great excitement on board when she found us in port, with the Confederate flag flying at our peak. We saw the telescopes brought to bear upon us, and their evident delight at what no doubt seemed to them their nearness to a long-desired capture. On board the little *Sumter* there was a fiery spirit of resistance manifested. Every man looked after his side arms, and made application for putting in order their short Roman swords with which they were armed as boarders. It was remarked on board that "so nice an edge was put upon these swords that they might have been used to shave with," and by sunset every man was anticipating, if not desiring, being boarded. The *Sumter* was snugly moored with a long scope of chain ahead and the stern fast to a tree on shore. The *Iroquois* anchored and communicated with the shore. Upon being informed that if she

RECOLLECTIONS OF A NAVAL LIFE

anchored she would have to remain in port twenty-four hours after the departure of the *Sumter*, in accordance with international law, she got up anchor and stood out of the harbor. As night advanced, however, she drew in to the shore, and about 11 o'clock made evident demonstrations of boarding us, as she was heading for us under a low head of steam. All hands were called to quarters on the *Sumter*, the guns were cast loose and trained upon the enemy, and boarders called away. At this time the *Iroquois* rang a bell from her engine room and sheered off from us. It was only a feint, or possibly a change of purpose upon seeing we were not to be surprised, but ready to resist. She rang her bell as signal to go ahead slowly, and steamed out of the harbor. This was our first night's experience, and in the morning Captain Semmes communicated to the governor her strange proceedings. The governor then communicated to Captain Palmer, of the *Iroquois*, that he should require him to observe the neutrality of the port and keep beyond the marine league. We noticed the boats of the *Iroquois* plying between that vessel and an American schooner at anchor in the harbor, and learned from acquaintances on shore during the day that an officer from the *Iroquois* was stationed on the little schooner to give signals of our movements. This was also reported to the governor, but no action taken on it, and the espionage continued.

We were now through with our coaling ship and repairing and were anxious to get to sea. Every evening at sunset all officers and men were required to be on board and steam gotten up, in readiness to make good our escape if the opportunity offered. We had one drawback, the moon and stars were not in our favor, and not until the ninth day of waiting did we find that the night would be sufficiently dark for us to attempt to get out. On the night of the 23d of November everything was in readiness and all hands called to get the ship under way—the armorer with tools for slipping the cable, the quartermaster

164   RECOLLECTIONS OF A NAVAL LIFE

with axe to cut the hawser from the stern, and the engineer with steam up, the firing of the 8 o'clock gun being the signal to go ahead. All this was promptly done, and at firing of the gun the little *Sumter* bounded off like a thing of life. Captain Semmes had a little stratagem of his own to carry out. He steamed across the city lights so that he could easily be seen at full speed steering south. Our lookout, instructed to report signals from shore, now reported two red lights, which we interpreted as going south. After running a short distance out southward we got under the shadow of a very prominent boulder, stopped the engines, and while so concealed changed our course to the northward. Our glasses on the *Iroquois* showed her steaming rapidly southward, and before morning we were many miles apart! Poor Palmer, we heard, paid for his want of success by being relieved of his command. After this night of great anxiety we shaped our course for the broad Atlantic. The enemy's cruisers in the land-locked waters of the Gulf were active in pursuit of us, as we found from captured papers, and Captain Semmes now decided to make our way to European waters.

Our frail bark was built and intended for only one night at sea in the run from New Orleans to Havana and the voyage across the Atlantic was a severe test of her seaworthiness. Our course was now to the northward and eastward, which soon put us in the track of commerce between Europe and the West Indies. We were changing from the temperate to the tropic zone, in which latitude we experienced much changeable weather. The second day out we sighted a large ship standing in our direction and evidently of American build. We fired a gun across her bow and hoisted the American flag. She hove to, with Stars and Stripes at her peak, and upon the captain being brought on board with his papers she proved to be the *Montmorency*, of Bath, Maine, from England, loaded with coal for the English mail steamers that touch

RECOLLECTIONS OF A NAVAL LIFE

at St. Thomas. She was bonded and allowed to proceed on her way, as she was carrying neutral property from a neutral port.

The following day we took the *Arcade*, a schooner from Portland, Maine. There being no papers to prove the property neutral, we applied the torch to her and she burned finely. By this prize we learned of "Dupont's grand naval victory at Port Royal," where a fleet of war vessels nineteen in number, with at least thirty transports containing fifteen thousand men, captured two mud forts and a few hundred raw recruits! We now let our fires go down, lowered the smoke-stack and uncoupled the propeller, and put the *Sumter* under sail, as our coal was becoming exhausted and we were not half way across the ocean. On the 3d of December we sighted another prize. As she was running down to us we had no chase to make, and hoisted the French colors. When under our guns we hove her to with a blank cartridge, and sending an officer on board she proved to be the *Vigilant*, of Bath, Maine. We got late papers from the North by this ship, containing full accounts of "the blockade of the pirate *Sumter* by Captain Palmer," but no account of his want of success! There was also a graphic description of Commodore Hollins's gallant exploit in introducing the ironclad ram at the mouth of the Mississippi (in October) into the enemy's fleet, which consisted of the *Preble*, the *Water Witch*, the *Richmond* and the *Vincennes*. While these vessels all escaped except the concussion to the *Richmond* (which was the ship assaulted), the experiment proved of great benefit to the enemy, whose unbounded resources enabled him to introduce the *Monitor* with more favorable results later in the war. The crew of the *Vigilant* were equally divided as to color, and were messed accordingly, all seated at the same mess-cloth. This making no distinction as to color was very amusing to our crew, but seemed to make no difference to our prisoners.

166 RECOLLECTIONS OF A NAVAL LIFE

Our next prize was the *Eben Dodge*, from New Bedford, a whaler, bound for the Pacific Ocean. From this prize we took a good supply of fresh water, of which we stood greatly in need, also took stores, clothing and provisions. We took her two fine whaleboats during a rough and tempestuous sea, and after the arduous work of transferring cargo, burned the ship. The weather continued changeable and the falling barometer indicated a coming storm, which we prepared for by sending down light spars and sails, and on the night of the 11th of December the gale broke upon us in all its fury. We now put the *Sumter* under close reefed top-sails and try-sails. The wind and fury of the storm increased to such a degree that I was called by the officer of the deck. Some of our bow ports were being stove in. I summoned the carpenter and his crew and barricaded the ports, and strengthened her in such a manner as to resist the violence of the waves and prevent our gun deck from being flooded. For several hours the gale was furious, but as day dawned the wind and sea moderated sufficiently for us to bear away under our fore-sail, and we ran before a fast following sea. This experience in the *Sumter*, from the unseaworthiness of the little craft, surpassed in danger even the violent typhoon I experienced many years before in the China Seas in the United States Steam Frigate *Mississippi*, of which I was master at the time. The bad weather continued and we were buffeted about with heavy westerly gales, and spent our Christmas Day in mid-ocean, nothing to mark it to poor Jack but an extra "tot of grog," which is known to the sailor as "splicing the main brace." It was so disagreeable that we did not even have muster and inspection, holiday occasions on board ship. After passing through about two weeks of this monotony we had a change of wind from the eastward. Being in the track of the European trade, we sighted and boarded a number of vessels bound west, but not an American among them. On the 30th day of De-

RECOLLECTIONS OF A NAVAL LIFE

cember we spent the entire day boarding ships of various nationalities. The only compensation for this trouble was that we learned what was going on in the outside world, from which we had been so cut off of late, and through the courtesy of the many ships we received many late and interesting newspapers. The *"Trent* affair" was largely discussed in most of them. American war news was occupying the press of the world. We then learned of England being called upon to mourn the sudden death of "Albert the Good," the lamented Prince Consort.

Chapter V

Our next port of entry was the beautiful and commodious harbor of Cadiz, which we reached early in January, 1862. We put the ship under steam, and after getting a pilot on board proceeded up this beautiful bay, passing a strong fortification on our starboard side. We had our colors flying, and were saluted by many vessels at anchor in the harbor. We were soon boarded by the health officer, reporting our ship clean and our men well. Captain Semmes communicated with the United States Consul through letter conveyed by the health officer, that we had a number of prisoners on board, crews from the different ships we had destroyed, and he desired, after paroling them, to turn them over to his care. The consul at first refused to take them, but after communicating with the American Minister at Madrid he was instructed to receive them. We were glad to free our decks of the additional numbers that crowded and inconvenienced us.

After getting rid of our prisoners, Captain Semmes applied for permission to go into dock, as we were in a leaky condition. This was refused, with peremptory orders to "leave the port within twenty-four hours." The captain positively declined to do this, and urged that he be allowed to put his ship in seaworthy condition before venturing to sea again. Another communication with Madrid, and we were allowed to go into dock. Next day we proceeded up the bay about eight miles, where we found everything in readiness, and in a very short space of time we had the little *Sumter* in dock. Upon close inspection we were pleased to find we had not suffered as much as we thought from running on the reefs entering Maranham. There was no injury done to her bottom except displacing a por-

RECOLLECTIONS OF A NAVAL LIFE

tion of her false keel and rubbing off some of her copper. The troublesome leak proved to be at the journal of the propeller, and was soon repaired. While in dock we had a great deal of trouble with our crew. Cadiz proving very charming, and the inveterate Yankee Consul putting in his work, several of our crew were induced to desert, and we left the port of Cadiz minus half a dozen men. On our return to our anchorage off the city the captain made application to the authorities for the return of our men, as we were informed that they were sheltered at the American Consulate; but we could get no satisfaction, and on the 17th of January we set sail for Gibraltar. As we left the port of Cadiz we saw a Spanish boat with an officer in her bow waving a formidable looking yellow document. It was reported to Captain Semmes. He gave orders to take no notice of it, but increase the speed of the ship. We had been so coldly received in Cadiz that we cheerfully took leave of that port, with no regret at leaving. During the night we ran far enough out to hold on to the light, but after midnight we got up steam for our run to Gibraltar. In all my cruises in the old Navy it had never been my good fortune to enjoy the charming cruise in the Mediterranean. The Pacific, the South American waters, the Gulf, and the far-distant China Seas,—all but the very enjoyable Mediterranean,—had fallen to my lot. As we passed the Pillars of Hercules before entering the strait, I found much to interest and charm me.

We made the light at Gibraltar just at day dawn. As soon as we had light enough to use the telescope we scanned the horizon to see in what company we might shortly find ourselves—whether friend, foe, or neutral. We soon discovered two sails that looked very inviting for a chase—too inviting, indeed, to be resisted. We chased one for about two hours. It proved to be the Bark *Neapolitan*, of Kingston, Mass., with a cargo of sulphur for Boston. The cargo was protected in a measure by being consigned by Baring Bros. to their agent in Boston, but

170   RECOLLECTIONS OF A NAVAL LIFE

sulphur was contraband of war, and possibly the reputed agent a partner. So Captain Semmes very wisely decided to burn the ship. We transferred the prisoners as quickly as possible, for there was another sail in sight, of Puritanical whiteness, the "cut of whose jib" we thought we recognized. We took time, however, to transfer some of the beautiful fruits belonging to Baring Bros. to our various messes. Figs, raisins, oranges, and other fruits fresh from Sicily were very tempting! The second sail was the Bark *Investigator*, of Maine, her cargo iron ore. She was bound for Wales. Finding her cargo British, we released her under ransom bond. The chase of these vessels had consumed many hours, and lured us away miles to the eastward of Gibraltar. Between two and three o'clock we turned our head in the direction of the rock, and about seven o'clock in the evening, under the full blaze of Europa Point light, we steamed in and anchored under the shadow of the renowned historic rock. It had been a day of fatigue to all on board, and we were only kept up by the excitement of chase and our surroundings of activity, so the night of rest was gladly welcomed. If I may be forgiven the liberty, instead of using my own descriptive powers (which are poor, at best), I will here give a pen picture of this point in the words of an eminent divine, Rev. Robert Barrett, of Atlanta, who is also a great traveler, and I imagine a great lover of Nature:

We entered the Bay of Gibraltar at daybreak. Jupiter seemed to rest on the crown of the great rock that loomed above the sea. Below, like sleeping sea birds, lay the dark hulls of many a steamer, ship and gunboat. I was amazed at the marvelous beauty of Gibraltar. Grim as it appeared from the water, we found it a flower garden where we began to drive along the tortuous road that winds up to the top. Every crevice in the rock seemed to blossom. Such fuchsias, such geraniums I never saw before! At the foot of the rock is a town of 20,000, Spaniards and Moors. The shops and streets present a most novel and interesting appearance. The garrison is composed of 6000 red coats. This great rock, 1400 feet high, is hollowed out. A series of galleries or tunnels are cut on the inside, about ten feet back from the outer wall

RECOLLECTIONS OF A NAVAL LIFE 171

of the precipice. These galleries are pierced every forty feet, for cannon and for light. Still further in the rock are great chambers full of ammunition and provisions sufficient for five years. Thus while this vast mountain of stone is covered with flowers, it fairly bristles with unseen guns. Between Gibraltar and Spain is a strip of neutral ground, flat, unused, barren, useless, like all neutrality! The view of the bay and of the sea from the top of Gibraltar is quite as fine as the Bay of Naples. The snow-crowned summits of the Sierra Nevadas are distinctly seen. The solemn, far-off mountains of Africa suggest mystery. The Mediterranean seems to say, "I mean History." The Atlantic, vast and majestic, stretches toward the West.

If Cadiz tried to freeze us out and gave no hospitable hand to "the stranger at her gates," we were fully compensated for the mortification by the warmth of our reception at Gibraltar. Our "English cousins" warmly welcomed us. Even while obliged to observe a strict neutrality, this did not interfere with the social enjoyment of our sojourn among them. We were not unexpected visitors at the port of Gibraltar, for the news of our trouble at Cadiz had preceded us, and the chase we made for the *Neapolitan* had drawn crowds to the signal station to witness the capture, and subsequently our little bonfire had created a great excitement. Soon after anchoring we were made the usual tender of service from the admiral of the port, and had sent a boat to report ourselves to the health officer. By ten o'clock the next morning officers · of the Army and Navy, and citizens, began to call on us. At an early hour Captain Semmes went on shore to pay his respects to the military commander of the rock, Sir Wm. J. Codrington, K.C.B. He gave permission to land our prisoners, who were paroled and sent on shore immediately. We were treated with all the courtesy due to our rank, and but one stipulation made, "that we should not pursue the enemy from British neutral territory." This, of course, we could not do in the face of international law, in which our leader was so well learned. Communicating

172   RECOLLECTIONS OF A NAVAL LIFE

with our minister in England, Mr. Mason (he had just relieved Mr. Yancey, who from ill health gave up his position), we were allowed to draw upon Messrs. Fraser, Trenholm & Co. for repairs to our little craft, sadly in need of them. We then entered heartily into the enjoyments of the port. The clubhouses were opened to us, and we made many pleasant acquaintances. It gives me great pleasure here to record that in those days of recreation I formed a very pleasant friendship, which has not ceased (but grown warmer with the passing years), for a young Canadian, an Army officer, Brown Wallis, a lieutenant in the "Prince of Wales 100th Regiment of Royal Canadians," then stationed at the Rock. Here we also met Major Fremantle, who afterwards, later in the war, visited our Southern States, and was a warm Confederate sympathizer, writing and publishing very interesting accounts of the same. In writing of my friend, Captain Brown Wallis, a late English paper makes this statement: "Mr. Brown Wallis was one of the original Canadian officers of our regiment. His commission in the 100th bore date July, 1858. During the time he served in the old 100th he was one of the smartest officers and a thorough soldier. He took the greatest possible interest and trouble in promoting and furthering everything for the welfare of the regiment. He left the 100th to take a very responsible and highly important appointment under the Government of Canada. His retirement from the old corps was universally regretted by his brother officers and the rank and file, amongst whom he was so deservedly popular. That he should some years before have given up the profession of the law, for which he was studying, the comforts and luxuries of a home of affluence, to embrace the military profession, won for him the admiration of his friends, and are the best evidence that the spirit of loyalty and patriotism is as strong in the hearts of Young Canada as in any portion of Her Majesty's dominions." He is still

RECOLLECTIONS OF A NAVAL LIFE

a faithful and loyal subject of Her Majesty, being in the Department of Interior, at Ottawa, Canada, and still faithful and loyal to the friendships of his youth,—a noble, earnest English gentleman. Some of my happiest hours of leisure were spent with him at Gibraltar and I review that time with unfeigned pleasure in memory.

Chapter VI

A few days after our arrival at Gibraltar we were invited to partake of one of their greatest sports and pleasures—a grand fox chase. An English nobleman, who owned them, allowed the 100th Regiment to keep his pack of fifty hounds at the Rock of Gibraltar, and it was worth seeing these splendid creatures in twenty-five couples, under full control of their keepers,—hunters, keepers and all in gay attire and eager for the chase. I had often heard and read of the vigor of English women, but saw proof of it at that time. Sir Wm. Codrington, with Lady Codrington and their two young daughters, joined our party. We crossed the little narrow strip of land that joins the Rock to Spain, and a few miles' ride brought us into the cork woods. The early part of the day we enjoyed the chase through this forest, the echoes of which resounded with the baying of the hounds. The ladies entered keenly into the sport, rode their horses beautifully, with no apparent fatigue, though it must have been a ride of between thirty and forty miles, and returned quite fresh to a seven o'clock dinner! Imagine an American lady doing the same! The cry of the fifty hounds was music, and although on so grand a scale it brought to memory other fox hunts over, the red clay hills of Georgia. The dogs ran so admirably that, to use the huntsman's parlance, you "could cover them with a blanket." We got up two or three of the wily, treacherous, little beasts, but carried none in as trophies. Our ride was over a very broken country. We were fond of riding through the cork woods, but were warned to avoid them. The rough men who barked the trees for the cork of commerce were a set of banditti willing to venture anything for money.

RECOLLECTIONS OF A NAVAL LIFE

They would not have scrupled to capture us had any reward been offered for our heads by our enemies. The cork tree somewhat resembles the oak, though it does not grow so large or have as luxuriant foliage.

After a few days in Gibraltar, and much effort made to procure it, we began to realize the impossibility of securing coal. The captain decided to send the paymaster, Mr. Henry Myers, to Cadiz for it. In accomplishing this duty he was accompanied by a friend, a former United States Consul at Cadiz, Mr. Tunstall. They took passage on a little French steamer that plied between the Rock of Gibraltar and Cadiz, stopping at the Moorish town of Tangier on the route. Arriving at Tangier, they found the steamer would be delayed an hour or two, and so decided to walk up to the hotel. Upon their return to the steamer the ever-watchful Yankee Consul informed the authorities that there was a pirate on shore for whom a large ransom would be paid, thus arousing their cupidity. The two unfortunate gentlemen were set upon by a Moorish mob of soldiers, overpowered and seized, placed in double irons and imprisoned at the American Consulate.

As soon as the news of this high-handed and unjust act reached the Rock, Captain Semmes made every effort for their release. He wrote to the English Minister, asking his immediate influence in the name of civilization and humanity! Mr. Hay refused to interfere, simply declaring the neutrality of his government, and Messrs. Myers and Tunstall were hurried off on board the enemy's Sloop of War *Ino*. From this vessel they were transferred to the Federal Merchant Ship *Harvest Home*, on board of which they were treated with the greatest insult and indignity. Their heads were shaved like felons, they were heavily ironed, and put below hatches and kept in this condition till they reached Boston. There they were imprisoned for awhile, but treated as prisoners of war, and finally released on parole. Paymaster Myers was a most efficient officer and a high-toned gentleman. The treatment he received aroused in the hearts of his brother offi-

RECOLLECTIONS OF A NAVAL LIFE

cers and shipmates a feeling of righteous indignation. I have at times the pleasure of extending to him the hand of friendship in these more peaceful days.

The career of the doughty little *Sumter* was drawing to a close; dangers seemed to beset her at every turn. We were unable to purchase coal, and could not make the necessary repairs. It would have been absolutely necessary to have had new boilers put in to make another cruise or prolong this one, and we could not have done this short of the shipyards of England. In the face of all these difficulties,—to say nothing of being watched by from three to six Federal cruisers, each one greatly her superior,—Captain Semmes made up his mind, after much deliberation, and with much regret, to lay up the *Sumter* in ordinary, in charge of Midshipman Armstrong, Master's Mate Hester, and ten seamen. To pay off his officers and crew, with instructions to make the best of their way to the South and report to the Government at Richmond, was his next step, and the hour of parting came, upon which we need not dwell.

I have always felt that the little *Sumter* has never had full justice done her, or been accorded her high meed of praise! She was the first vessel to unfurl the flag of the young Confederacy to the nations of the world on the high seas. Frail and unseaworthy at best, her career was a marvel. In the hands of a commander as daring as any Viking in seamanship, she swept the waters of the Caribbean Sea as she moved silently on her career of triumph. No ship of her size, her frailness, and her armament ever played such havoc on a powerful foe! Within the six short months of her brief career she had captured, ransomed, or destroyed seventeen of the enemy's ships, and so alarmed the commercial world as almost to drive their flag from the thoroughfares of the ocean. When Captain Semmes made known his intention of giving up the little craft there was a feeling of sadness among officers and crew. Of course she had done what she could, and there was pride and satisfaction in feeling she had accomplished

RECOLLECTIONS OF A NAVAL LIFE

a great deal, but it seemed to sailor hearts like desertion and abandonment to leave her to an unknown fate! There was no use, however, in the face of the frowning circumstances, to attempt to run the blockade. After consulting by telegram our minister, Mr. Mason, and coming to a decision, the captain gave orders to disband and seek other work for their cause and country. In less than a couple of months the little *Sumter* was sold, and sailed under the British flag as a merchant ship. We afterwards heard she had gone into the port of Charleston, South Carolina, as a blockade runner, the new owner having given her the name *Gibraltar*. After some little time and service she found a watery grave in the North Sea, where two years later her far-famed successor, the *Alabama*, was doomed to sink after an unequal combat, to be seen no more "till the sea gives up her dead!"

About the middle of April we took passage on the English mail steamer for Southampton. She was on her regular trip from India, and had as passengers many Englishmen who had worn out health and strength in the East in search of fortune, and were now returning to Old England with well-filled pockets to recruit broken health and spend their declining years in affluence and comfort. The steamer was fitted up with every luxury and comfort for the East India traveler and we made ourselves very comfortable. As we passed out of the harbor of Gibraltar we cast a lingering look at the little vessel that had been our "home on the rolling deep" during those last exciting months. Many of our hospitable friends and entertainers of the regiment at the Rock were there to wish us a very pleasant voyage home. We were fully prepared to enjoy the voyage as passengers, and not actors, on the magnificent mail steamer, and were delighted with the beautiful scenery on the coasts of Spain, Portugal and France. After six days' pleasant steaming at this charming season of the year, we entered the harbor of Southampton, and after a few hours' rest took rail for London.

12

Chapter VII

Captain Semmes and I took rooms together in Euston Square, a very convenient and central part of the great city. A parlor and two bed-rooms furnished our suite, and we gave ourselves up to rest and enjoyment for a few days. While in London we met many brother officers, some resident in England at the time, and others, like ourselves, birds of passage. We also learned all the Confederate naval news and plans on this side of the water. The new Gunboat *Oreto* (afterwards named the *Florida*) had just sailed, without armament, under the British flag, for Nassau, New Providence, where her brave and gallant commander, dashing John N. Maffitt, was waiting for her. Another new ship, the *290*, was nearing completion, but no officers yet assigned to her command. We were all delighted with our minister abroad, Mr. Mason, who had succeeded Mr. Yancey (who on account of failing health had returned home). Mr. Mason was a typical Southern gentleman, a fine representative of the old Virginia school of that day. When we called on him to discuss affairs we were invited to clay pipes and old Virginia tobacco, with true Southern hospitality. While in London we had the pleasure of attending Mr. Spurgeon's tabernacle, by invitation of one of his church dignitaries. He offered to provide seats for us. According to appointment we met him the following day (which was the Sabbath) at the door of the tabernacle. He escorted us into the building by a private way, and up a flight of stairs, which opened upon Mr. Spurgeon's platform, in the rear of which were a number of pews. In one of these pews sat Mrs. Spurgeon and family. Opposite them we, with the church officials, took our seats. The enormous building was filled to overflowing, but the greatest order and

RECOLLECTIONS OF A NAVAL LIFE   179

decorum prevailed. The wonderful speaker was listened to with breathless silence. I was more impressed with his earnestness than his eloquence. I had so lately heard the celebrated Dr. Palmer, of New Orleans, that I think I was mentally comparing the two speakers and giving the palm of eloquence to the latter. At the conclusion of the services the immense throng quietly dispersed. We had heard that Mr. Spurgeon preached to the masses— the working classes of London—and if this was true it was a pleasure to witness their reverence in the tabernacle and upon retiring from it.

At our boarding place in Euston Square we had the pleasure of a visit from a genial English clergyman, Rev. Francis W. Tremlett, in charge of the church at Belsize Park. He was an ardent sympathizer with the South and her cause. He invited us to his house, a beautiful English home presided over by his mother and sister. We accepted this kind invitation and met there many Confederate and English Navy officers. The friendship for Mr. Tremlett and his family here formed has been earnest and life-long.

There was no apparent work for us abroad, and we resolved to turn our faces homeward to the Confederacy. For this purpose, late in May, we took passage in the Steamer *Melita* for Nassau, intending to run the blockade from that point into Norfolk, Virginia. The *Melita* was loaded with arms and ammunition and belonged to the English firm of Isaac Bros. Accompanying us on our passage to Nassau was my friend and relative, Hon. John E. Ward, returning from China, where he had been as United States Minister. He had left his family in Europe and was making his way into the Confederacy. He was full of his late mission, and very entertaining. I recollect an amusing anecdote of him in this connection. At his first reception in China, having no official dress (indeed, none was required) yet wanting to impress the high Celestial officials with his personality, he donned his Chatham

180 RECOLLECTIONS OF A NAVAL LIFE

Artillery uniform, of which honored company he had been captain in Savannah. Through the interpreter the Chinese wished to know the meaning of the letters "C. A." on his belt. With ready wit he told them "China and America." This satisfied their curiosity and their sense of honor and dignity. They were very much flattered, and it had the effect the minister desired.

Arriving at Nassau, we found it a live seaport town, crowded with blockade runners and shipping. The hotels were swarming with Confederates and Federals, the latter driving a lively trade in furnishing arms and equipments to the Confederates. Here we met the gallant Maffitt at work before the Colonial Court getting the *Oreto* cleared of the charge of violating English neutrality, which he was at last, after much effort, successful in doing. While here Captain Semmes gave up one of his officers, Lieutenant Stribbling, to become the executive officer of Maffitt's ship. Among the guests at the Victoria Hotel were many ladies from the North and South. Among them shone conspicuously Maffitt's young daughter, handsome and just grown up. The inspiring war song, "Maryland, My Maryland," we heard for the first time from her young lips, and sung with great expression and pathos it made one of the events of the evening at the hotel, and always met a round of applause.

Maffitt after great delay got his ship out of this harbor and proceeded to his appointed rendezvous to receive his armament. He had many misfortunes. Yellow fever attacked his crew and he lost many men; poor Stribbling died; his young stepson, Laurence Reed, died; he had the fever himself and his life was given up by all on board. As he lay apparently unconscious (as his physicians thought) he opened his eyes, and, looking around him, said feebly: "Don't give me up; do all you can for me; I haven't got time to die now, there's too much for me to do." He recovered to do grand service in the *Florida*. Maffitt seemed to hold a charmed life—he dashed through

RECOLLECTIONS OF A NAVAL LIFE

the nine ships of the enemy's blockading squadron, and flew into Mobile like a meteor, and when recovered and recruited as to health and acquisition of men, dashed out again, meteor-like, fearless and brave. His notable career on the high seas belongs to the history of the war between the States. Maffitt lived in his life the truth of the lines:

> "The bravest are the tenderest,
> The loving are the daring."

Though I may have cause to refer to his career again in these annals, I cannot help now saying, with a benediction: "Peace to the ashes, and rest to the soul of one so brave and true!" Maffitt lived many years after the war, and has left a very interesting family to inherit his virtues and his great name.

While at Nassau Captain Semmes received a letter from Mr. Mallory, Secretary of the Confederate Navy, brought by an officer just from the South, assigning him to the command of the new steamer just finished in England, the *290*. He had instructions to gather up the officers of the *Sumter*, but this it was not possible to do, as they were now too widely scattered and some of them assigned to other duties. We were to make our way back to England, resigning on the altar of patriotism, when almost within sight of home, all hope of reunion and domestic happiness, for another and longer cruise of danger and peril, and, as it proved, with loss of everything save life and honor. But I will not anticipate.

Chapter VIII

I have been perusing some of a batch of old letters written from Nassau and England at that most stirring and enthusiastic period of my life. It makes an old man's pulses quicken and the fires of pride and patriotism rekindle on the altar of a dear lost cause. Under date of July 2d, 1862, Nassau, N. P., I write:

As two steamers leave to-day I will write by each, hoping some among them all may reach home safely. Cousin John Ward left here a week ago in the *Memphis*. He promised to see you and tell you of our movements. We were going to link our fates together, when, as I have written in previous letters, the severe trial came to me in the orders to return to Europe and give up all hope of seeing home and loved ones! God grant it may be for the best! At least the sacrifice is made for our beloved country, and it must be done with a good will and a cheerful spirit. The fortitude with which you and my dear mother bear this separation sustains me through it all, and for every duty. We have just received news of a great victory for us near New Orleans, with the capture of 8000 prisoners. We can but hope the city has been recaptured, for the feeling of the people must have been intense against the brutal Butler, and cries aloud for vengeance! We anxiously await news from Richmond, as the near approach of the two armies must ere this have resulted in a battle. I leave for Europe in a few days now, in company with Captain Semmes and some other officers, and as soon as practicable after our arrival across the water we will take charge of our new vessel (said to be a superior one), and we will be better able to do good service for our country, than in the little *Sumter*.

We have just heard of the capture of the *Cecile,* by which I sent letters, a package, and late English papers. It is truly disheartening to see so many of our arms, and ammunition falling into the enemy's hands. We risk a great deal to obtain small advantages. I have just had returned from England yours of the 19th of March, the first and only letter since running the blockade, now wanting ten days of being a year! Could we have run the blockade, what compensation in the

RECOLLECTIONS OF A NAVAL LIFE

joyous home-coming! But it is ordered otherwise, and a cheerful acquiescence must be given to our duty. Our beloved Southland requires my services abroad, and they must be given. I would not be worthy of your love if I could ever flinch from duty. As I have written (but you may never have received the letters) two months ago, we laid up our good little ship, the *Sumter*, at Gibraltar as unfit for further service. We left Midshipman Armstrong in charge of her, with ten or a dozen men. All other officers detached with orders to make the best of their way home to report for duty. The captain and I came on together and reached this place a week ago. To our surprise he has received orders transferring him with his officers to a superior new ship, in which I trust we will be able to do good service for our country and her sacred cause. Do tell Mrs. Armstrong that her son is in fine health, left at Gibraltar in charge of the *Sumter* on account of his efficiency. He will be promoted, and join us in our new ship with the rank of lieutenant. Congratulate her for me. I enclose her letters to him from England to Gibraltar.

Under date of Liverpool, August 12th, 1862, I write:

We sailed from Nassau on the 13th of July and arrived here on the 5th of August. Met here the news of several blockade runners getting safely into Charleston and Wilmington. I hope you have my many letters, the boxes and packages. I will try to write from the unfrequented ports into which we go, but I can not even hope to hear from home again till the close of this dreadful war. We go on board ship in two hours, and sail early to-morrow morning to meet our new ship at the appointed rendezvous. She is said to be a beautiful gunboat, and very fast. I hope before very long you will get good accounts of us and our work. She will be christened the *Alabama*. Young Armstrong is to be second lieutenant, tell his mother. I am glad of his promotion, as he is very efficient. God grant this war may close this winter, but should it continue longer we must be brave and bear up cheerfully till we have driven the invader from our soil and established our beloved Southland free and independent among the nations of the earth. God grant it!

We were three weeks on our passage from Nassau to Liverpool, where we were detained some days in making arrangements for our cruise. Our ship had preceded us on the voyage, and we hoped was now safely anchored off the Island of Terceira, our rendezvous, where a sailing

184 RECOLLECTIONS OF A NAVAL LIFE

ship with our battery and stores had gone before her, and both should be awaiting us if no accident had befallen them. Captain James D. Bulloch, who superintended the building of the *290*, as she neared completion was much annoyed with Federal spies. He conceived the idea of running her out as soon as finished on a trial trip, and in order to avoid suspicion he invited a large party of ladies and gentlemen to accompany him, at the same time chartering a little steam tug to follow the new ship out. The gay party made their appearance at the dock for the excursion at the appointed time, and with all on board for the festive occasion the *290* dropped gracefully down the Mersey and steamed across the Irish Channel, shaping her course to the northward. After the enjoyment of a pleasant run, with music and dancing and an elegant luncheon, the new ship being now opposite the Giant's Causeway, Captain Bulloch made signal for the little tug to come longside, and the merry party, with himself, were transferred to the tug to return to Liverpool. Captain Butcher, a fine young Englishman, in command of the *290*, received his last instructions from Captain Bulloch, and wishing him God-speed and a safe voyage, the ship proceeded on her way around the north end of Ireland, bound for the Western Islands.

On the 13th of August we left Liverpool in the Steamer *Bahama*. Captain Bulloch felt a laudable pride in his work, and desiring to see the opening of the career of the *290*, accompanied us. We were some days, possibly a week, on our trip to Terceira. On the morning of the 20th of August we sighted the land, and to our great delight we were not long in catching sight of our two ships safely anchored. By 11 o'clock we steamed into the harbor and found the work of transferring had begun. The stores were easy enough to transfer, but the heavy guns were not so manageable, and Captain Semmes quickly decided that we had best go around to Angra Bay, on the western side, to a more sheltered place. The anchorage was very

RECOLLECTIONS OF A NAVAL LIFE

much exposed to the prevailing winds, and the captain communicated with the ships to heave up their anchors and follow the *Bahama* to leeward of the island, and that afternoon we came to anchor with the three ships in Angra Bay. In order to avoid trespassing on the laws of neu trality, the captain decided to take the sailing vessel that had the armament on board outside the marine league. Lashing her securely to the *290*, and providing good fenders to prevent chafing, we got under way and proceeded along the coast to the required distance. We had prepared, before leaving port, heavy purchases for hoisting these large guns out of the hold of the ship to the deck of the *290*. This work required very careful management, for even the natural motion of the sea made it a difficult job. To our great satisfaction it was successfully accomplished in two days, we running in at night to our anchorage, casting off our lashings for the two ships to ride comfortably at their anchors.

The name with which our ship left England was the *290*. This was a mystery in itself, apparently. A Yankee, writing an attempt at history in those times, explains for the benefit of the public that "290 rebel sympathizers among the moneyed English people had built this Confederate pirate," when in truth she was the 290th ship built by the firm of Laird Bros., shipbuilders, of Birkenhead. I do not know that they took special pride or pains in her construction, but they certainly made "a thing of beauty" in a perfect ship of her! She was built rather for speed than battle, though her means of defense were very good. She was of 900 tons burden, 230 feet in length, 32 feet in breadth, and about 20 feet in depth. Her engine was 300 horsepower, and we carried a condenser by which to get all the fresh water required for the crew. Her sailing qualities were perfect, and when under full sail, from her long lower masts, she had the appearance of being much longer than she really was. Her propeller was so constructed as to be easily detached and hoisted in a well

186   RECOLLECTIONS OF A NAVAL LIFE

made for the purpose. We could at our pleasure have a steamer or a sailing vessel. She had never the very great speed accredited to her, though when under both sail and steam she could be made to run fifteen knots an hour. Her armament consisted of eight guns—six thirty-two pounders in broadside, one Blakely hundred-pounder rifled gun pivoted forward, and one eight-inch solid-shot gun pivoted abaft the mainmast. The Blakely gun was not very satisfactory. It became easily heated, from deficiency in metal, and the powder charge would have to be reduced on account of the recoil. The crew consisted of about one hundred and twenty men and twenty-four officers—that is, the captain, five lieutenants, surgeon and assistant surgeon, paymaster, marine officer, captain's clerk, and three midshipmen. We had four fine engineers, boatswain, gunner, sailmaker and carpenter. Chapman, Evans and Stribbling, our lieutenants on the *Sumter*, being out of reach when we arrived in England, we made lieutenants of our midshipmen. Armstrong was called from Gibraltar and appointed second lieutenant, J. D. Wilson, of Florida, was third, John Lowe, of Georgia, was fourth, and Arthur Sinclair, Jr., of Virginia, was fifth. The acting master was Irvin D. Bulloch, of Georgia, a younger brother of Captain Bulloch. Francis L. Galt, of Virginia, was surgeon, and David Herbert Llewellyn, a young Englishman, assistant surgeon. Becket K. Howell, our marine officer, was of Mississippi, and the younger brother of Mrs. Jefferson Davis. Our midshipmen were Eugene Maffitt, of North Carolina, a son of Captain John N. Maffitt; Edward Anderson, of Georgia, and George T. Sinclair, of Virginia, all mere youths, most of them just out of the Naval Academy at Annapolis. None, with the exception of the captain, the surgeon, and myself, had even reached the prime of life, and while they may not have had "old heads on young shoulders," they had all the alacrity, enthusiasm and bravery necessary for our haphazardous cruise and steady, ceaseless work. Our engi-

RECOLLECTIONS OF A NAVAL LIFE

neers were skilful and efficient. As for the crew, they were a mixture. With some very fine, adventurous seamen, we had also about fifty picked-up sailors from the streets of Liverpool, that looked as if they would need some man-of-war discipline to make anything of them, but we had hope in the old adage, "time will show" (as time did show), that we had some good material to work upon. We were some days transferring battery and stores from the ship sent out ahead of us, and by Saturday night we were ready to take charge of the *290*. We steamed out to sea, six miles, in company with the *Bahama*.

On a lovely Sunday morning (strange fate that Sunday should have been her birthday and also the day of her sad sea burial!)—Sunday morning under a cloudless sky, with the soft breeze blowing upon us across the Island of Terceira—we unfurled from the peak of the ship the banner of the Confederacy. The ceremonies were appropriate and imposing. By order of Captain Semmes all hands were summoned aft to the quarter deck. Mounting a gun carriage the captain read aloud his commission as captain in the Confederate Navy, followed by his orders from the Secretary of the Navy, Hon. Stephen R. Mallory, to take command of the ship we were now to christen the *Alabama*. All officers stood with heads uncovered, as in the presence of Sovereign Authority, and while this ceremony was going on slowly ascending to the peak and royal mainmast head were the ensign and pennant of the new man-of-war. At the conclusion of the captain's words and a wave of his hand a gun was fired, officers and men gave a deafening cheer and the band played "Dixie," the anthem of the new-born Confederacy. The *Bahama* then fired a gun and cheered our flag. The captain in his speech had explained to his listeners the object of the cruise, the war that was going on between the States, also the work and dangers before them; but he offered good pay for the work, and if successful in our cause the extra compensation of the Confederate Government, and invited

188   RECOLLECTIONS OF A NAVAL LIFE

all who wished to go to the paymaster and sign for enlistment. Of the crews of the two ships—the *Alabama* having taken out sixty and the *Bahama* thirty men—eighty men joined us.

The following day the *Bahama* (Captain Butcher) was to sail for her return to England. Captain Bulloch and he took leave of us, wishing us "bon voyage and Godspeed," and the *Alabama* and *Bahama* parted company. After some necessary work the *Alabama* sailed away to begin her brief but brilliant career on the bosom of the trackless deep!

CHAPTER IX

OUR new ship was now commissioned, christened, and set sail on a cruise. Of course there was a great deal of work to be done before the *Alabama* would be in shipshape for her memorable cruise in search of Federal merchantmen, with strict orders from the Confederate Secretary to "avoid all engagements with the enemy's ships of war, but to destroy all their commerce that we could in the shortest space of time." We had been out almost ten days and were less than a hundred miles from the point where we put the ship in commission, when we sighted and afterwards captured our first prize—a fine whaling ship, named the *Ocmulgee*. All hands were hard at work with a whale alongside, "trying out the blubber." The amazement of the captain at being taken prisoner was so great as to be really amusing, but he bore it as philosophically as a true sailor could, and that is saying a great deal. We transferred the officers and crew and their personal effects, and burned the ship. We did not do this, however, till the following morning, as Captain Semmes thought that a bonfire at night would proclaim our whereabouts and the work we had begun. We took from her a good supply of beef and pork and some small stores.

We now shaped our course for the Island of Flores, the most western of the Azores. We had spent all our spare time in organizing and disciplining the crew, messing them, stationing them at quarters, exercising them at the great guns, and all the minor work on board a man-of-war, which is of the first importance, so that we were prepared for an excellent muster, our first since going into commission. This muster was not simply a calling of the roll, but reading the Articles of War, inspection of dress, of

190 RECOLLECTIONS OF A NAVAL LIFE

neatly trimmed sails, of polished brass and iron works, of white decks, and everything pertaining to the health, comfort and cleanliness of a well-kept man-of-war. The Island of Flores rises like a lone sentinel in mid-ocean, and is very fertile and picturesque. As we approached it there seemed to be a succession of hills with lovely valleys between, and little cottages peeping out from the beautiful foliage, looking very cosy and homelike, and all presenting a high state of cultivation and contentment. I think the habitual cheerfulness on board our ship was due in a great measure to the youth of our officers, and their ardor and patriotism were unfailing. They never flagged or wearied, but were always on the alert to meet every duty, and any pleasure that presented itself was eagerly enjoyed. No matter how hard the day's work, the crew would gather around the forecastle and enliven the evening air with amusing nautical ditties, often of their own improvising, but generally closed the evening's entertainment with the national songs of our own beloved Southland.

Our second prize was the Schooner *Starlight*, of Boston, from Fayal with passengers. She gave us quite a chase, for her captain seemed determined not to submit to capture, but our speed proved too much for him, and a round shot across his bows made him heave to with the Yankee flag flying at his peak. The lady passengers were greatly alarmed, but being informed that they were soon to be landed at Flores, their anxieties were relieved. The following day we ran in so near to land passengers and crew that we were visited by the governor of the Island and most of the prominent citizens. This prize we burned. The same afternoon, continuing our course around the Island, we captured a large whaler, the *Ocean Rover* by name. This ship had been three years out, and was on her return home filled with several hundred barrels of sperm oil. The following morning we captured the *Alert*. She had just left New London with a good supply of winter clothing, and it being just what our crew stood most in need of,

RECOLLECTIONS OF A NAVAL LIFE 191

it was turned over to the paymaster. Their fresh rations also came in good time to fill our larder. We paroled the officers and crew and sent them ashore. Before sunset of this day we discovered another sail standing in for the Island, a large schooner of Yankee rig. She was about three miles distant, but after half an hour's chase was within range of our guns. We fired a blank cartridge and she hove to, an easy prey. She was the *Weathergauge*, a whaling ship, six weeks out from Yankeedom.

I have often been asked by persons interested in the cruise of the *Alabama* of the treatment of prisoners by Captain Semmes. The late files of papers taken from these captured ships brought us news of the harsh treatment of our prisoners in Federal hands, among them our former paymaster of the *Sumter* and his companion, Mr. Tunstall, two very innocent victims, and Captain Semmes resolved upon taking some retaliatory measures for this treatment. He accordingly put the captains of the *Starlight* and several other captured vessels in irons, as a counterbalance to the treatment of our officers. The captains were very indignant, as they said, "on account of their positions," but Captain Semmes replied that "Mr. Myers held a high position also, and was a gentleman, an officer of unblemished character and great worth, and should not have been treated like a felon." When opportunity offered, however, they were paroled speedily and released, so their harsh treatment was never of long duration. The prisoners were otherwise well treated, and after six or eight captures the captain concluded to desist retaliatory measures, and treated them only as ordinary prisoners of war. We had a respite of several days before we heard again the welcome cry of "sail ho!" Our next capture was the Whaling Brig *Altamaha*. After taking all her boats and crew we burned her. The following night we captured the Whaling Ship *Benjamin Tucker*, from New Bedford. By ten o'clock we had taken crew and boats and burned this ship. The next morning we made an early capture in the Whal-

192   RECOLLECTIONS OF A NAVAL LIFE

ing Schooner *Courser*. These ships gave us seventy or
more prisoners, and we were much inconvenienced on
board ship in consequence, so we thought best to go
back to Flores for the purpose of landing them.

We now stood to the northward and westward, and soon
sighted and gave chase to a sail. She proved to be the
American Whaling Ship *Virginia*. After three long hours
of chase we took her. She bore a proud name, "Virginia,"
mother of States, mother of statesmen! How dear the
name to our Southern hearts, but she (the whaler so mis-
named) soon fell a prey to the rules of war. A few hours
brought us great change of weather, and our next capture
was almost in the face of a storm, but we braved it and
took the Whaling Ship *Elisha Dunbar*, which made our
tenth capture in two short weeks! The stormy season was
now approaching, and September gales and the later and
more to be dreaded autumnal gales made us prudently
resolve upon a change of base and new fields of operation.
The teeming harvests of the great Northwest would by
this time be ready for transportation to Europe, and bountiful Nature had no doubt enough and to spare from her
capacious arms, not only for the swarms of Irish, German,
Dutch, and other nationalities that had gone over to help in
the subjugation of the South, and the establishment of the
"great and glorious Union" (for the money found therein,
and not for honor or glory), but also for the trade abroad,
so we entered upon the ocean highway of that trade.

It was now October, the most beautiful month of the
year. When in the lovely Southland the gorgeous Indian
summer sets in, and the skies are blue beyond description,
and life seems so beautiful to dream, to love, to live! To
the seaman it is often a month of perilous adventure, and
especially is it one of danger in the waters to which we
were wending our way, and before many days had elapsed
we were to experience some very heavy weather off the
Newfoundland Banks. Early in October we captured
the *Brilliant* and the *Emily Farnum*, both from New York,

RECOLLECTIONS OF A NAVAL LIFE

bound for England, loaded with flour and grain. The *Emily Farnum* showed a neutral cargo, so we made a cartel of her, placing our prisoners on board and sending her on her way. We burned the *Brilliant.* We sighted many ships, but they were all foreigners. We continued our way northward and westward, heading towards New York, where Captain Semmes had planned a surprise for the Board of Trade. He intended to enter Sandy Hook anchorage and set fire to the shipping in that vast harbor. We might have accomplished our plans—we certainly would have tried to carry them out—but for the violent gale, amounting to a cyclone, which we encountered, and which left us in a very disabled condition. But of this hereafter.

On the 7th of October we captured and burned the Bark *Ocean Wave,* and in the light of her bonfire gave chase to another sail. It was a beautiful moonlight night and the chase was exciting in the extreme, and consumed some hours. She was the *Dunkirk,* bound for Lisbon. Two days later we fell in with the *Tonawanda,* of Philadelphia, a large packet ship, which carried a cargo of grain; but she had passengers, mostly women and children. As we had no room for these we were forced to release this ship on ransom bond, but detained her a day or two, lest we should need to put other prisoners on board. This was a prudent move, as we soon took the *Manchester,* a fine ship, grain cargo, bound for Liverpool. We transferred the passengers and crew and burned the *Manchester.* The weather now began to show decided danger of approaching gales, which reduced us to reefed topsails. In this condition our next prize came running down to us under all sail. We fired a blank cartridge across her bow, which brought her to leeward of us. She was the *Lamplighter,* of Boston, with a cargo of tobacco. Captain and crew were brought on board and the ship fired. A wilder scene I never witnessed. The flames ran up the tarred rigging like demons to the mastheads, with burning lanyards flying to the gale!

13

194   RECOLLECTIONS OF A NAVAL LIFE

Each hour of the night the gale increased in fury, and by morning we were overtaken by one of ‹the most violent storms that ever blew across the Atlantic. The wind blew with such force (though we had taken every precaution to have our sails in readiness for it) from southward and eastward as to press our little ship almost under the waves. We battened hatches to keep the seas that were breaking over us from going below, and passed life lines along the decks to keep the men from being washed overboard. Our main brace was carried away, the main yard snapped in two like a pipestem, and the main topsail torn into shreds! It was a time of desperation, but the brave sailors were equal to the work. They secured the main yard and lowered the spars to the deck without loss of life. Suddenly the gale ceased and we lay in a dead calm. Captain Semmes, who was watching the storm, turned to me and said, "Mr. Kell, in a few minutes we will get the wind with renewed violence in the opposite direction." I at once braced the yards and secured the storm staysail to receive the storm from the northwest, and we were prepared to receive the gale that came with greater violence, if possible, than it did before the calm. It lasted two long hours. The little ship labored heavily, but weathered it. In a constant sea service of nearly twenty years I had seen but one gale that could equal this one. That gale we encountered in the United States Steam Frigate *Mississippi*, returning from Commodore Perry's Expedition to Japan. We were out a week from Jeddo Bay. I was master of her at the time. Grand old ship that she was, she rode out that gale magnificently. In the storm to which the *Alabama* was exposed the vortex passed more immediately over us, which made it seem more violent while it lasted.

CHAPTER X

IN OUR crippled condition we had to abandon our brilliant plans of surprising New Yorkers by setting fire to their shipping, and find our way by sail to milder latitudes. We sailed along the coast of the United States, and two or three days after the gale captured the Ship *Lafayette*, bound for Ireland with grain. We transferred officers and crew and burned her. On the third day after the burning of the *Lafayette* we sighted to the windward of us a tapering, rakish schooner, of unmistakable American build. We brought her to with solid shot, after a short chase, examined her papers, and finding her a legitimate prize, consigned her to the flames. She was the *Crenshaw*, grain laden, three days out, and bound for Scotland. The weather was still rough and disagreeable, but trade in grain ships was too good to be abandoned for rough weather, and we could not seek our mild latitudes very rapidly. Our next capture was the Bark *Lauretta*, disposed of in the usual way. Our next prize was the Brig *Baron de Castile*, loaded with lumber. We made a cartel of her, as our prisoners were getting inconveniently troublesome again, and sent her to New York. Being in the direct line of trade, and so actively employed, we had to keep our fires banked and be in readiness for the enemy's men-of-war, should any put in an appearance. Our rather limited supply of coal must soon give out, and it became necessary for us to seek our rendezvous, where by this time a coal ship sent to us by Captain Bulloch should be in waiting to supply us. As we were making our way to the southward, we fell in with a large whaling ship, bound for a long cruise to the Pacific Ocean, the *Levi Starbuck*. She had on board all the necessaries to be desired for such a

196 RECOLLECTIONS OF A NAVAL LIFE

voyage, besides many articles for trade with the islanders in that distant ocean. After supplying all our wants we burned the ship. We got very late news and papers by her, which were of great interest to us. Our next capture was the *T. B. Wales*, an East Indiaman, bound for Boston. She had on board as passengers the United States Consul to Mauritius, with his wife, three little daughters, and a lady friend. At first the ladies were alarmed at being taken prisoners, but the fright soon wore off, and the children were very contented and happy. They were made great pets of by the officers and parted from us with regret. The consul's wife was an Englishwoman of culture and refinement. We gave up our best staterooms to them, and they fully appreciated our efforts to make them comfortable. We secured from the *Wales* a main yard, which replaced our loss by the gale on the Newfoundland Banks. After getting it aloft in place we were complete again in our sailing capacity.

The *T. B. Wales* had been five months on her homeward journey. Besides getting her main yard, which was almost precisely the dimensions of our ship's lost one, we took a lot of spars, of which we stood in need. We were obliged to destroy some articles of East India workmanship that were highly prized by our lady prisoners, among them some elegantly carved ebony chairs. They seemed deeply to regret the loss of these treasures. They bore us no malice, however, for the fortunes of war. The consul, Mr. Fairchild, after the close of the war, when Captain Semmes was arrested and thrown into a Federal prison, wrote to him and offered to be a witness for him against the many false charges brought against him, among them "cruelty to prisoners." In the admiral's interesting book, written some years after the war, he takes occasion to thank the consul for "this act of a Christian gentleman in those troublous times of malice and unrest." The *Wales* gave us several fine seamen as recruits, and we now numbered

RECOLLECTIONS OF A NAVAL LIFE

about one hundred and ten men—our full complement should have been one hundred and twenty.

We now made our way to Port de France, on the Island of Martinique. As soon as we arrived in this port I was sent by Captain Semmes to call on the French Admiral to present his regards and report the arrival in that harbor of the Confederate States Steamer *Alabama*. The jolly Frenchman received me very pleasantly, but while sending his very kind regards to Captain Semmes, asked me to say that he advised the captain to bring his ship under the guns of the fort, as the Scotchman of the *Agrippina* (our coal ship) had, under the influence of too much Scotch whiskey, communicated on shore that he was there waiting for the *Alabama*, and that he would not be surprised at any moment at the appearance of American men-of-war in search of us. I thanked him, and delivered the message. Captain Semmes summoned the Scotchman, and in one hour's time the *Agrippina* was under way, standing out of the harbor with orders to proceed to Blanquilla, on the coast of Venezuela.

At Port de France we had a most amusing experience with our men, and at the same time the nearest approach to a mutiny we ever had on board the ship. Late in the afternoon, having landed our prisoners and received the usual amount of visitors, the "bumboats" put in an appearance, loaded with fruits, pipes, tobacco, orange water, and sundries; but as night approached we had reason to believe something stronger than "orange water" had also been smuggled in. Suddenly some of the men became noisy and boisterous, a most unusual thing under our discipline. Upon my going forward to quell the disturbance on the forecastle, a sailor threw a belaying pin at me that, but for the drunken aim, might have been serious, and others threatened violence. Some of the men directed to seize their disorderly comrades refused to do it, and there was a general defiance of authority. Just at this juncture Captain Semmes appeared on deck. He said quickly, "Mr.

RECOLLECTIONS OF A NAVAL LIFE

Kell, give the order to beat to quarters." The drum and fife were gotten up and they fell in mechanically, some of them so drunk they scarcely knew what they were doing. "At quarters" all officers appear armed as if going into battle, and twenty-five or thirty armed officers were a match for a hundred or more men with belaying pins and knives. We then passed among them as they stood at their guns, the eagle eye of Captain Semmes pointing out the most disorderly and riotous to be ironed. There were about twenty of the culprits. He then ordered them taken to the gangway, and called out for the quartermasters to provide themselves with draw-buckets, and beginning with the most drunken culprit to douse them thoroughly with water. The buckets full came down on them in quick succession. At first they were very derisive, and cried out, "Come on with your water, we're not afraid of water," but before long they began to gasp for breath and shiver with cold. Then they began to beg for mercy and to promise loudly "never to do the like again." This ceremony took about two hours, all officers and men standing at quarters, when the captain turned to me and said, "Mr. Kell, give orders to beat the retreat." There were none who were not sufficiently sober now to go below and change their wet garments, take to their hammocks, and sleep away their troubles. From that time there was a saying among them that showed the novel mode of discipline was not forgotten (to say the least of it): "Old Beeswax [the captain] is hell when he waters a poor fellow's grog!"

It was well that the captain got the *Agrippina* away on such short notice, for the first call of the lookout in the morning reported a United States man-of-war off the harbor. She was the notorious *San Jacinto*, of Wilkes and Seward fame. She saw us as soon as we saw her. We were amused at her preparation for combat. Her battery of some fourteen guns, her men double the number of ours, we never for a moment thought of engaging her, or of anything but eluding her giant grasp. We remained at

RECOLLECTIONS OF A NAVAL LIFE

our anchors all day, such of the officers as desired going on shore; the stewards of the different messes all busy laying in fresh stores and fruits. The evening set in dark and rainy. The weather was more kind to us than it was when, almost a year before, the little *Sumter* dodged the *Iroquois* at St. Pierre. Knowing the harbor well, we determined upon taking a southerly direction out. When we had gotten up steam and made all other preparations (having no lights) we passed out without even a glimpse of the *San Jacinto*, but we saw by the papers later that she remained some days off the port, still watching for us, unable to credit the fact that we had really escaped!

After a day and night's run we came to anchor with our coal ship off the barren little Island of Blanquilla, off the coast of Venezuela. In this out-of-the-way little coral reef we found a Yankee whaling schooner. As we were running under United States colors, the master of the whaler came out to us, delighted to see one of his own gunboats, and offered to pilot us in. He was quite carried away with our guns and battery; said he "thought we could give the Pirate Semmes fits if we met him, and hoped we would." Imagine his state of collapse when he found we were the veritable pirate's ship! The captain invited him to an interview—he was aghast and overcome. The captain told him that "out of respect for Venezuela he had no idea of violating maritime law and jurisdiction, and would not burn his ship (though he had called him a pirate), but he must insist upon his 'making us a visit,'" which meant that he would be detained on the *Alabama* till we were ready to depart. He readily agreed to these terms, and his visit was of some days' duration. During our stay here the mate of the little schooner sighted a whale off the harbor, and immediately all boats were sent in pursuit of him. They came up with him and had a beautiful chase, which we all enjoyed very much as "lookers-on." In a few hours they had killed him, and taking him in tow brought him to shore, where they tried him out.

RECOLLECTIONS OF A NAVAL LIFE

We had a pleasant stay here, and took advantage of our opportunity to break out the hold, whitewash, and do many useful jobs, while the officers enjoyed many little fishing frolics, as well as happy sports on shore. Everybody enjoyed the week or ten days' stay at Blanquilla. The crew had liberty days in quarter watches, and bathing on the beach was a favorite amusement. There were flocks of sea birds, flamingo, pelican, gull, sand-snipe, and plover in abundance, and those who went on shore usually came back laden with game. Sharks were not scarce, but being a cowardly fish they seldom attacked a party, usually reserving that sport for a lone fisherman or bather. As a health motive these "liberty days" were always given the crew, and they greatly improved by it. When we had finished coaling and were otherwise ready for sea, we let our visitor depart in peace, but Captain Semmes cautioned him "not to allow himself to be caught a second time, as it might not fare so well with him." We sent the *Agrippina* to the Arcas Cayes for our next rendezvous, having still a supply of coal on board of her.

Through the capture of late papers we found that General Banks was fitting out a great expedition for the invasion of Texas, to rendezvous at Galveston, which city had fallen into the enemy's hands some weeks before. Our vigilant commander laid his plans accordingly. He knew the Galveston bar, and knew that the transport ships required to carry a vast army of thirty thousand men or more would not be able to proceed far into a harbor that held but twelve or fourteen feet of water. He designed to surprise this fleet, fire into them, set fire to the shipping, and make his escape before they could recover from their astonishment, as the late Northern papers had reported the "*Alabama* on the coast of Brazil on her way to the East Indies." Closely calculating the time, we thought the expedition could not reach the city of Galveston before the 10th of January, and it was now only the last week

RECOLLECTIONS OF A NAVAL LIFE   201

in November. We had plenty of time to make a few more captures, and possibly we might take a California steamer and fill our strong box with gold enough to help us out!

On the morning of the 29th of November we were coasting along the south side of Porto Rico, enjoying the beautiful scenery, smooth sea, and gentle breezes, when we passed a large French steamer, also a little English bark, which latter saluted us in passing by dipping her colors to the United States flag at our peak. By nightfall we entered the Mona Passage between Porto Rico and St. Domingo. We did not know but that we should find a man-of-war here, as the papers stated that there were many in search of us. Finding none, we decided they must all be busy blockading the Southern ports. We boarded a little Spanish steamer just from Boston and procured late papers from her. They were filled, literally crammed, with Banks' great expedition, which had given life and activity to all New England, and from revival of trade must have made the war very popular there. We requested the steamer to report us the United States Steamer *Iroquois*. What did it matter? "A rose by any other name would smell as sweet," and we might not arouse such an army of sea hunters if we committed the depredation of a name only! The following bright Sunday morning, while most of the officers were on deck enjoying the atmosphere and scenery so suggestive of history and Christopher Columbus, with his early dreams and realizations, and the men were gathered in groups amusing themselves in their own sailor-like ways, we were startled by the cry of "sail ho!" from the lookout. All eyes were scanning the horizon, and soon discerned the snowy sails and tapering masts of the unmistakable American. A few hours' run brought her within our clutches. The bark was the *Parker Cook*, of Boston, bound for Aux Cayes, south side of St. Domingo. She had everything we needed, Boston bread and crackers of the freshest, beef and pork, cheese

202 RECOLLECTIONS OF A NAVAL LIFE

and good butter, dried and canned fruits and sundries. With the sun's setting rays we fired our opportune and ample provider and left her to her fate. A little Baltimore schooner was our next capture. She was of little value and her cargo neutral, so we transferred the prisoners of the *Cook* to her and let her go on ransom bond. She had not even given us a chase, and like many things in life what is most easily won is little valued!

Chapter XI

We sighted many neutral vessels within the next few days, and one Spanish frigate that at first gave us quite a scare, not knowing but she might be the enemy about to "gobble us up" in the dead hour of midnight. As she took no notice of us we concluded she was a Spanish frigate bound for Cuba. We sighted and afterwards overhauled a French bark, that took no notice of the blank cartridge we fired. The boarding officer asked the Frenchman "why he took no notice of the cartridge, but waited for the shot?" The angry monsieur replied: "I and my government are not fighting anybody! There is no war going on with my people" (a most astonishing fact with his mercurial race!), and he shrugged his shoulders with a Frenchman's disgust. In the early part of December the boatswain had called out "all hands in white frocks and trousers for muster," when suddenly came the prolonged and ringing cry, "sail ho!" "Where away?" cried the officer of the deck. "Broad on the port bow, a large steamer, brig rigged." I took the trumpet and called out, "All hands work ship!" In twenty minutes we were ready. Unfortunately, she was in the wrong direction for a California steamer, such as we wanted. She was northwest instead of southeast. We scrutinized her closely. She had no guns, so must be a packet ship. All her awnings were set, and under those on the upper deck were a crowd of passengers, male and female, and as we drew nearer we could see that there were officers in uniforms and soldiers in groups. The scene was stirring and beautiful. The steamer must have suspected our nationality, and she evidently hoped to reach the marine league, and steered for the Cuban coast. We gave chase, but finding she

204 RECOLLECTIONS OF A NAVAL LIFE

would not stop we threw a solid shot over her deck. It was an excellent shot and took a chip out of her foremast, and she stopped instantly. We then steamed up to her and sent a boarding officer on board. He soon returned and reported her the American Steamer *Ariel*, from New York, with five hundred passengers, besides one hundred and fifty marines and some naval officers going out to join the Pacific Squadron. She was a prize of the white elephant style and dimensions, except the prisoners to be paroled. We held her a day or two, in hopes of getting a smaller ship to take passengers and crew, that we might burn her. To secure her we sent our engineer to take out a part of her machinery and disable her temporarily. Our boarding officer, Lieutenant Armstrong, reported all alarm on board among the ladies, but when Captain Semmes sent him back to take charge of her with the promise and assurance that no ill should befall them, they were so won by his courtesy that the fairest among the prisoners began to ask for his bright Confederate buttons as souvenirs of this occasion, and he came back with very few buttons on his uniform and fell into the tailor's hands!

The night we were in company with the *Ariel* we sighted a sail, which proved to be a foreigner, but in returning from the chase, stopping our engine suddenly, a part of the machinery snapped and totally disabled us from moving by steam. This we kept a secret, however, for our prize could easily have escaped us had she known it. At daylight the next morning Captain Semmes sent for the captain of the *Ariel* and told him that the chase we boarded the night before reported to him that the yellow fever was raging in Kingston, Jamaica, where he had intended to land his prisoners and burn the *Ariel*, but humanity forbade his landing helpless women and children in a pest-stricken city, so he preferred releasing him on proper ransom bond, return his machinery, and allow him to proceed with his ship. This he gladly assented to, and the papers were drawn up to that effect. When he returned to the

RECOLLECTIONS OF A NAVAL LIFE 205

ship the ladies called for "three cheers for Captain Semmes and the *Alabama*," which were heartily given, with a waving of handkerchiefs and adieus. I find the following letter in my old package, written at this time, that may be more graphic than my memory:

We found no trouble in running clear of the *San Jacinto* the night we left Martinique, from whence we steamed quietly down to an island on the Spanish Main, where we filled up with coals from the Bark *Agrippina*, which preceded us, sailing again in a few days. Since then we have captured one bark and a California steamer outward bound. She had no gold aboard, but we had the greater satisfaction of placing on parole one hundred and fifty United States Marines, besides several prominent Navy officers on their way out to join the Pacific Squadron. Among these officers was Captain Sartori, whom you may remember commanded the little steamer on which my friend Gillis was lieutenant, at the Pensacola Navy Yard. I saw him, but had no talk with him. He was honest enough to tell Mr. Low, who was prize master of the *Ariel,* that he "should state to his Government the erroneous reports in circulation about the *Alabama,* for himself and every passenger on board—amounting in all to about seven hundred—and received the most courteous treatment." Holding the place he does as an officer in the Navy, I am compelled to place confidence in his voluntary proffered statement. We have, however, had statements before of prisoners who, upon reaching their homes, have falsified themselves; but we care not for their report of us, so long as we conscientiously serve the righteous cause of our country. The latest news we have of the war was by that steamer, which brought us dates up to December 1st. The two armies were then on either side of the river at Fredericksburg, our forces under General Lee and the enemy under General Burnside. We doubt if the great battle will be fought there, as it gives the enemy every advantage in ready communication for supplies and reinforcements. That a battle has been fought, and one of great importance, during the past month, I think there is little doubt. The North seem impatient to have their new favorite, Burnside, lead his army into battle, and I hope General Lee will give him a good drubbing (if he has not already done so). I have great fears for our poor seaboard, where their gunboats can operate so effectively. Charleston and Mobile have no doubt been attacked by their ironclads, with what result it is difficult for us to conjecture! I also notice in the papers their raids on our salt-works and lumber mills, when the McIntosh County Dragoons peppered them sharply on two occasions. Once upon going up Sapelo

206 RECOLLECTIONS OF A NAVAL LIFE

River past Belleville they must have gone within three miles of our place, and perhaps have abducted more of our negroes; and again I notice they went up to the Ridge in a couple of steamers, landing a hundred or two armed negroes to reconnoiter (they say) while their boats loaded with lumber. They were fired upon sharply from the undergrowth and the armed negroes made a masterly retreat to the boats! Upon reading this I concluded that we had no force there, but a few of our friends and relations with shotguns and rifles must have taken shelter in the undergrowth and frightened them off. What an outrage on the civilization of the nineteenth century! Arming our own negroes to murder our families! We hear that Mr. Lincoln's fiat has gone forth liberating four million slaves on the first day of January. Truly he is a mighty man!

Our young boarding officer was struck with the conduct of the male passengers of the *Ariel*. Their watches disappeared like lightning! They flew to their trunks and began overhauling them in the most anxious, secretive manner. "I really believe," said he, "they think us no better than their Northern horde of thieves plundering dwelling houses and robbing defenseless women and children." We spent a day or two at repairs, then being in no hurry we sailed to the southward and westward and carefully feeling our way along the Yucatan Banks we entered the Gulf of Mexico. We sighted a bark standing in the same direction as ourselves. Who should it be but the old Scotch captain and the good Ship *Agrippina*. We had made the voyage from the east point of Cuba without sighting a sail. The ocean seemed lonely indeed. The day after sighting the *Agrippina* we both stood in to the anchorage together at the Arcas Cayes, our rendezvous. It was now the 22d day of December. Here we passed the holy season of Christmas. The time so full of home delights and good cheer was to be to us but a time of memories and work. I find a letter written at that time.

ARCAS CAYES, C. S. Str. *Alabama.*
December 25th, 1862.

I take advantage of a quiet Sunday (the last of the old year) to write you, not by a mail steamer, and you may never get the letter; for it

RECOLLECTIONS OF A NAVAL LIFE

no doubt puzzles even the Yankees to fix our whereabouts at the present time, but look on the chart of the world that hangs in your father's library, and in the Gulf of Mexico you can find where I spent my Christmas—latitude 26° 12' north, longitude 91° 53' west—which spot you will find on the Yucatan Banks, west coast. A snug harbor, formed by the little industrious insects of the sea. Three small islands, or cayes, as they are called, form our harbor. Each a few hundred yards only in circumference, and the largest of them not over ten feet above the level of the sea. These coral reefs, although they do not shelter us from the force of the wind which blows violently during the frequent northers at this season of the year, yet form a complete breakwater, so that we may ride safely at our anchors, having a distant view upon the horizon to watch the approach of an enemy. Upon the largest of these cayes is a fisherman's hut, unoccupied at this season, but containing nets and all the implements for taking turtles during the summer, when they abound. We have taken the liberty of using the nets and have succeeded in taking a few turtles. The most interesting sight on shore, however, are the sea birds, which flock here in great numbers to rear their young. It is beautiful to witness the anxious defense the old birds make for the protection of their young ducklings; nor will the old ones be drawn or driven from their nests, unless forcibly removed or killed. This fearlessness, however, is to be attributed in a measure to their ignorance of the depravity or wickedness of man, of which I have no doubt they will be taught a lesson before we leave, for our men, so long at sea, are feasting on fresh eggs and young ducklings, notwithstanding their fishy flavor.

January 1st, 1863. Another New Year has rolled around, but alas, how few the inmates of unbroken homes in our beloved Southland that are permitted to-day to greet each other with the time-honored salutation, "A happy New Year!" Let us not sorrow or despond, but rather lift up grateful hearts that we are still able to defend our homes and firesides from the wicked invasion of the hordes of the enemy and their vandal minions, and God grant that ere another year rolls around our land may rejoice in peace and acknowledged independence!

In one of the early days of the new year, having coaled ship abundantly and gotten everything in trim, we got under way from the Arcas Cayes and began our cruise to Galveston harbor. We gave ourselves five days for the trip, and but for a calm that delayed a day we should have reached our destination on the 10th of January. As it was, the afternoon of the 11th found us with the ship

208   RECOLLECTIONS OF A NAVAL LIFE

headed for the Galveston lighthouse. The man at the masthead was instructed to look out for an immense fleet anchored there. After what seemed a season of weary waiting to us, the cry came, "Land ho! sail ho!" But what a damper! No fleet; five vessels of war only. Presently a shell or two, thrown by one of the steamers, burst over the city. "Well," said the captain in astonishment, "they would not be firing on their own people. Galveston is recaptured and Banks's great expedition a failure!" And this proved true. General Magruder, with the assistance of Captain Leon Smith and a couple of river steamboats, with a number of sharpshooters on board, had driven the fleet to sea. The recapture of the city had changed the plans of the great expedition. Banks afterwards made the invasion of Texas by the Red River Valley, and was met and repulsed by the gallant Dick Taylor.

While we were talking over the changed condition of affairs, deciding that it would not be safe to tackle five men-of-war, each one of which was doubtless more than a match for us, the lookout cried from aloft, "One of the steamers is coming in chase of us." This was a new rôle for the *Alabama!* She had done a good deal of chasing, but never been chased before. What was to be done? We must show our heels till we got out of sight of the fleet. In ten minutes we had up steam and started on our decoy. We furled sails and cleared ship for action. We were now about twenty miles from the fleet. The enemy, approaching on our starboard bow, took position on our starboard quarter. We were now within a hundred yards of each other, heading in the same direction, when both engines stopped. The enemy hailed, "What ship is that?" We replied, "Her Britannic Majesty's Ship *Petrel.*" We demanded, "Who are you?" but only heard United States Ship ——," name lost to us. The stranger said, "If you please, I will send a boat on board of you." Captain Semmes turned to me and said, "Are you ready for action?" I replied, "The men are only waiting for the

RECOLLECTIONS OF A NAVAL LIFE

word." He said, "Don't strike them in disguise; tell them who we are, and give the broadside at the name." I took the trumpet and sang out, "This is the Confederate States Steamer *Alabama*—fire!" Away went the broadside. The wind was blowing in the direction of the fleet, and the Federal Admiral must have heard the guns and realized that the vessel he sent in chase had a fight on hand.

The *Alabama* fought starboard broadside and her antagonist port broadside, and each ship under steam it became a running fight. Our men handled their guns well. The action was sharp and decisive, and did not last long. Just thirteen minutes after the firing began the enemy fired an off gun, a signal of defeat. Our men sent up a wild cheer. We steamed close to the vanquished steamer and asked if they surrendered. The captain replied that he did. We then offered assistance, and he said his ship was sinking, and he needed our boats. They were promptly sent. In his report Captain Blake says: "After considerable delay [it no doubt seemed so to him] caused by the report that a steamer was coming from Galveston, the *Alabama* sent us assistance, and I have the pleasure of informing the Department that every living being was conveyed safely from the *Hatteras* to the *Alabama*."

Immediately after our fight with the *Hatteras* we made sail. When clear of all chances of pursuit we hoisted the propeller and put sail on, as we were running before a northerly gale of wind. The next morning I was on deck very early, looking after the clearing up of ship and putting things in order after the fight, when Captain Blake came up on deck. Having known him in the old service, he saluted me, "How do you do, Mr. Kell? Fortune favors the brave, sir." I thanked him and replied, "We take advantage of all fortune's favors." We ran on with a spanking breeze, and that day sighted and came up with a ship. It was our coal ship, the *Agrippina*. The old Scotchman dipped his colors by way of saluting, and we

210   RECOLLECTIONS OF A NAVAL LIFE

returned the salute.   He little dreamed what work we had
accomplished since we parted from him•a few days before.
We continued our course with favorable winds till we approached Kingston, Jamaica, when we lowered our propeller and steamed into the harbor.   Here we met the
English admiral of the West India Squadron.   Captain
Semmes reported his arrival with a number of prisoners.
After communicating with the authorities on shore we
were permitted to land them, which we did after paroling.
Captain Semmes, feeling the want of rest and relief from
the life on shipboard, accepted the invitation of a friend
on shore and visited him at his bungalow on the heights,
leaving me in charge of the ship to coal and repair damages received in the fight, which amounted to a few shot
holes and some rigging cuts, all of which was soon attended
to and the men given liberty.   In the company of our
recent prisoners all were "hail fellow well met!"   Our
men, carried away with victory, many of them got gloriously drunk, and gave me a good deal of trouble to get
them back and properly sobered.   After reporting all
things in readiness, Captain Semmes returned on board,
quite refreshed from his rest, giving us a glorious description of the difference of temperature he had enjoyed up in
the hills.   We then got the ship ready for sea and proceeded on our way.

Chapter XII

We left Port Royal harbor late in January—about the 25th—bound for the coast of Brazil. We passed through a heavy sea, with a stiff northeaster blowing, but by morning the wind had moderated and the sun rose bright and clear. The first business on hand was a few trial cases and courts-martial of our delinquents and culprits of the few days' stay at Jamaica. These were scarcely disposed of when "sail ho!" greeted the morning air and our listening ears from the mast-head. The tapering masts and fluttering sails in the idle breeze proclaimed her nationality. She was the *Golden Rule*, for Aspinwall, and belonged to the Atlantic & Pacific Steamship Company. We had the satisfaction of burning with this prize a complete set of masts, rigging, etc., meant for the United States Brig *Bainbridge*, that had lately been swept of everything of the kind in a gale off the coast of Aspinwall. We also destroyed a lot of patent medicines. Salt air is very healthy and bracing, and we did not expect to need any of them in our voyage to the distant Cape of Good Hope and the East. The weather was not good at this time; we had head winds to labor against, with diminished speed, and sometimes stiff northeasters blowing—great trials to the mariner. We boarded a brig, but she was Spanish, bound for Havana. Later in the night we hove another sail to with a shot, and sent a boat on board of her. She was the *Chatelaine*, of Boston, just from Guadalupe, where she had discharged a cargo, and was now on her way to Cuba for sugar and rum for the Bostonians. We saved her the trouble of another cargo, and she lit up the heights of Alta Vela, a mountain of rock about fifteen miles from the mainland of San Domingo, and frightened the sea

RECOLLECTIONS OF A NAVAL LIFE

birds, if there were no other eyes to witness the conflagration.

We steamed eastward and anchored off the old town of San Domingo. Here we landed our prisoners of the two captured ships. There is no city in the world of more historic interest than this old city of San Domingo. It was the temporary home of Christopher Columbus, and his last resting place for two and a half centuries. Here his son, Diego Columbus, was sent to enjoy a position of vice-royalty. The ruins of the Palacio of Diego are still to be seen, and also those of the Dominican Monastery, that once sheltered three hundred monks. Who can conjecture at this late period, or what imagination picture, the sorrows of their loveless, homeless, human lives! Yet the self-abnegation with some devout souls must have found its compensation in the comforting love that sometimes fills the hearts of those that "have left all to follow Him." On the cession of the Island of Haiti to France, the remains of Columbus and his brother, Bartholomew, were removed to Havana. San Domingo was founded by Bartholomew Columbus in 1496. The great earthquakes of 1684 and 1691 are responsible for the ruin of the magnificent buildings that once adorned this historic ground, though there has also been much vandalism in later periods, when Sir Francis Drake took the city by assault, and in the years 1822 to 1825, when the Haitians themselves occupied the city for its spoliation and desecration. At the time of our visit its greatness was but a memory and a dream. There were but three craft in its waters, our own one of them. Haiti has been truly called the "Paradise of the negro." Here fruit abounds the year round. Fish is always abundant. The generous sunshine allows them to do with very little clothing, which the Yankee skipper can supply at small cost, and the people revel in idleness. We tried to make an early start from this land of ease, but the usual supplies of the market, butchers and fruit vendors, all on board for the last refreshing supplies,

RECOLLECTIONS OF A NAVAL LIFE

detained us. Finally getting rid of the motley crowd we turned our head to the eastward and steamed away. The day's run was quiet, and after nightfall we entered the Mona Passage.

Our first capture after leaving San Domingo was the Schooner *Palmetto*, bound from New York for Porto Rico. We had a chase of some hours to get her, but her papers concealed nothing, made no attempts at neutrality, and her cargo being provisions we helped ourselves to all articles needed, and burned her. The next day we descried four sails. The first we gave chase to, but she was to windward and a long way ahead. To secure her we might lose the other three. We abandoned her and gave chase to two of the others. We felt sure they were both Americans, they were so tall and white. One was steering to the eastward and one to the westward. The first was evidently drawing us on to allow the other to escape. Taking her, we put a prize crew on board and started in pursuit of the other. She was less obstinate than her confrère and hove to at the first gun. She was the Bark *Olive Jane*, wine laden from Bordeaux for New York. Not a bottle of brandy or a basket of champagne saw the decks of the *Alabama!* The sea maidens and their lovers must have drank a libation to the God of War if the flames left any to go down to their seashells and coral homes beneath the waves! We then turned to our first prize. She was the *Golden Eagle*, for San Francisco from the Pacific Islands, cargo guano. We burned her. Though she was the *Golden Eagle*, she (or her cargo) must not be allowed to make the golden grain for our enemies when we had hardly enough for the helpless women and children at home! A day or two after the capture of these two ships we sighted four more sails, all bound for Europe. One was French, the other three English. The next day a lone Portuguese passed us. The following day we came along with a Dutch brig and an English bark, also an English four-master—in none of these did we take special interest.

214   RECOLLECTIONS OF A NAVAL LIFE

The next morning the lookout reported seven sails, all bound for Europe, all neutral. Truly we were getting into good company. Our dear Maury had so marked the pathways of the sea that they were like the highways of the land, easy to pass by his charts, the lighted lanterns of the deep!

We next sighted an English ship, and an American almost in her company. The English one saluted us in passing. The American was very chary, and evidently tried to get out of the way. We sent her a shot that made her yield. The boarding officer found her with a cargo of guano from the Chincha Islands, belonging to the Peruvian Government, bound for Antwerp. She was the ship *Washington* (great only in name). We released her on ransom bond on account of her neutral cargo, and put our prisoners on board of her to be landed. On the 1st day of March we found ourselves in the early morning most unexpectedly (for the night had been dark) within a mile or two of a tall American. A gun was all that was required to bring her nearer to us, and we certainly wanted her mail or late newspapers. She was the *John A. Parks*, of Maine, and had lumber on board, bound for Montevideo. We helped ourselves for our carpenter, who was transported with delight. With all our captures we had never had anything in his line. He had to be remonstrated with, lest he should want it all, as we could not accommodate a cargo of lumber on our little ship all at one time. We burned the *Parks*. The coveted mail both amused and aggravated us. In these papers came news that the "new rebel pirate *Florida* had put to sea to assist the British pirate *Alabama* in her work of destruction to American commerce," etc.

At this time, while the *John A. Parks* was still burning, we came up with an English bark that kindly took our prisoners, the Captain of the *Parks*, his wife and two nephews, to land them in England. Our next capture was the *Bethiah Thayer*, from the Chincha Islands, with

RECOLLECTIONS OF A NAVAL LIFE

guano for the Government of Peru. We ransomed her. We were now nearing the equator. We met a number of sails, but all were neutral. About midnight on the 15th of March (the weather was very thick and cloudy) the lookout roused us with "sail ho, close aboard!" We hailed, but she flew on the wings of the wind. We wore ship and made sail in pursuit, and used all the expedition we could, but by the time our preparations were made she was nearly out of sight. Between three and four o'clock we had gained on her so effectually as to heave her to with a gun. She was the *Punjaub*, of Boston; cargo, jute and linseed oil. The cargo being properly certified English property, we released her on ransom bond and sent the prisoners from the *Bethiah Thayer* on board of her to be landed. On the morning of the 23d of March we made two captures, *The Morning Star*, of Boston, and the *Kingfisher*, of Fair Haven, Massachusetts. We released the first on ransom bond and burned the latter. She was a little whaler, and her crew of twenty-five or thirty men all Portuguese. We were now in sight of the commerce of the world and never out of sight of sails. At the crossing of the equator (as all mariners know) the weather is apt to be capricious. Sometimes a thunder storm, followed by light airs and calms. Two days after burning the *Kingfisher* we made two captures, the *Charles Hill* and the *Nora*, both of Boston, bound for liverpool. We took forty tons of coal and half a dozen recruits from these ships and then burned them.

On the 19th of March we crossed the equator. There was a dense and blinding rainfall, and the great equatorial current was setting to the westward. We had to abandon a chase at this juncture, losing her in the gloom and darkness. The weather continued raining, with fitful gusts and calms, for several days. The 3d of April the clouds lifted in the early morning watch and showed us a tall, fine ship going to the southward. The wind died away, which was a great help to us, but towards noon a heavy

216 RECOLLECTIONS OF A NAVAL LIFE

rain set in, when we lost sight of her for a time. We steered in her supposed direction, however, chased all day, and about five o'clock in the afternoon we sent a whaleboat out to find her and halt her, and a boarding officer to take possession. Night was setting in. We hoisted a light to guide them in our direction. In two hours more she was alongside of us, a prize. She was the *Louisa Hatch*, of Maine, with a cargo of coal for the Island of Ceylon. What a godsend in mid-ocean! Hundreds of tons of coal nearing the Brazilian coast, where coal, from its scarcity, always brings from fifteen to twenty dollars a ton. Our old Scotchman and the *Agrippina* were to meet us at Fernando de Noronha, but we could not let the *Louisa Hatch* slip, or destroy her valuable and needed cargo, so we put a prize master on board and directed him to keep in our company. By the 9th or 10th of April we came to our anchorage off Fernando de Noronha. The Ship *Agrippina* had never put in an appearance. We concluded the old Scotch sinner had grown to regard us as veritable pirates, or become afraid of our powerful enemy. We knew he had been dispatched to us by our faithful friend Captain Bulloch. No doubt he sold the cargo of coal elsewhere. We now saw the wisdom and foresight of Captain Semmes in holding on to the cargo of the Ship *Louisa Hatch*.

Chapter XIII

To the mariner in these waters the solid peak of granite that marks and adorns the Island of Fernando de Noronha is nothing new, but it must always excite wonder and admiration as one of the marvelous freaks of Nature in this volcanic region of the earth. The Island is made use of by Brazil as a penal settlement. It is well guarded by troops, and has a Brazilian army officer in command, but having very little trade and little communication with the outside world a more lonely, out-of-the-way rendezvous could not have been chosen for us. It has some little farming interest, worked by the convicts, and we were able to get some fresh supplies. We went through the usual custom of communicating our arrival to the Governor of the Island and he sent an aide to call. The Island is in some parts quite fertile, and I remember that we ate there the young cocoanut in its custard-like stage, when it can be dipped out of its shell with a spoon, and is very delicious. Captain Semmes and Dr. Galt called upon the governor and found him at a late breakfast, which he insisted upon their partaking of, after which they had cigars, and then horses were ordered that they might accompany the governor in his "'morning constitutional." His family were, to say the least of it, "caste," but we were not expected to take notice of so small a matter as that in foreign countries!

It took us some time to coal, and while we were lying in port with the *Louisa Hatch* beside us, two ships (evidently whalers) came in, hove to, and lowered boats. Their object was to barter sperm oil for supplies. As we had no flag in sight they could not know our nationality. They innocently inquired, and our prize master told them "we

218 RECOLLECTIONS OF A NAVAL LIFE

were a Brazilian steamer bringing convicts." They seemed suspicious of us. We quietly got up steam and moved outside and reconnoitered. They were outside the marine league. We fired as we drew near, and they made no resistance. One was the Bark *Lafayette*, of New Bedford; we made short work of her. The other was the *Kate Cory*, of Westport. We were going to make use of the latter to convey our prisoners (now quite numerous) to be landed, but a Brazilian schooner that had come to anchor offered to take the prisoners to Pernambuco if we would reward them for their trouble by giving them a few barrels of flour and pork. This we consented to do, and so we burned the *Cory*. We remained some days after coaling, hoping the *Agrippina* would come, but finally giving her up, we went to sea. This was now the latter part of April, and with our bunkers filled and all hands refreshed by a season of rest, we steamed forty or fifty miles to the eastward, let the steam go down, raised the propeller, and quietly began our usual work of watching for the enemy's ships.

We had been but twenty-four hours out when the signal was given, "sail ho!" Another whaler, thoroughly saturated with oil, returning home after a three years' cruise in the Pacific Ocean. She was the Bark *Nye*. We burned her. The next day we took the *Dorcas Prince*, of New York, bound for Shanghai. The *Prince* was forty days or more out and her newspapers were old. We transferred the master, his wife and crew, and burned the ship. For some days we overhauled nothing. We received through courtesy some papers from a St. John's, New Brunswick, ship, but they had nothing interesting in them. On the 3d day of May we gave chase to a fine clipper ship and took her, the *Union Jack* by name. While we were pursuing the *Union Jack* another sail hove in sight. She also became a prize—the *Sealark*, of New York, bound for San Francisco. Both ships were burned. From these ships we obtained late papers and found that

RECOLLECTIONS OF A NAVAL LIFE

the "Stars and Stripes were waving over half the slave States! In thirty days Charleston would be taken and the Mississippi opened." All very discouraging news to us, but only the greater inducement for vigor in our work. We were making our way toward Bahia with the crews of our prizes, four in number, that must be gotten rid of, as they were more than we could hold with comfort. We reached the anchorage off this city on the 11th of May. The bay and city of Bahia are beautiful and imposing. The city is divided into two parts—upper and lower Bahia. The harbor is so commodious as to take in vessels of any size. Bahia was originally the Capital of Brazil, but about the year 1763 the viceroyalty was transferred to Rio Janeiro. There are few cities of its size that have as many fine public buildings, or as much natural beauty. When one ascends into the hills upon which beautiful residences, as well as public buildings, are situated, the eye takes in the scene below like a vast amphitheatre with the lovely bay in front of it. I think the people of Bahia were disposed to be very kind to us, though we had been preceded in our visit there by very condemnatory articles in their papers, complaining of our destruction of the two ships outside the marine league at the island off their coast. The captain with his command of international law soon set them right about that matter. We were a week or more in Bahia, enjoying all the hospitalities of its citizens and the salubriousness of its climate. The men had their runs on shore, and a British merchant gave a very handsome ball to the officers of our ship.

The morning after this entertainment a steamer of war made its appearance in the bay, but showed no colors, it not being the hour for hoisting them. We showed them our colors, and quickly in reply was the Confederate flag thrown to the breeze. It was the *Georgia*, commanded by Wm. L. Maury. She had come in to meet her coal-ship, ordered here to rendezvous. Our old brother officers of the *Sumter*, Chapman and Evans, were on board

220   RECOLLECTIONS OF A NAVAL LIFE

of her.   It was a joy to meet again and hold pleasant intercourse with them in a brotherly way,•to exchange our experiences in the time we had been parted, and express our hopes of meeting again at home in brighter times.   In a few days we were ready for sea again.

On the 25th of May (a day or two out of Bahia) the shout of "sail ho!" from the masthead served to remind us that we had regained the track of commerce on the pathway of the deep.   We were preparing to chase, when "sail ho!" rang out again.   The ships were in the same direction.   We had a rough time boarding and overhauling them.   They were the *Gildersleeve*, a New York ship, from London, with coals for some navigation company; the other, the *Justina*, a Baltimore ship.   We put the prisoners of the first ship on the *Justina* and released her (as some of her cargo was neutral) on ransom bond and burned the *Gildersleeve*.   The next evening we began a chase that consumed the night and amounted to nothing, being only a Dutchman!   The next evening we had a successful chase of the *Jabez Snow*, of Buckport, Maine, from Cardiff, with coals for Montevideo.   We took provisions and cordage and consigned her to the flames.   Our next capture was the Bark *Amazonian*, of Boston, bound for Montevideo.   We turned over our prisoners to an English brig to be landed in Rio Janeiro, where he was going, paying well for the courtesy in provisions.   The next capture was the Clipper Ship *Talisman*, from New York, bound for Shanghai.   She made no pretense at neutrality, and we burned her.

The coast of Brazil is at all times and in all weathers a dangerous coast, being coral bound, and coasting there can never be a pleasure to the seaman from the amount of anxiety it involves.   We were now in the winter season of this country, for their June is as our December, and we experienced some miserable weather.   In the middle of June we were compelled to put on our winter clothing to be comfortable.   On the 20th of June we captured the

RECOLLECTIONS OF A NAVAL LIFE

Bark *Conrad*. She was a very pretty little vessel, and Captain Semmes resolved to make a cruiser of her. We had captured and taken from the *Talisman* two rifled 12-pounders (brass), which we transferred to our cruiser. Acting Lieutenant Low was made captain, Midshipman George T. Sinclair, first lieutenant; Adolphe Marmelstein, second lieutenant, and two young seamen watch officers, and we gave them ten men. Twenty rifles and half a dozen revolvers completed the armament. We called her the *Tuscaloosa*, being the offspring of *Alabama*. When the *Tuscaloosa* hoisted the Confederate colors three cheers were given by the *Alabama*. The cheers were heartily answered by the small crew of the newly-commissioned ship. The youthful captain and crew made sail on their cruise, our first appointed meeting to be at the Cape of Good Hope.

We now passed some little time of inactivity. We overhauled a good many ships, but all were neutrals. Either our enemy were learning the "tricks of trade," or were too much engaged at home to take care of their commerce abroad, or possibly they were "gaining wisdom by experience" and were daily growing more wary of the few little Confederate cruisers that were trying to do what they could for their blockaded homes and country. It was late in June or the first of July that we next sighted an American. We were actually by this time in search of food. The ship's bread had become both stale and weevil-eaten, and we were hoping daily to fall in with a well-provisioned ship. This only could prevent our going all the way to Rio Janeiro for breadstuffs. As Captain Blake, of the *Hatteras*, had once facetiously observed, "fortune favors the brave," and the shot we sent across the bow of our next capture made the ship heave to speedily. She was the *Anna Schmidt*, from Boston, for San Francisco; cargo, sundries, which means everything—food, clothing, medicines, all required for the use of man, and "Boston notions" thrown in for good measure! Such Boston

222   RECOLLECTIONS OF A NAVAL LIFE

bread, biscuits, and crackers, and all so fresh and good!
There was no attempt at protection papers, so we helped
ourselves hugely (with thankful hearts) and burned her,
after our task of lightening her cargo was finished. We
had grown so accustomed to these duties that the days
were very monotonous when such work did not present
itself. We next took the Ship *Express*, of Boston, from
Callao, for Antwerp; cargo, guano from the Chincha
Islands. The papers were not satisfactory and the ship
was burned. The master of the *Express* had his wife and
a lady friend on board, and though they were just from
Cape Horn there seemed no alternative but that we must
take them to the Cape of Good Hope. In the travel of
several hundred miles we now made we sighted but one
ship.

Captain Semmes thought it best to go first to Saldanha
Bay, as we did not know how many Yankee men-of-war
we might find waiting for us at the Cape of Good Hope.
We arrived at Saldanha Bay on the 28th of July, 1863.
Saldanha Bay is in Cape Colony, South Africa, fifty or
sixty miles north-northwest of Cape Town. It has a fine
anchorage at all seasons of the year, and is the station in
this part of the world for the Dutch East India Squadron
on the west side. It seems hard to understand or appreciate that it should not hold the place in the commercial
world that Cape Town does. It is really a land-locked
harbor, where ships of any size may ride at anchor safely,
while the gales at Cape Town sometimes cause even the
sailor's stout heart to tremble and his cheek to blanch with
fear. Arriving at Saldanha Bay we were surprised to find
nothing at anchor. We communicated with the shore for
supplying the ship with fresh provisions, and sent the
seine for securing fish. The fishermen had fine success
and reported the bay "grand fishing ground." The original settlers of Saldanha were exclusively Dutch, but the
country has for many years past been in the hands of the
English. At the time of our arrival there, late in July, we

RECOLLECTIONS OF A NAVAL LIFE

might have expected bad weather, as the month of August would correspond with February in the northern hemisphere, but their winter had not set in, or rather was unprecedentedly mild, and to us delightful. We set to work with a hearty good will to overhaul ship, to look after her machinery, rigging, caulking, repainting, etc. Those not required for the necessary work were given all the delight of going on shore in search of pleasure and amusement, and "Jack" had in turn his "liberty days" to idle and frolic. Although immediately at the anchorage the shore looked barren and rocky, with immense granite boulders and precipices on every hand, proceed a little and Nature asserts her right to deck the earth in verdure, and affords excellent grasses for sheep, that are abundant, and cattle, that are plentiful, but rather undersized. Far back in the interior game is fine and hunting a grand sport. Pheasants are abundant, the deer is native in several varieties, rabbits and quail in bountiful supply, to say nothing of the wilder sport, for the ostrich in its native plains, the lion and tiger in their jungles, and still further inland the majestic elephant is at home.

We were thronged with visitors. All came with extended hands, for the English papers had proclaimed our "piratical deeds," and all seemed anxious to welcome the sea-rover to their shores. The captain had many timely presents to express his gratification over—wild peacock to dine on, ostrich eggs fresh for breakfast, one enough for breakfast for the mess; pheasants and quails, and a superb bunch of ostrich feathers (worth several hundred dollars) as a souvenir of his visit. We were kept busy, notwithstanding our other work, in showing the Boers, and sometimes their families, over the ship, to their great pleasure and admiration. When my work was done in superintending the overhauling of the ship I took a little jaunt and recreation, feeling the need of rest and diversion for mind and body.

224   RECOLLECTIONS OF A NAVAL LIFE

Having been invited by one of our young visitors (a very prominent Boer) to visit him at his home a few miles distant and join him in an ostrich hunt, we made our preparation for the same. Leaving the ship early in the morning, we took horses and rode to his farm, where we found a sumptuous breakfast awaiting us. We had no idea such delicious dishes could be made of the fish which cling to the rocks on these shores, the shells of which we had been collecting as specimens for their great beauty. Everything was abundant and delightfully served, and greatly enjoyed by those who had been three months at sea, and with appetites sharpened by a horseback ride in the early morning. After breakfast we prepared for our hunt. Our friend and host was greatly disappointed that we had brought shotguns instead of rifles. We thought buckshot would be best to secure the birds, but he told us "that they would have very little effect on the hard bones of these enormous birds." Four of us got into what he termed his "African spring cart" (though we failed to find much spring), he taking the driver's seat and driving four horses. We drove several miles, when he pointed out a little rising ground, where he said he had sometimes seen the birds feeding. We began our lookout and in a few minutes sighted three fine ostriches. He explained to us his mode of approaching them. He drove as if to pass them, and made several circles around the birds. They took very little notice of us, only raising their heads occasionally to look at us as they fed. As our circles drew in and nearer to them, he stopped the cart and told us to get out, "as this is a fine opportunity for a shot." We quietly got out, took deliberate aim and fired—without ruffling a feather! The call to "heave to" was disregarded and the majestic birds trotted off, apparently in a slow gait, but making such strides that they covered ground very rapidly in a straight line, and as far as the eye could reach they were going as fast as a horse could run! By this time our "buck ague" began to pass

RECOLLECTIONS OF A NAVAL LIFE

off, and we realized all the disappointment and chagrin of a lost opportunity. We consoled ourselves with shooting at some little spring-bok (a small deer peculiar to those regions), and returned to a grand dinner, after which we drove back to the shore and found our boat in waiting to convey us to our ship-home. If we could have remained long enough our young friend wished to give us an elephant hunt and many other pleasures; but the *Alabama* like "time and tide [and duty] waits for no man," and work gotten through we must ere long leave the beautiful waters of Saldanha Bay.

CHAPTER XIV

THE creeping shadow that throws its gloom athwart the sunshine was in store for us, and grim death (without our knowing it) was soon to look into the face of one of our fine young officers and claim him as his own. Death is at all times a sad and gloomy thing, but when it comes—dreadful, accidental death—in a foreign land, to one young and full of all life's gladness, it is doubly saddening and full of horror! We had faced a great deal of danger, but grim death kept far away till now. Among the last of a party of young hunters to set out for sport and enjoyment on shore was our third assistant engineer, Cummings. The party were just returning at sunset, when in the act of stepping into the boat his loaded gun struck against its side and the load was discharged in Cummings' body near the heart, and he fell back dead upon the shore. His friends and comrades lifted him tenderly into the boat and brought him to the ship to be prepared for his interment. We got permission to lay him to his last repose in the family graveyard of a farmer, who promised that the grave should always be cared for, and with ship's boats amounting to six forming a procession, with funeral stroke and drooping flags we carried his body ashore. I read the beautiful service for the dead over him from my prayer-book, and we buried him and left him to his dreamless rest, the waters of Saldanha Bay his ceaseless dirge till the morning of the resurrection, when the grave (like the sea) "shall give up its dead!" His brother officers raised a subscription among themselves to erect a monument to mark the spot where he sleeps the quiet sleep of death in the land of the friendly stranger. Many years afterwards I had a call in my office in Atlanta from an

RECOLLECTIONS OF A NAVAL LIFE

uncle of Mr. Cummings, and gave him all these details, which seemed to comfort and gratify him, and he remarked that he would be so glad to recount it to his family, who had mourned long and deeply for the youth who had so sadly passed away from them in his early manhood.

While at Saldanha Bay Captain Semmes received by a little schooner that came in from Cape Town several letters from the merchants there welcoming us to the Colony and offering to supply us with anything we might need, especially coals. Early in August we got under way for Table Bay. I find an old letter in the packet, which I here give, written at that time:

C. S. STR. *Alabama*, AT SEA,
July 29th, 1863.

We are now but forty miles from the Cape of Good Hope, and will probably run into Simon's Bay to-morrow to land prisoners, learn the news, etc. I will take the opportunity of writing, hoping some wave of good fortune may attend the receipt in due time of my occasional letters, this one among them. My last was written from Bahia two months ago. It is now over one year since I have heard from home. We have had no news from the United States since the 2d of May. You can imagine our anxiety to learn the result of the spring campaign; how Fighting Joe Hooker fared in his advance upon Richmond; whether our army in the West holds Tennessee, and has beat Rosencrans; indeed, if our arms throughout have been victorious, and conquered a peace. If not, then must this cruel, dreadful war continue till the end of this Administration, when the Yankees may begin to see that the South can never be conquered, and a new President may come in on the popular cry of peace measures.

SIMON'S BAY,
August 12th.

I began this letter two weeks ago, but experiencing a gale of wind that night, we put into Saldanha Bay. Finding we could not do all the repairs necessary, and doing all that we could effect within ourselves, we steamed to Cape Town, fifty miles to the southward, and had the good fortune of taking our fifty-sixth prize, the *Sea-Bride,* just as she was steering in for the land bound for the same port as ourselves. We threw a prize crew on board of her, with orders to stand off the

228 RECOLLECTIONS OF A NAVAL LIFE

coast and meet us at an appointed rendezvous, and continued our way into the harbor. As we approached it was wonderful to behold the people congregated on shore. The hillsides were covered with an excited populace, and no sooner was our anchor down than hundreds crowded on board to see the far-famed *Alabama* and Captain Semmes. Their enthusiasm was beyond description, and their hearty welcome and sympathy for our cause truly gratifying. The day following, from early dawn "till dusky eve," was a brilliant, gala day, and our visitors can only be enumerated by thousands! The two days following bad weather prevented as much visiting on board, yet a few of the more daring ones battled with the winds and waves to say they had been on board the *Alabama!* At daylight the next day we got under way and steamed around the Cape of Good Hope to this Bay, where we anchored early in the afternoon (the 9th), and have been busy at work ever since making the necessary repairs; so busy, indeed, that I have not been able to leave the ship, and in consequence have declined many pressing invitations of the most kind and complimentary nature.

August 13th.

The late news of our glorious victory over Hooker near Fredericksburg, and the gallant defense of Vicksburg, is most cheering, and fills our hearts with gratitude to God, and love for our brave and chivalrous brothers of the South. The death of our good and noble Stonewall Jackson must have caused mourning throughout the land, but his last words teach us not to be disconsolate at his loss, since it was God's will that he should be taken from us! We are looking hourly for the steamer from England, which should bring us news from the United States up to the first of July. No doubt important news from Vicksburg, which place has been so formidably attacked by General Grant. God grant us victory! I wrote you all about our putting into commission as a cruiser a little prize we took, naming her the *Tuscaloosa*. Armstrong is well, tell his mother, though I hope she will hear from him at the same time this' reaches you.

The capture of the *Sea-Bride* caused a great commotion at Cape Town. She was of Boston, from New York, with a cargo of provisions and notions for trading on the east coast of Africa. We sent an officer on board to procure the ship's papers, and bring on board the *Alabama* the captain and crew, with instructions to "lay off and on the port" till further communication with him. Just below Table Mountain, as it sloped to the sea, the shores were

RECOLLECTIONS OF A NAVAL LIFE

covered with the entire population of Cape Town. We now steered for the anchorage in the bay. As we started for the bay the crowds returned to the wharves in the city to secure boats for visiting our ship. No sooner had we dropped anchor than the visitors began to crowd our decks. The officers and crew took delight in receiving them and in extending to them the hospitality of our little vessel. Captain Semmes sat in his cabin receiving the ovation tendered him by an admiring populace. Bartelli, his faithful and devoted steward, stood at the cabin door and received all visitors with laudable pride. The captain, with pen in hand, was kept busy writing his autograph at the request of his lady visitors. The following day was a gala day. Army officers and their wives, all the city officials and their families called, and we numbered visitors from every class and station in life. The captain took time, however, to arrange for the sale of our prize and cargo for one-third of her value. A speculative Englishman was purchaser, whereupon we got up steam and communicated with our prize, ordering her up the coast to Angra Pequena Bay, situated in the Hottentot country, beyond the limit of the British possessions.

We steamed around the Cape of Good Hope to Simon's Bay, the military station of the colony, where we found Admiral Sir Baldwin Walker's flagship and other English men-of-war. They received us cordially, and we exchanged many pleasant courtesies, they inviting us to dine, etc. We remained in port a few days, and then left to join our prize and conclude our sale. We found her at the place appointed, safely anchored. We went to work to break out the cargo, and took such things as we needed for provisioning our ship. The *Sea-Bride* was loaded with all the luxuries of the New York market. After satisfying our own needs we turned over the remaining cargo and the ship to the purchaser. He transferred the cargo to little coasters, running them into ports in the colony, and no doubt realized a good profit. The ship (as

RECOLLECTIONS OF A NAVAL LIFE

we learned afterwards) was an elephant on his hands. Taking in ballast he ran her around the Cape on the east coast of Africa and tried to get clearance papers from Portuguese ports. Failing at that, or to make sale of the ship, the last we heard of her she was seen as the "Flying Dutchman" off the Cape. So far as we know, thus ended the career of the *Sea-Bride*. We returned to Simon's Bay and received as warm a welcome as upon our first visit.

Admiral Sir Baldwin Walker lived in comfortable style in a neat cottage on the bay. He invited Captain Semmes and I to dine with himself and staff. While at table the admiral informed Captain Semmes that "if he intended remaining any time he had better change his anchorage nearer the shore, to avoid any conflict with the United States Vessel of War *Vanderbilt*, as Captain Baldwin, who had dined with him a few days previous, had stated that he 'was in pursuit of the *Alabama*, and did not mean to fire a shot at her, but to run her down and sink her!'" Captain Semmes quietly replied that "it would take two to play at that game; that the *Vanderbilt* had the speed, being four times as large as the *Alabama*, but he could turn his ship in a very small space, whereas the *Vanderbilt*, from her great length, would require much more room,—which reminded him of the chase of the greyhound and the hare. The greyhound was with his great speed about to overtake the hare, when the hare would turn suddenly and dodge out of the way, and the greyhound would go tumbling on, and lose his game." Admiral Walker, however, impressed upon Captain Semmes that "this was the second time the *Alabama* and *Vanderbilt* had visited his port within a day or two of each other, and possibly the third time they might come into collision." After dinner we joined the ladies of the family, and found the admiral's wife and daughter very charming. At a late hour we took leave and returned on board ship, whereupon the captain gave orders to "get under way and stand to sea."

RECOLLECTIONS OF A NAVAL LIFE

The next morning we were fifty miles from the Cape, and continued under steam and sail that day till we struck the "brave West winds" described so graphically by Commodore Maury in his "Geography of the Sea."

We now hoisted our propeller, banked fires, and the next land we sighted was the Island of Java, in the far East, and we never afterwards heard of the *Vanderbilt* and her various pursuits of us till after our return home. She chased us very persistently, from all the newspaper accounts, but apparently it was a chase to keep up appearances, with no intent to capture. We were constantly hearing of her previous to this time, a day or two ahead of us, or a day or two following after us, sometimes almost near enough to see each other's smokestacks, but the face-to-face meeting did not come! I cannot say that we regretted it, for she was much more than twice our metal, and no doubt had greatly the advantage of us in speed. It was late in September when we left the Cape of Good Hope, I think about the 25th of the month. We had a great deal of trouble with our men here about their "liberty days," and had to leave some dozen or more behind us; but having the offer of some of his "boarders" by a landlord, who was quite tired of them, feeling that he could not well spare so many men, Captain Semmes began to consider how he could make good his losses by accepting the landlord's offer of taking the rollicking gentlemen on a pleasure trip, as passengers on board our steamer, awaiting a chance of their offers of enlistment. We could not, of course, enlist men in Her British Majesty's dominions! We left the Cape in a gale of wind, but then the Cape that divides the Eastern and Western world is acknowledged by mariners to be a very "stormy point."

It took but a few hours' run to find ourselves in the Indian Ocean. Our "gentlemen boarders," when recovered from their drunken debauch and made decent and respectable by a deal of scrubbing and a call upon the paymasters' stores for clothing, made a "virtue of neces-

232   RECOLLECTIONS OF A NAVAL LIFE

sity" and gave their valuable services in return for our hospitality and payment of their bills at the Cape, and some of them proved very good seamen. In our voyage to the East (as contradictory as the terms may seem) we struck the "brave West winds" again, had continual rainsqualls and thick weather, and were often in danger; but we did not meet the dreadful icebergs which are sometimes in these regions the terror of the sea. Nothing can be more dangerous than to meet these drifts of ice, unless it be the avalanches that come down the Alps, burying everything in their way. In the year 1856 I was associated with Lieutenant de Haven on the coast survey of Texas. He was an officer who had been in the famous search for Sir John Franklin and party in Arctic waters. His thrilling narratives of danger and distress, his snow or ice-blind eyes and frost-bitten hands and feet bearing witness to the truth of his assertions, made on me a strong impression in its sickening detail of suffering! While I had volunteered in every service that had even a dim foreshadowing of a fight, the blood of my Highland ancestry giving me, I freely acknowledge, a love for the same, I frankly say I would never have volunteered as an Arctic explorer, or chosen a death by freezing! But this is a digression.

We missed the icebergs, but rode ahead of two or three threatening cyclones. The constant entries in my logbook (which I am sorry to say found its grave in the *Alabama*), I well remember, had such entries as these: "rough weather," "quantities of rainfall," "furious, turbulent winds," "meeting a ship would be a bad thing for us now; such blinding rains we would run into each other," etc. It is astonishing, the loneliness of the ocean as to sails. In a run of seven or eight hundred miles, as I mentioned before, we only sighted one sail; so in our present run of more than four thousand miles we have met but three or four ships. About the middle of October we passed the little islets of St. Peter and St. Paul, but did

RECOLLECTIONS OF A NAVAL LIFE

not stop, as the weather was very bad. We were trying to make the Straits of Sunda, the passage into the China Seas. Late in October we boarded a Dutch ship from Batavia. They informed us that the United States Ship *Wyoming* had boarded them a little way out of Batavia. As we drew near the Straits of Sunda we fell in with several ships and chased and boarded three English and one Dutch ship. A day or two later, while we were giving chase to two English ships, a third ship hove in sight. It was too American to be allowed to elude us. We fired across her bow, and the flag of the United States went up, our first prize in East India waters. She was the *Amanda*, from Boston; cargo, sugar and hemp. The papers were not satisfactory, so we burned her, after taking off necessary articles for our ship. We soon after came to anchor off the north side of the Strait, a mile or two from Sumatra, where we hoped to procure the fresh food needed for the good health of our crew, for we had been a long time at sea.

Chapter XV

Having been warned of her near vicinity to us, we tried to keep "our weather eye" open for the U. S. Steamer *Wyoming*. We took the narrow and most unfrequented channel to the Strait, passing Stroom Rock and the small garrison town of Anjar. Our next prize in these waters was a beautiful new ship, *Winged Racer*. She was a New Yorker, of graceful, symmetrical mold, known in the shipping world as a "clipper." She was returning from Manila with a cargo for New York of coffee, Manila tobacco, sugar, jute, etc. We found just what we wanted, and made havoc in the coffee, sugar and tobacco. We thought the *Winged Racer* too handsome a ship to burn, but what could we do? Our tenders were not a success; our only sale, the *Sea-Bride*, was a failure. We could run nothing into our own ports, and to fire our prizes seemed the only thing to do. We made the master of the *Winged Racer* a present of his boats and all he could stow in them, and he took our prisoners of the *Amanda* and proceeded to Batavia, the little fleet of boats looking very pretty as they pulled away. By the lighted bonfire of the *Winged Racer* we steamd out of sight of Java and Sumatra, made a little island called Lone Watcher, here meaning to wait till daylight for further action. Scarcely was the propeller hoisted when "sail ho!" rang out, and we made sail in chase. If the breeze had freshened at all we would have lost her, but fortune favored us and the failure of the wind acted greatly in our favor. It made the capture more possible each moment, and finally complete. The speed of the *Alabama* made her shorten sail and heave to. The ship proved to be the *Contest*, from Yokohama for New York, a fine clipper ship; cargo, Japanese goods,

RECOLLECTIONS OF A NAVAL LIFE

curios, etc. Among other things some elegant hand-carved ebony armchairs that it seemed a shame to burn, they were so beautiful. We made the night brilliant with her destructive conflagration. We sighted and boarded a great many vessels in these waters, but American commerce had dwindled into very small dimensions! The sails were mostly Dutch and English, but Dutch predominated.

Of all the waters that cover the face of the earth none are so beset with dangers as the China Seas. The surveying expeditions that have been going out to these waters since the time of Commodore Perry's great expedition have seemed to make little headway, and with the best of modern charts to light the ocean a ship stands in danger during the changing of the monsoons, or drifting with the terrible under-currents upon coral reefs so abundant on every hand, and shoals and breakers. Winds, weather and the very elements conspiring against us, we now considered it best to make some point to do our necessary repairing. We were some distance from Singapore, so made for the small Island of Condore (claimed by the French), a very pretty, fertile spot. We had availed ourselves of no rest since leaving the Cape, and not having much fear that the *Wyoming* would find us in this far-away harbor, we anchored and gave ourselves up to enjoyment and relaxation. Here game and fish were abundant, bathing a luxury, and life delightful. Insects, birds, reptiles and the celebrated vampire bat were all here, a deer of small size, and even a small species of bison. Apes, too, abounded, sufficiently fearless and intelligent-enough looking to tempt the followers of Darwin into credulity—some looking old and venerable enough to have been patriarchs. I think it was on this island that a party of our men captured a lizard between three and four feet in length. The serpents, we were glad to hear, kept to the jungles. I doubt if they could have been any more dangerous than the rattlesnakes that inhabit the lagoons and

RECOLLECTIONS OF A NAVAL LIFE

sun themselves on the savannas of our own Sea Islands on the Southern coast. But one never grows accustomed to rattlesnakes, or snakes of any kind, and while the mother of mankind in fearless innocence was beguiled into converse with the Tempter "in the form of a serpent," her descendants I have usually found ready to give a wide berth, with a shudder of horror, to all serpent kind.

The young governor of the Island of Condore was a Frenchman about five-and-twenty years of age. He paid us every attention, and enjoyed our visit as heartily as we did. We spent two weeks or more there, and then turned our heads in the direction of Singapore. We crossed the Gulf of Siam, and on the 19th of December anchored under Palo Aor, a little island whose forests are cocoanut trees and the inhabitants Malays. These people were a merry, careless set, who enjoyed life to its fullest extent, lived on fish and fruits, were too near the equator to care for clothing, and gave no thought to the morrow. Simple children of Nature, knowing nothing of civilization, living their quiet, happy island lives, with no knowledge or thought of the bustling unrest of the great world outside the limit of their horizon. The city of Singapore, our next port of landing, is situated on an island of the same name in the Malay Peninsula, and is the seat of commerce in that section of the globe. It has 100,000 inhabitants, and a more motley, mingled multitude of the nations of the earth could hardly be found anywhere. Persians, Hindoos, Javanese, Chinese, Japanese, Malays, Sumatrans, Tartars, Siamese, Bornese, all mingled in the crowded streets, while the shipping—European and American— made the picture complete. We found here upwards of twenty American vessels laid up. The destruction of the Ship *Amanda* off the Strait of Sunda had decided the American East Indiamen to get out of harm's way, or at least to "lay up" until our departure from the China Seas.

We were treated with great consideration and hospitality by the people at Singapore. They were almost as

RECOLLECTIONS OF A NAVAL LIFE 237

glad to see us and fête us as the kind people at the Cape of Good Hope had been. The governor of the colony at Singapore was a British colonel. We sent an officer to call upon him and report our arrival and our needs. An English merchant came on board and offered to supply us with everything in his line. Shortly after he urged Captain Semmes to make him a visit (which he did) of a day or two at his semi-English Oriental home. It is astonishing how rich these Englishmen grow in the East, but they never lose their English habits and tastes, no matter where they locate. We had the usual trouble with our rollicking tars, and half a dozen were left behind at Singapore; but their places were supplied by fellows eager to take a trip with us till such time as they could safely enlist without the consent of Queen Victoria, or with no condemnation of her Government for our infringement of neutrality.

The morning we left Singapore, when our little ship was sailing through the Strait of Malacca, "sail ho!" was cried from the mast, and an American-looking ship being hove to showed us the English colors. Master's Mate Fulham was sent on board to examine papers. The master was requested to come on board the *Alabama,* but refused point blank to do so. Mr. Fulham (a young Englishman himself) was very suspicious of the craft. When he returned and reported facts, Captain Semmes, for the first time in the cruise, resolved that he would assume the rôle of boarding officer under the circumstances, and had rather an amusing experience. He soon satisfied himself that the ship was American, if the cargo was English, or purported to be. When the master of her saw the gleam of decision fatal to his hope of escape in Captain Semmes's eagle eye, he began to remonstrate, and said to him, "You hadn't ought to burn this ship," for such and such reasons. His phraseology was quite sufficient, and the doom of the ship was sealed. She was freshly painted the *Martaban,* but a fortnight previous she had

238 RECOLLECTIONS OF A NAVAL LIFE

been the *Texan Star*. The master made frank acknowledgment of his change of plan; said "all things were fair in war," and rather boasted of the shams and ruses he had used (so unsuccessfully) to save the ship. We ran into the little town of Malacca to land our prisoners, or get permission to do so. It was early morning—the morning of Christmas Day. The little town just waking from its sleep, the friendly lighthouse throwing its light on our deck, all reminded us of distant towns and homes and lights so far away!

In a little while boats came off to us filled with officers and citizens and a few ladies, all urging us to spend the Christmas Day with them. The captain excused himself, saying "there is no holiday in time of war," and in two or three hours we were on our way, the only outward observance of the day being that the crew "spliced the mainbrace" in honor of festivities consequent upon the season. The following day the lookout called out "sail ho!" twice very hurriedly from the masthead, and our flag seemed to strike two Yankee skippers dumb, as they were not polite enough to show their bunting in return. They were both large ships, of 1100 or 1200 tons burden, one named the *Highlander*, from Boston, the other the *Sonora*, also from the land of the Puritan. We gave them their boats, and as they were captured at the western entrance to the Strait of Malacca they found it easy sailing to Singapore. One of the captains when he reached our deck told Captain Semmes, with a long-drawn sigh of relief, that "he had been trying to keep out of his way for nearly three years, but now the suspense was over, and he was relieved that there was no more running to be done." Captain Semmes replied that he "was very glad the long search was over."

The last day of the year we cleared the Sumatra coast and crossed to the Bay of Bengal, toward the Island of Ceylon. We doubled this island and found ourselves on the coast of Malabar. The middle of January we captured

RECOLLECTIONS OF A NAVAL LIFE 239

the *Emma Jane*, of Maine. We took the provisions we required from her, transferred the crew and burned the ship.

Coasting eastward a short distance, we made the little Portuguese town of Anjenga and came to anchor. There were no English in this town, but a mixture of Portuguese and Hindoo, the presiding official a Portuguese. We arranged to land our prisoners, and the officer sent his son to call upon us. Captain Semmes returned this call of ceremony through one of his lieutenants. This officer was so long in returning that Captain Semmes sent me with an armed boat's crew to rescue him in case of danger. I found it was only a feast or fête day, and all officials were devoutly attending church, which delayed our officer's call of civility. Both Spaniards and Portuguese are great nations for keeping saints' days and religious festivals of all kinds. They never allow worldly business or secular employments to interfere with their religious calendar of saints' days. They seem as happy and exultant in their priest-ridden superstitions and idolatry as the Puritans, who turned their backs on home and country and sought new lands with the privilege of "freedom to worship God" in their own way.

The conquest of India by Great Britain is surely one of the "special Providences" in which we are taught to believe, and the "Empress of India" has a right to think with pride of her vast cotton fields that help so largely to clothe the world; but dearer far must be to her the knowledge of the grand religious influences brought to bear upon her heathen subjects. Schools have sprung up everywhere, the printing press, the railroad, all modern appliances of utility and civilization have usurped the place formerly held by despotism. Now a beneficent Government is displaying the happy rule and reign of justice and humanity!

Having coaled ship at Singapore we left. Passing through the chain of islands adjacent to the Malabar coast, we stretched across the Arabian Sea in the direction of

240   RECOLLECTIONS OF A NAVAL LIFE

the eastern coast of Africa. The weather was perfectly delightful. For a fortnight or three weeks we had serene skies and gentle breezes, with scarcely even a change of sail; and fleecy, gauze clouds, such as make children dream such "fairy dreams" as Hans Christian Andersen has given in his very charming books to delight the world. The beautiful dolphin peopled the Arabian Sea, passing near the ship in great schools, and some flying fish were caught by the sailors. On the last day of January we crossed the equator, and the latter part of the first week in February we made the Cormora Islands, and getting up steam ran in and anchored at Johanna. This is quite a stopping place for ships passing to and from the East Indies by way of the Mozambique Channel. Johanna at the time of which I write was ruled by an Arab, who called himself a Sultan. The Sultan sent his commanding officer to call upon us, and we made contracts with him for supplies of fresh meats, etc.

We spent a quiet week among the Johanese, and enjoyed it, they being very friendly. Having taken in fresh vegetables, fruits, and plenty of beef, we got under way and turned our faces to the southward. The lovely weather we had in the Arabian Sea did not follow us into the Mozambique Channel, and as we drew near the south of Madagascar we encountered some of the most terrific rain squalls and thunder storms I have ever seen. The lightning played about us with wild fury, as though opening the very heavens above us, and the thunder crashed and rolled with deafening volume till it seemed as if the heavens and earth, the mountains and the deep, were being broken into eternal dissolution! It was a relief to leave the channel and pursue our way, pointing to the Cape of Good Hope. The "stormy Cape," as it is known to mariners, might equal, but could never surpass, the sublime glory of the storms of such frequent occurrence in the waters of the Mozambique Channel. Early in March we took soundings on the dangerous Agulhas

RECOLLECTIONS OF A NAVAL LIFE 241

Banks, where the ground swell and the angry currents seem to meet each other, and the battling billows fight themselves into fury, like contending armies. "Men who go to sea in ships" can realize in the wonderful power of the elements the hand of Him who guides and rules the storm, and yet whose watchful, tender love "heeds even the sparrow's fall."

After an absence of six months we found ourselves anchored at our old cruising ground off the Cape of Good Hope. We met as warm a welcome as we had received on former visits. Captain Semmes was very indignant to find our cruiser, the *Tuscaloosa*, had been seized under the pretext that she was an uncondemned prize and not a ship of war, and that having been brought into British waters regardless of British neutrality, she should be seized and returned to her original owners. It did not consume much time (with his legal knowledge and ability) for Captain Semmes to set matters right, and after some very spirited correspondence with the authorities the *Tuscaloosa* was ordered released and turned over to Captain Semmes, or his lieutenant in charge of her. But for this useless detention our little cruiser would have done efficient work. Low was an able young officer, who had George Sinclair as his first lieutenant and Adolphe Marmelstein (who had been a quartermaster on the *Alabama)* as second officer, and was fully equal to his duty—loyal and true. By the time, however, that the orders reached the Cape we had left that part of the world, and possession of the *Tuscaloosa* was never resumed. Doubtless she was reclaimed by her owners, or the Federal Government.

We spent several days at the Cape and there met the equinoctial storm March 20th. We had a great influx of visitors, to whom we tried to play the part of agreeable host, though we were very busy all the while coaling and provisioning ship. We received a bountiful supply of newspapers at the Cape, and they were very welcome, for we had been cut off from our part of the world for many

16

242 RECOLLECTIONS OF A NAVAL LIFE

long months. All news was depressing and discouraging. It was very apparent that our cause was daily growing weaker. We could but see that after the Battle of Gettysburg and the surrender of Vicksburg defeat seemed to stare our struggling people in the face, and with the failing finances and shut-in ports ruin seemed inevitable!

By the middle of April we had reached the track of homeward bound American ships from the Pacific. On the 22d of April we sighted and gave chase to a ship and chased her all night by the light of the moon, on a smooth sea. At daylight a gun brought her to. She was the *Rockingham*, her cargo guano, from the Chincha Islands, bound for Cork. We made a target of her and then burned her. Two or three days later we took the *Tycoon*, from New York for San Francisco, with a valuable cargo, much of it clothing. We took what we needed, got plenty of newspapers, dates a month back, and burned her. On the 1st of May we recrossed the equator. We entered the Northern Hemisphere with the usual amount of calms and storms. The late papers made us sick at heart. There was gloom and disaster on every hand, and our poor Southland in her single-handed fight against the world was giving out! We passed through the Azores, bringing vividly to mind the opening of our career, when the beautiful *290*, fresh from her builders' hands, was christened and received her armament, and full of life and spirit was ready for the fray! Now worn and jaded officers, men and ship—what a contrast! We had done valiant work and had nothing to regret in our brief and brilliant career.

I found from his talks with me that Captain Semmes had fully made up his mind to seek rest and refitment of ship in some friendly port where we could go into dock and allow the little ship that had been our home for twenty-two months to be made anew. The mental strain and excitement through which we had lived was really more wearing upon natural energy and powers of mind

RECOLLECTIONS OF A NAVAL LIFE

and body than labor could have been. We stretched over from the Western Islands to the coasts of Spain and Portugal, thence to the historic British Channel; on the 10th of June made Cape La Hague, on the French coast, and a few hours later were boarded by a French pilot, and at noon were anchored in the port of Cherbourg. A few miles from these shores, later in the month, the valiant *Alabama* was destined to sink in mortal combat, to rise no more!

Chapter XVI

Soon after our arrival at Cherbourg an officer was sent on shore to ask permission of the port admiral to land our prisoners of the two captured ships. This being obtained without trouble or delay, Captain Semmes went on shore to see to the docking of the ship for repairs. Cherbourg being a naval station and the dock belonging to the government, permission had to be obtained of the emperor before we could do anything. The port admiral told us "we had better have gone into Havre, as the government might not give permission for repairs to a belligerent ship." The emperor was absent from Paris at some watering place on the coast, and would not return for some days. Here was an impediment to our plans which gave us time for thought, and the result of such thought was the unfortunate combat between the *Alabama* and the *Kearsarge*. The latter ship was lying at Flushing when we entered Cherbourg. Two or three days after our arrival she steamed into the harbor, sent a boat on shore to communicate, steamed outside and stationed off the breakwater. While Captain Semmes had not singled her out as an antagonist, and would never have done so had he known her to be chain-clad (an armored ship), he had about this time made up his mind that he would cease fleeing before the foe, and meet an equal in battle when the opportunity presented itself. Our cause was weakening daily, and our ship so disabled it really seemed to us our work was almost done! We might end her career gloriously by being victorious in battle, and defeat against an equal foe we would never have allowed ourselves to anticipate.

RECOLLECTIONS OF A NAVAL LIFE

As soon as the *Kearsarge* came into the harbor Captain Semmes sent for me to come to his cabin, and abruptly said to me: "Kell, I am going out to fight the *Kearsarge*. What do you think of it?" We then quietly talked it all over. We discussed the batteries, especially the *Kearsarge's* advantage in 11-inch guns. I reminded him of our defective powder, how our long cruise had deteriorated everything, as proven in our target-practice off the coast of Brazil on the Ship *Rockingham*, when certainly every third shot was a failure even to explode. I saw his mind was fully made up, so I simply stated these facts for myself. I had always felt ready for a fight, and I also knew that the brave young officers of the ship would not object, and the men would be not only willing, but anxious, to meet the enemy! To all outward seeming the disparity was not great between the two ships, barring the unknown (because concealed) chain armor. The *Kearsarge* communicated with the authorities to request that our prisoners be turned over to them. Captain Semmes made an objection to her increasing her crew. He addressed our agent, Mr. Bonfils, a communication requesting him to inform Captain Winslow, through the United States Consul, that "if he would wait till the *Alabama* could coal ship he would give him battle." We began to coal and at the same time to make preparation for battle. We overhauled the magazine and shell rooms, gun equipments, etc.

The *Kearsarge* was really in the fullest sense of the word a man-of-war, stanch and well built; the *Alabama* was made for flight and speed and was much more lightly constructed than her chosen antagonist. The *Alabama* had one more gun, but the *Kearsarge* carried more metal at a broadside. The seven guns of the *Kearsarge* were two 11-inch Dahlgrens, four 32-pounders, and one rifled 28-pounder. The *Alabama's* eight guns were six 32-pounders, one 8-inch and one rifled 100-pounder. The crew of the *Alabama* all told was 149 men, while that of the *Kear-*

246   RECOLLECTIONS OF A NAVAL LIFE

sarge was 162 men. By Saturday night, June 18th, our preparations were completed. Captain Semmes notified the admiral of the port that he would be ready to go out and meet the *Kearsarge* the following morning. Early Sunday morning the admiral sent an officer to say to us that "the ironclad Frigate *Couronne* would accompany us to protect the neutrality of French waters."

Many offered to join us. William C. Whittle, Jr., Grimball, and others; also George Sinclair and Adolphe Marmelstein, officers of the *Tuscaloosa*, and others who were in Paris came down to join us, but the French authorities objected, and they were not allowed to do so. Between 9 and 10 o'clock, June 19th, everything being in readiness, we got under way and proceeded to sea. We took the western entrance of the harbor. The *Couronne* accompanied us, also some French pilot-boats and an English steam yacht, the *Deerhound*, owned by a rich Englishman (as we afterward learned), who, with his wife and children, was enjoying life and leisure in his pleasure yacht. The walls and fortifications of the harbor, the heights above the town, the buildings, everything that looked seaward, was crowded with people. About seven miles from the land the *Kearsarge* was quietly awaiting our arrival.

Officers in uniforms, men at their best, Captain Semmes ordered them sent aft, and mounting a gun-carriage made them a brief address: "Officers and seamen of the *Alabama:* You have at length another opportunity to meet the enemy, the first that has presented to you since you sank the *Hatteras*. In the meantime you have been all over the world, and it is not too much to say that you have destroyed and driven for protection under neutral flags one-half of the enemy's commerce, which at the beginning of the war covered every sea. This is an achievement of which you may well be proud, and a grateful country will not be unmindful of it. The name of your ship has become a household word wherever civilization

RECOLLECTIONS OF A NAVAL LIFE

extends. Shall that name be tarnished by defeat? [An outburst of Never! Never!] The thing is impossible. Remember that you are in the English Channel, the theatre of so much of the naval glory of our race. The eyes of all Europe are at this moment upon you! The flag that floats over you is that of a young Republic that bids defiance to her enemies, whenever and wherever found! Show the world that you know how to uphold it. Go to your quarters!"

We now prepared our guns to engage the enemy on our starboard side. When within a mile and a-quarter he wheeled, presenting his starboard battery to us. We opened on him with solid shot, to which he soon replied, and the action became active. To keep our respective broadsides bearing we were obliged to fight in a circle around a common center, preserving a distance of three quarters of a mile. When within distance of shell range we opened on him with shell. The spanker gaff was shot away and our ensign came down. We replaced it immediately at the mizzen masthead. The firing now became very hot and heavy. Captain Semmes, who was watching the battle from the horse block, called out to me, "Mr. Kell, our shell strike the enemy's side, doing little damage, and fall off in the water; try solid shot." From this time we alternated shot and shell. The battle lasted an hour and ten minutes. Captain Semmes said to me at this time (seeing the great apertures made in the side of the ship from their 11-inch shell, and the water rushing in rapidly), "Mr. Kell, as soon as our head points to the French coast in our circuit of action, shift your guns to port and make all sail for the coast." This evolution was beautifully performed; righting the helm, hauling aft the fore-trysail sheet, and pivoting to port, the action continuing all the time without cessation,—but it was useless, nothing could avail us. Before doing this, and pivoting the gun, it became necessary to clear the deck of parts of the dead bodies that had been torn to pieces by the

248   RECOLLECTIONS OF A NAVAL LIFE

11-inch shells of the enemy. The captain of our 8-inch gun and most of the gun's crew were killed. It became necessary to take the crew from young•Anderson's gun to make up the vacancies, which I did, and placed him in command. Though a mere youth, he managed it like an old veteran. Going to the hatchway, I called out to Brooks (one of our efficient engineers) to give the ship more steam, or we would be whipped. He replied she "had every inch of steam that was safe to carry without being blown up!" Young Matt O'Brien, assistant engineer, called out, "Let her have the steam; we had better blow her to hell than to let the Yankees whip us!" The chief engineer now came on deck and reported "the furnace fires put out," whereupon Captain Semmes ordered me to go below and "see how long the ship could float." I did so, and returning said, "Perhaps ten minutes." "Then, sir," said Captain Semmes, "cease firing, shorten sail, and haul down the colors. It will never do in this nineteenth century for us to go down and the decks covered with our gallant wounded." This order was promptly executed, after which the *Kearsarge* deliberately fired into us five shots! In Captain Winslow's report to the Secretary of the Navy he admits this, saying, "Uncertain whether Captain Semmes was not making some ruse, the *Kearsarge* was stopped."

Was this a time,—when disaster, defeat and death looked us in the face,—for a ship to use a ruse, a Yankee trick? I ordered the men to "stand to their quarters," and they did it heroically; not even flinching, they stood every man to his post. As soon as we got the first of these shot I told the quartermaster to show the white flag from the stern. It was done. Captain Semmes said to me, "Dispatch an officer to the *Kearsarge* and ask that they send boats to save our wounded—ours are disabled." Our little dingey was not injured, so I sent Master's Mate Fulham with the request. No boats coming, I had one of our quarter boats (the least damaged one) lowered and

RECOLLECTIONS OF A NAVAL LIFE

had the wounded put in her. Dr. Galt came on deck at this time, and was put in charge of her, with orders to take the wounded to the *Kearsarge*. They shoved off in time to save the wounded. When I went below to inspect the sight was appalling! Assistant Surgeon Llewellyn was at his post, but the table and the patient on it had been swept away from him by an 11-inch shell, which made an aperture that was fast filling with water. This was the last time I saw Dr. Llewellyn in life. As I passed the deck to go down below a stalwart seaman with death's signet on his brow called to me. For an instant I stood beside him. He caught my hand and kissed it with such reverence and loyalty,—the look, the act, it lingers in my memory still! I reached the deck and gave the order for "every man to save himself, to jump overboard with a spar, an oar, or a grating, and get out of the vortex of the sinking ship."

As soon as all were overboard but Captain Semmes and I, his steward, Bartelli, and two of the men—the sailmaker, Alcott, and Michael Mars—we began to strip off all superfluous clothing for our battle with the waves for our lives. Poor, faithful-hearted Bartelli, we did not know he could not swim, or he might have been sent to shore—he was drowned. The men disrobed us, I to my shirt and drawers, but Captain Semmes kept on his heavy pants and vest. We together gave our swords to the briny deep and the ship we loved so well! The sad farewell look at the ship would have wrung the stoutest heart! The dead were lying on her decks, the surging, roaring waters rising through the death-wound in her side. The ship agonizing like a living thing and going down in her brave beauty, settling lower and lower, she sank fathoms deep— lost to all save love, and fame, and memory!

After undressing with the assistance of our men we plunged into the sea. It was a mass of living heads, striving, struggling, battling for life. On the wild

RECOLLECTIONS OF A NAVAL LIFE

waste of waters there came no boats, at first, from the *Kearsarge* to our rescue. Had victory struck them dumb, or helpless—or had it frozen the milk·of human kindness in their veins? The water was like ice, and after the excitement of battle it seemed doubly cold. I saw a float of empty shell boxès near me, and called out to one of the men (an expert swimmer) to examine the float. He said: "It is the doctor, sir, and he is dead." Poor Llewellyn! Almost within sight of home, the air blowing across the channel from it into the dead face that had given up the struggle for life and liberty. I felt my strength giving out, but strange to say I never thought of giving up, though the white caps were breaking wildly over my head and the sea foam from the billows blinding my eyes. Midshipman Maffitt swam to my side and said, "Mr. Kell, you are so exhausted, take this life-preserver" (endeavoring to disengage it). I refused, seeing in his own pallid young face that heroism had risen superior to self or bodily suffering! But "what can a man do more than give his life for his friend?" The next thing that I remember, a voice called out, "Here's our first lieutenant," and I was pulled into a boat, in the stern sheets of which lay Captain Semmes as if dead. He had received a slight wound in the hand, which with the struggle in the water had exhausted his strength, long worn by sleeplessness, anxiety and fatigue. There were several of our crew in the boat. In a few moments we were alongside a steam yacht, which received us on her deck, and we learned it was the *Deerhound*, owned by an English gentleman, Mr. John Lancaster, who used it for the pleasure of himself and family, who were with him at this time, his sons having preferred going out with him to witness the fight to going to church with their mother, as he afterwards told us.

In looking about us I saw two French pilot boats rescuing the crew, and finally two boats from the *Kearsarge*. I was much surprised to find Mr. Fulham on the *Deerhound*, as I had dispatched him in the little dingey to ask the

RECOLLECTIONS OF A NAVAL LIFE

Kearsarge for boats to save our wounded. Mr. Fulham told me that "our shot had torn the casing from the chain armor of the *Kearsarge*, indenting the chain in many places." This now explained Captain Semmes' observation to me during the battle—"our shell strike the enemy's side and fall into the water." Had we been in possession of this knowledge the unequal battle between the *Alabama* and the *Kearsarge* would never have been fought, and the gallant little *Alabama* have been lost by an error. She fought valiantly as long as there was a plank to stand upon. History has failed to explain, unless there were secret orders forbidding it, why the *Kearsarge* did not steam into the midst of the fallen foe and generously save life! The *Kearsarge* fought the battle beautifully, but she tarnished her glory when she fired on a fallen foe and made no immediate effort to save brave living men from watery graves! Both heroic commanders are now gone—before the great tribunal where "the deeds done in the body" are to be accounted for but history is history and truth is truth!

Mr. Lancaster came to Captain Semmes and said: "I think every man is saved, where shall I land you?" He replied, "I am under English colors; the sooner you land me on English soil the better." The little yacht, under a press of steam, moved away for Southampton. Our loss was nine killed, twenty-one wounded and ten drowned. That afternoon, the 19th of June, we were landed in Southampton and received with every demonstration of kindness and sympathy.

Chapter XVII.

I find among my old letters one written at Cherbourg on the 16th of June, that is not only a contribution to history, but an honest statement of the sentiment of the times.

C. S. Str. *Alabama,* Cherbourg, France,
June 16th, 1864.

We are on the eve of going out to engage the enemy's Gunboat *Kearsage,* now lying off this harbor. We arrived here on the 11th inst., seventy-eight days from Cape Town. On the passage we burned two of the enemy's merchant vessels—making fifty-three that we have destroyed, released one, ransomed nine, sold one, and commissioned one, making our total captures sixty-five vessels, including the *Hatteras.* We are now much in want of repairs, and came here for that purpose, the captain immediately upon our arrival applying to have the work done. From the delay of official correspondence we have been put off from day to day, when the *Kearsarge,* happening to be at Ostend and hearing of our arrival here to undergo extensive repairs, thought she could insult us with impunity, and came steaming into the harbor a couple of days ago, and has since been laying off, communicating twice with the shore by her boats. Captain Semmes at once determined to give her battle, and applied for permission to purchase coals. This at first was refused, but afterwards granted, and we are now taking them in, and may go out to-morrow or the day following. We expect to have a hard fight, for she is fully our match, having to our knowledge two 11-inch guns, four 32-pounders, and 1 30-pound rifle gun, with a crew of 160 men. She is just out of dock and in thorough order, while we are sadly wanting in repairs, with a crew of 120 men only—but they are ready for the fray, and, God willing, we hope to come out victorious!

In the year 1886 I was solicited by the *Century Magazine* to contribute to their pages an article on the fight, afterwards embodied in "Battles and Leaders of the Civil War." I did so. Some years afterward I received some letters that had been in the possession of a relative that had recently died. I copy a letter herewith, written a few hours

RECOLLECTIONS OF A NAVAL LIFE

after the sinking of the *Alabama*, which though brief is very graphic.

KELWAY'S HOTEL, SOUTHAMPTON, ENG.,

June 20th, 1864.

MY DEAR H——: I have just received your telegram of J. H. A. & Co. Captain Semmes and Mr. Smith are here and much obliged, but need no funds. We shall have our money and accounts from Cherbourg in a day or two, which we landed before coming out. We left Cherbourg at half-past nine yesterday morning expressly to engage the *Kearsarge,* she laying off the port. We began the action a few minutes before 11 o'clock, about nine miles distant from the land, and had sharp work of it for an hour. We commenced the action about one mile distant, knowing the enemy had the advantage of us in his 11-inch guns, although we had the advantage of range in our 100-pound rifle (Blakely) and 8-inch solid shot. We at once discovered that the enemy had the speed of us and chose his own position, which was from three to five hundred yards. His 11-inch shell had terrific effect upon us, which, striking about the water-line, caused us to fill very rapidly. The action lasted about one hour and ten minutes, during which time we had made seven complete circles. When I found the water gaining so rapidly upon us I reported to Captain Semmes that we could not float much longer, and he ordered the course shaped for the land. We made what sail we had available to assist the engines, carrying on a running fight; but the water gained so rapidly as to put out the fires, when the engines stopped, and humanity demanded that we should haul down the colors and save the wounded. Fortunately, two of our boats were not too much injured, and we had time to lower them and get the wounded off for the *Kearsarge,* when the ship commenced to settle. Then the order was given for every man to take to an oar, or spar, and jump overboard, which was hurriedly done, and the ship went down about twenty minutes after the colors were hauled down. We were in the water about half an hour when a boat from the English Steam Yacht *Deerhound,* belonging to Mr. John Lancaster, picked us up, took us on board and kindly treated us—fifteen officers and about twenty-seven men—and steered away for this port. We left a French pilot boat and two boats from the *Kearsarge* picking up the remainder. We had nine men killed, twenty wounded, and one officer—Dr. Llewellyn— and several men drowned. We learn from the officers who took the sick and wounded alongside of the *Kearsarge* that her midship section was completely protected by chain bighted from her rail to the water's edge, which was broken and indented in many places by our shot, but did not penetrate her, so that we were in fact fighting an ironclad!

RECOLLECTIONS OF A NAVAL LIFE

They also report that she is damaged in her upper works and quarter, and was pumping and plugging up shot-holes when they were alongside, so that it is likely she will be obliged to make some harbor near at hand. If so, I trust our officers and men on board will be paroled. Please return the letters sent for my wife and mother from Cherbourg, as I shall endeavor to get off to the Confederacy as soon as possible. Let me hear from you. I shall not be able to see you probably for a week or so, as I have a number of our men to look after, besides setling up our accounts before leaving.

Affectionately yours,

Jno. McIntosh Kell.

I do not mean in these simple annals of my life and work to turn back and try to recall the feelings and sentiments of those "times that tried men's souls." I believe I have said that I am "writing for posterity," that those of the younger generation may know, and all that come after them may know, the part it was my privilege to act in the war that left my country desolated and myself penniless, with broken health and broken spirit in middle life, and without a profession. I feel that the generation that is passing away (my own contemporaries) are well versed in the history of that time thirty-odd years ago. That all who could read that grand book of Admiral Semmes's, "Service Afloat," which dealt so largely of law and science, and our deeds, that it seems presumptuous for any one else to take up his well-handled themes that left nothing unsaid. There may be some of the present generation, however, who have not read this book, and there may be friends of mine who will take an interest in my less able narrative, so for the pleasure of these friends and my family I have told the story of the cruises once again.

The press of the world at that time teemed with the combat. The Yankee papers, of course, gloated over the victory,—but what had they gained? An ironclad had sunk a wooden ship, but except the shot that remained to them unexploded in their sternpost to tell "what might have been" but for defective fuses, etc., there was no trophy! There were many beautiful notices of the loss of

RECOLLECTIONS OF A NAVAL LIFE 255

the *Alabama* in the papers, a few of which I here insert, as papers are perishable things and often only kept on file in their own offices.

[From the *London Times*, June 21st, 1864.]

Fathoms deep in Norman waters lies the good Ship *Alabama,* the swift sea rover, just so many tons of broken-up iron and wood, and wearing away in the huge depository of that genuine and original marine store-dealer, Father Neptune!

Should any painter conceive a fantasy of the ocean akin to that of Raffet in "Napoleon's Midnight Review," the famous Confederate cruiser would be one of the first ships that his imagination would summon from the depths of the sea, and amongst the spectral fleet of high-beaked Danish galleys, of antique Spanish caravels, of bluff and burly British three-deckers and saucy British frigates, there would be room for this quick and cunning craft that raced so swiftly and roamed the deep so long. The waves wash to and fro about her, as if in mockery of the dead mass that could once almost outstrip the hurricane, and the fish swim in and out of the port-holes and round the muzzles of the guns that will never again burn powder. For yet a day or so to come corpses of brave men killed in battle or miserably drowned will float to and fro on the summer waves—a strange and horrible sight, perchance, to French fishers busy with their nets or English yachtmen taking their pleasure in the Channel. The skipper, a wounded man, is safe on English ground, but many of his strange crew will nevermore tread a deck or answer to the boatswain's call. The *Alabama* could have found no more fitting grave, for she had lived on the waters, their child and playmate. She hailed from no Southern harbor, she was warned off from many a neutral port, and went away to her wild work amid the loneliness of the watery waste. It was well, then, that she was not destined to be laid up in ordinary, or daubed with dock-yard drab at Charleston or Savannah, while idle gossips wandered over her and talked glibly about her deeds. Beaten in fair fight, she went down in the open sea, whilst her crew, leaping from the sinking ship, swam manfully for their lives. Her career was a strange one. She was an outlaw; men called her a "corsair," and spoke of "Semmes, the pirate captain" as though he had been some ruffianly Blackbeard sailing under the black flag with skull and cross-bones for his grisly ensign. To-day we do not care to quote Puffindorff, Grotius, or Wheaton; we do not concern ourselves with legal quibbles; we decline to take a lawyer's view of her. She was a good ship, well handled and well fought, and to a nation of sailors that means a great deal.

256 RECOLLECTIONS OF A NAVAL LIFE

Since Philip Brooke captured the *Chesapeake* there has been no more chivalric encounter between single ships than that of Sunday last off Cherbourg, not far from the old battleground of Cape La Hague, It was a deliberate challenge. The contest did not take either crew by surprise. Semmes might have stuck to Cherbourg Dock, or trusted to speed for his escape, but he resolved to fight it out. So on a bright June morning, whilst the French folks were quietly at church, he steamed gallantly to sea and attacked his ready antagonist. The *Kearsarge* had more men, carried heavier metal and was chain-plated under her outside planking. Of this latter fact Semmes is said to have been ignorant. At any rate, he knew that a hard day's work was before him and he lost no time in grappling with his work. The story reads like a page from James's "Naval Chronicle," but with some new features about it that remind us how much the conditions of maritime warfare have changed. For instance, we see that this was at first an artillery duel at long range, the two steamers wheeling round and round as falcons might, careless of the wind. Ere long they came to closer quarters, whilst an English yacht cruising in the offing watched the fight. Twice the *Alabama* was struck heavily; the third shot carried away the blade of her fan, shattered a part of her rudder and disabled a gun. The water rushed into her engine-room and she filled rapidly. The *Kearsarge* also suffered severely, but it was plain that the battle was over, and that the *Alabama* was about to sink. Not till the very muzzles were under water would the Southern captain discontinue the action; even then he disdained to surrender, but lowering his boats and placing his wounded in them he waited till the moment before she sank, and then, bleeding as he was, jumped into the sea. His gallant and chivalric enemy sent boats to save the crew and claimed the assistance of the English yacht in the same charitable office. He enquired after Semmes's fate and was told that he was drowned, but Semmes meanwhile, although sorely suffering, was safe in the *Deerhound,* which got up steam and bore away as swiftly as possible. From thirty to forty of his comrades were killed or wounded; the rest are either in England or prisoners on board the Federal Ship.

So ends the log of the *Alabama*—a vessel of which it may be said that nothing in her whole career became her like its close! Although a legitimate and recognized form of hostilities, the capture and destruction of peaceful merchantmen is one barbarism of war which civilized society is beginning to deprecate. Yet for many reasons one can impute no moral guilt to Semmes. His enemy—the United States—specially and distinctly refused adhesion to the Paris Declaration against privateering; and his own country, "Secessia," is the weaker in the present contest. Possibly if he had been cruising with letters of marque under

RECOLLECTIONS OF A NAVAL LIFE 257

ordinary circumstances, with twenty ports upon a friendly seaboard eager to receive him, few would care about his fate. It was his peculiar fortune to keep the sea, almost alone, against a hostile navy, running the gauntlet of countless cruisers with no southern harbor of refuge under his lee, and carrying on the conflict without any of the usual forms of recruitment. And well did he fulfil his adventurous duties. The *Alabama* seemed ubiquitous. If suddenly on the Indian Ocean a red light was seen in the distance, and dim clouds of smoke rolled away before the wind, men knew that Semmes was at work, and was boarding and burning some Yankee trader to the water's edge. American captains homeward bound with a precious freight caught sight of the strange craft and rejoiced that they sailed under the Union Jack and not under the Stars and Stripes. The Federals tried hard to catch her, for indeed she and her sister ships threatened to paralyze their commerce, and even underwriters murmured when they heard of cargoes burned and vessels destroyed. She had many a narrow escape, had often to show a clean pair of heels and run for it, often to change her guise, to give her sides a fresh coat of paint and hoist some foreign flag. In all the sea subtlety and stratagem Semmes was as cool and crafty as even old Francis Drake himself, but also like Drake he could fight when fighting was required. Gradually men came to think that the *Alabama* bore a charmed life, that nothing could hurt her, that to all purposes she was like Vanderdecken's barque—a phantom ship coming when she listed, but never to be caught. No really mortal ship, however, can keep the sea forever, and the two-years' cruise began to tell upon the *Alabama*. She was compelled to bear up for some neutral port and sue for leave to repair. Cherbourg was the selected port, and then whilst her crew stretched their legs ashore up came the *Kearsarge* and waited obstinately. Semmes might perchance have slipped out and passed her at night, a game he has often tried successfully with other cruisers, but he may have been somewhat tired of what, after all, was hardly the pleasantest work for a gallant Southern gentleman, or, more probably, he learned that the watch on board the enemy was too good. For the last time, then, the *Alabama* got up steam and made sail. At a few minutes past eleven she was again in blue water, and by one o'clock, riddled with shot, she had sunk, never again to leave her spreading wake on the dancing waves. Beaten in fair but unequal combat by a gallant foe she has disappeared from the field of ocean to take her place in history; and destined to singular luck even at the very depth of calamity, the still formidable Semmes is spared capture and sentenced by fate to nothing worse than to be for a time the guest of England.

While the *Kearsarge* was anchored off Tybee a few years ago, Mr. Stanhope Sams interviewed me for an account of

17

258   RECOLLECTIONS OF A NAVAL LIFE

the fight. I willingly gave him the narrative, and now quote from his gifted and beautiful pen:

While single combats have not been rare in naval wars there are but few instances of a pre-arranged duel at sea, and there is not another instance of such a duel as was fought off the coast of France more than twenty-eight years ago between the wooden Confederate Cruiser *Alabama* and the Federal armored Ship *Kearsarge*. When Captain Laurence on the blood-stained deck of his gallant ship gave the famous command, "don't give up the ship," he had gone out to meet an equal foe under like conditions. But when Admiral Semmes and his brave Executive left Cherbourg harbor for the fatal duel in the Channel, they went out naked before a steel-girt antagonist! What made the fight still more unequal was the fact that the *Alabama* did not suspect that her foe was sheathed in armor. The wooden cruiser fought the *Kearsarge* as if she had been a wooden hull like herself. Had they known these things the departure from the French harbor would have been to them but a ·certain passage to martyrdom upon the wave they had so often glorified by their heroic deeds. They went to certain death as cheerfully as though they were sweeping onward to accustomed victory. [Then follows a full account of the fight already told.] ‑Captain Kell remarked: "The *Kearsarge* was not quick to assist our struggling crew. Her boats did not come in time to save them. Had it not been for the help given by the *Deerhound* and French boats many would have sunk. I say this with no feeling now, but state the truth as it ought to appear in history. This cruelty sadly marred the gallantry of the fight made by our enemy." Captain Semmes took a stern view of the action of Captain Winslow of the *Kearsarge,* he regarding it almost as a meeting "under the code," certainly one to be governed by the highest sense of honor and courage. His enemy, he thought, did not act with honor in concealing the fact of her armor. Semmes would never have been guilty of such conduct himself. He did not imagine a soldier and a gentleman would willingly fight in concealed armor against an unarmored craft. But war and its animosities are past. We are concerned only with the sad but dear memories of the war, and the justice and truth of history. Whenever this story of the *Alabama* and *Kearsarge* is *falsely* told, as it is almost always told in our histories, it is the duty of a Southern man to "absent himself from felicity awhile to tell the story" of that daring ship which, for a season, alone drove from the seas the commerce of a nation furnished with fleets of war. Her record will be a proud one in the annals of American naval warfare in that she has contributed to the glories of our history and the most daring and eventful career ever run by a single ship upon the seas of the world.

RECOLLECTIONS OF A NAVAL LIFE 259

I was very much pleased with an editorial that appeared in the *Macon Telegraph* some years ago, and which I gave credit without really knowing the fact to the pen of an old and valued friend, Col. H. H. Jones, of the "Independent State of Liberty."

A REFLECTION.

The *New York Sun*, after giving a fairly fair résumé of the fight between the *Kearsarge* and the *Alabama*, as gathered from recent publications in the *Century*, says: "It is one of the strange reflections on this great duel, fought in the presence of thousands of spectators who lined the heights of Cherbourg, that Winslow is perhaps less widely known to fame to-day than Semmes, though the Yankee vessel in an hour's fight sank her renowned antagonist."

"Truth is stranger than fiction," and there is no power that can turn or control the natural impulses of the human mind. There is no record of any service beyond the fight referred to that should fix the name and fame of Captain Winslow in the popular mind. It even requires the pens of partial friends at this late day to accord him somewhat questionable credit. There was nothing particularly skilful or exciting in the manœuvring or fighting of the *Alabama* and the *Kearsarge,* and *accident* alone decided the result. The explanation of the surgeon of the *Kearsarge* as to the firing on the *Alabama* after her colors were struck, and she was sinking, cannot stand before the simple, straightforward statement of Captain Kell. If the surgeon had been at his proper post he could not have known anything of the details of the duel.

The failure of Captain Winslow to save drowning men is proof that he had been badly shaken by the fight, and that the *Alabama* did not cease to be an object of fear until she sought the bottom of the sea. Admiral Semmes had been a naval officer of distinguished service for years. But the cruise of the *Alabama* constitutes one of the great episodes of the war, and his own graphic pen has made it for all ages to come one of the most exciting "romances of the sea." He was no more a pirate than Robert E. Lee may be called a brigand. If he had been a buccaneer outlawed by the code of nations, Captain Winslow's name would last forever in the memory of men as the destroyer of a common enemy. The world at large does not sympathize with the feelings of the Northern people towards Admiral Semmes, and in this may be read one of the reasons why his name and fame tower above those of Captain Winslow. The Confederate cause for political, commercial and social reasons failed to secure the active and practical sympathy of other nations, but the respect and admiration of good men of every

RECOLLECTIONS OF A NAVAL LIFE

civilized clime clustered about it and its leaders. Fortune does not always favor the brave, and but few niches in the Temple of Fame might be filled if they all were reserved for victors in the strifes of the world. People remember and cherish the names of brave and honorable men who have highly illustrated these qualities. We present a couple of illustrations, both in point, one homely, the other heroic. Every American is familiar with the name of George Washington. There is not one in a thousand who can recall the name of the Virginia carpenter who bested him in a fisticuff. Where's the schoolboy who cannot tell you how Leonidas held the pass of Thermopylæ? Outside of a college professor or literateur, who cares to carry in his memory the name of the Persian officer who led the immediate assault upon it? The allied arms saved England at Waterloo, but the fame of Wellington has not obscured that of Napoleon.

Another tribute from the pen of the gifted and lamented poet, Dr. Frank O. Ticknor, a native Georgian, and I will to my narrative again:

THE SWORD IN THE SEA.

"The billows plunge like steeds that bear
    The knights with snow-white crests:
The sea winds blare—like bugles where
    The *Alabama* rests.

"Old glories from their splendor-mists
    Salute with trump and hail
The sword that held the ocean lists
    Against the world in mail.

"And down from England's storied hills,
    From lyric slopes of France,
The old bright wine of valor fills
    The chalice of romance.

"For here was Glory's tourney-field,
    The till-yard of the Sea—
The battle-path of kingly wrath
    And kinglier courtesy.

"And down the deeps, in sumless heaps,
    The gold, the gem, the pearl,
In one broad blaze of splendor, belt
    Great England, like an earl.

RECOLLECTIONS OF A NAVAL LIFE

> "And there they rest, the princeliest
> Of earth's regalia gems,
> The starlight of our Southern cross—
> The Sword of Raphael Semmes."

After landing in Southampton, Captain Semmes and I took a suite of rooms at Kelway's Hotel, Queen's Terrace. He was very much worn and jaded. Disappointment, too, had naturally broken his brave spirit, and he was greatly depressed. He had also been slightly wounded in the hand. After attending to all the business of the survivors of the lost ship, he accepted the kind invitation of the Rev. Mr. Tremlett and made him a visit at Belsize Park Parsonage. This dear "rebel home," as its inmates called it, had made very welcome many Confederates of renown. Here Commodore Maury was specially beloved, and here we all met the best of English society, and many English Navy and Army officers of note.

Captain Semmes and I parted at this dear English home of ours, I to make my way into the Confederacy to my family, and also as bearer of dispatches to the Government at Richmond. Our English friends made up a pleasant party to take Captain Semmes on the continent for his health. My dear commander, to whom I had grown greatly attached in these troublous times, was in need of rest and change, not so much of climate (for we had been in many climes), but change of scene and change of thought from the heavy responsibilities of his three years' life afloat. I believe I have told of the interest Captain Semmes took in me in my early youth—an abiding interest—for though I lost sight of him and did not meet him for many years, most of which I spent on the broad ocean, he kept me in mind, and no sooner did he gain a Confederate command than he applied for me as his first officer. Our friendship was life-long, and I trust will be eternal! In his own words of his little pleasure trip, they "landed at Ostend, passed through Belgium, visited the battlefield of Waterloo, spent a few days at Spa for the

262 RECOLLECTIONS OF A NAVAL LIFE

waters, passed on to the Rhine, up that historic, beautiful river to Mayence, thence to the Swiss lakes, resting at Geneva." Returning late in September, the 3d of October the captain began his journey home, determining to come by way of Mexico and Texas instead of making the effort to run the blockade, which had now become quite a dangerous experiment.

I sailed in the English mail steamer from Liverpool, bound for New York, stopping on her way at Halifax, Nova Scotia. Galt and I landed in Halifax, and while we were there the Roman Catholic Vicar-General paid us the honor of a call through his chief of staff, and invited us to a handsome entertainment given us as representatives of Captain Semmes and the South, he being a Southern sympathizer and our commander a devoted adherent of his church.

The following day we sailed in the little English mail steamer for Bermuda, from which point we were to venture on the rather difficult and dangerous task of running the blockade. We found the little side-wheel Steamer *Flamingo* ready to sail, and took passage on her. The sea was smooth, and beautifully adapted to our little vessel, which only drew three or four feet of water and skimmed the surface of the ocean like a bird. We began the voyage very well, but our first experience at nearing shore was disappointing. We failed to make the lighthouse, and could not ascertain by the bearings whether we were north or south of our port of entry, and ran into the shore almost within touching distance and shaped our course along it, hoping to discover our whereabouts, but failed to find any signal. As it was nearing three o'clock in the morning we held a consultation and decided it would be more prudent to stand off to sea and get an offing by day break, for fear of being shut in by blockaders. As the day opened up a little light to us we discovered two blockaders ahead, and three on our quarters We put on all the steam we could carry and proceeded eastward. The

RECOLLECTIONS OF A NAVAL LIFE

blockader ahead made every exertion to cut us off and fired on us, but the shot fell short, and we continued on our course—fairly flying—and soon our pursuers were out of sight and we greatly relieved to have made so narrow an escape. About eight o'clock we got out instruments to establish our longitude and at twelve o'clock we took our latitude, placed our position accurately on the chart, took our bearings on Fort Fisher, and as the evening drew on we got steam up and drew in with the land. Taking the bearings which were then open to us, we made all steam and passed in under the very guns of the blockaders, like a flash of lightning, and as quickly as it takes to relate it we were safely anchored under the guns of the fort. A basket of champagne was at once ordered up and a toast to our successful run was heartily quaffed. The cause of our first missing our bearings was due entirely to the drunkenness of the officers of the steamer. The risks they ran seemed to inspire the desire to get up a little "Dutch courage" as occasion required, and came very near precipitating us—after all our hair-breadth escapes—into the hands of the enemy!

In Wilmington I met a friend of the Anderson family, who informed me of the report that had reached them that their brave young son had perished in the fight off Cherbourg, being "literally torn to pieces by the explosion of an 11-inch shell." I had the great gratification of tele-. graphing them of his safety, he being one of the last to bid me good-bye in Liverpool. He seemed to them as one given back from the dead!

In August, 1864, Macon—my haven—was reached at last! After an absence of three years and nearly four months I found myself on her kindly soil, united to my wife and child. Death had come in my absence, while fighting the battles of my country, and bereft us of our first-born son, a manly, noble child of six years, and our one lovely daughter, a babe of three years (I left her three months old). I little feared at that time that I was

264 RECOLLECTIONS OF A NAVAL LIFE

never to see their fair, bright faces again! I think it due to their memories (that have influenced my whole life since their early removal) that even in this record of my public life I tell the sacrifice that was required of me on the altar of duty and patriotism!

Chapter XVIII

HAVING forwarded my dispatches, in ten days I left for Richmond to report and see what I could do for the failing fortunes of the Confederacy. I believe I have forgot to say that after the battle with the *Hatteras* I had been promoted to commander, of which I was not made aware till the commission was nearly a year old, and should not willingly have left Captain Semmes and the *Alabama* even to take a command. The commission read as follows:

COMMANDER JOHN KELL, C. S. A.

SIR: You are hereby informed that the President has appointed you, by and with the advice and consent of the Senate, a commander in the Provisional Navy of the Confederate States, to rank from the 4th day of October, 1863, "for gallant and meritorious conduct as First Lieutenant and Executive Officer of the C. S. Steam Sloops *Sumter* and *Alabama*, under the command of Captain Raphael Semmes." You are requested to acknowledge the receipt of this appointment.

S. R. MALLORY,
Secretary of the Navy.

C. S. OF AMERICA,
NAVY DEPARTMENT, *June 1st, 1864.*

Also this very gratifying letter:

CONFEDERATE STATES OF AMERICA, RICHMOND, VA.

COMMANDER JNO. MCINTOSH KELL, P. N. C. S., Macon, Ga.

SIR: Your letter of the 3d inst., reporting your arrival at Wilmington under orders from Captain Semmes to report to the Secretary of the Navy, was this day received. In congratulating you upon your return to your family and home, I deem it but just to you to say that the arduous duties which you have so long and ably performed as the Executive Officer of the *Sumter* and the *Alabama* are highly appreciated by your Government, and that they have achieved for you proud distinction in the naval service of your country, with whose history your name will ever be honorably associated. In recognition of your

266   RECOLLECTIONS OF A NAVAL LIFE

"gallant and meritorious services" I have the pleasure of handing you
enclosed a commission as commander in the Provisional Navy, by
direction of the President. Very respectfully,   •

Your obedient servant,

S. R. MALLORY, *Sec. Navy.*

August 8th, 1864.

I returned from Richmond for a little longer leave of
absence with my family, and in October was ordered to
the command of the new Ironclad *Richmond*, on the James
River. In the meantime, with the Yankee raids through
the country, and the threatened "march through Georgia,"
which was afterwards so effectually accomplished, I took
my wife and child and left Macon as a "refugee" for awhile.
I went to Commodore Tatnall, as I passed through Savannah, and told him where I would be, and asked him to call
for me if need be. He said, sadly, "Well, my son, it would
only be to shoulder a musket and go by my side. There
seems no work for us to do; the Navy has done all it
could, and you have done your share."

We went to my relatives, the McIntosh family, in
Thomas County, and there spent three quiet weeks. At
the end of that time I received orders to "proceed to Richmond without delay." I made three efforts to get off,
without success. The creeks and rivers were swollen to
danger point, and the railroads were cut or torn up in
many places by Yankee raiders. Finally I had orders
from Richmond to go to Thomasville, Georgia (the nearest town) and "impress a conveyance." I found a dilapi-
dated cloth-covered 'wagon there, which resembled the
old-time country "chicken trading" wagons. The ribs
across were too low for me, and I had to push back the
cloth for my head to come through; but my wife and
little son, John, Jr., and the nurse managed to sit comfortably, and we proceeded from Thomasville to Albany,
a journey, if I remember aright, of two days and two
nights (camping out), to the tune (for such a conveyance!)
of five hundred dollars! The camp fires at night and the

RECOLLECTIONS OF A NAVAL LIFE

very cool weather and exposure were a novel experience to the inmates of the wagon; but Southern women, even of extreme youth, bore everything heroically, and it was truly beautiful to witness the patriotism of their exalted souls, that rose so high above all discomfort or fatigue; that bore up the hearts of fathers, husbands, brothers and sons to achieve what they did. The deeds of valor on many battlefields were but the reflections of the brave hearts of women who loved home, honor and country better than life itself; and my countrywomen, though the cause failed for which you hoped and endured so much, your deeds will live in the memory of the Confederate veteran while life lasts, and they will teach their children's children the reverence and love due to Southen womanhood!

The second night of our "refugeeing voyage," about midnight, a carriage drove up and hailed us, and called for me. It was very startling. My wife roused first—she thought the enemy were upon us, but she answered bravely. Then the voice called out, "Uncle has sent me for Cousin Blanche and the boy; he saw the orders published for Richmond, and knew you would go; he is frantic about his children, and sent me for them." We rested the horses, and before daylight started for Albany to catch the earliest train for Macon, where we arrived safely, to the relief and joy of my wife's family. I had now to face the difficulties of a trip "on to Richmond." I find in my old letters the account of it:

SPARTA, GA., *December 25th, 1864.*

I have just arrived in a heavy rain! I had, however, a comfortable carriage with Mr. Habersham. He returns to Milledgeville to-morrow, having met his family in an open wagon eight miles from that town. He kindly insisted upon driving me through to this place, and in the morning I will take a seat in the regular hack to Mayfield, and hope to reach there by 10 o'clock to take the cars to Augusta, where I shall secure transportation and get on, I trust, without much delay to Richmond. Oh! what a gloomy Christmas to us, and throughout our beloved country!

268   RECOLLECTIONS OF A NAVAL LIFE

RICHMOND, *January 1st, 1865.*

I cannot wish you a happy New Year. It would be inconsistent and ironical! but I can and do thank God that you are safe in your father's house and under his loving care. Here I am with my dear Bob Minor, sharing his room for the day and night. Bob says he is just realizing, now that his eyes rest on me, that I am really in the Confederacy at last! My dear Bob, he will always be a boy, but he takes me back to the time when I was a boy, too. Yesterday I went down the river to report to Flag Officer Mitchell, who commands the Ironclad *Virginia.* Captain Roots has the *Fredericksburg,* and I am ordered to the command of the *Richmond,* which is a fine vessel. These three ironclads compose the James River Squadron—so change your present address to me, and address to the ship and James River Squadron. It was a terrible day on the water yesterday—a heavy, driving snow storm, and I did not get back till 7 o'clock. Shall be very busy to-morrow, as I take command the next day. I think we will be quiet for a while. The obstructions in the river and the great severity of the weather prevent the enemy moving by land or water, though we are in sight of the Yankee lines, and have picket boats out every night. I think Richmond is about the securest spot in the Confederacy at present. The ships lay about nine miles from the city. I called on Mrs. Mallory on New Year's day. She sent her love to you. I also met your friend Mrs. Clay. Eaneas Armstrong is attached to the *Fredericksburg.* I sent his mother's letter to him. Richard is in Charleston at his own request, on torpedo service.

C. S. IRONCLAD *Richmond, January 6th, 1865.*

I cannot give you a very glowing account of my new quarters. I had two staterooms knocked into one to give me room. The bed allows me to turn over on the mattress of sweetened hay with a few sticks in it; this is no disadvantage, however, as I should not sleep too sound these "war times." I borrowed six yards of Macon factory cloth to make the mattress from Colonel C., and it must be returned on his first visit South. I have a little pine table and an attempt at a set of drawers or bureau. I bought a tin basin and pitcher, and as they cost me eighteen dollars, I grew economical! I have also drawn from the ship seven yards of double-width gray cloth, and gave sixteen dollars a yard to the government for that; would have paid double or treble that price if bought on the market, and now that I have got the cloth it seems too expensive to have it made up, though I should like by doing so to keep in nice order the handsome uniforms made up in London—but enough of myself, and now of my ship. Her shield is covered with five inches of iron and she mounts four-inch rifle guns, all in fine condition; with a crew of one hundred and twenty men, exclusive of officers. This morn-

RECOLLECTIONS OF A NAVAL LIFE

ing I heard the Federal drums beating quite lively over the hills, but they do not seem disposed to make an attack on our works at present. I believe I would prefer good weather for a fight.

C. S. IRONCLAD *Richmond,*
JAMES RIVER SQUADRON, *January 26th, 1865.*

It is a month since I left home, and I have had no reply to my first letter. This may be the first news you have to relieve your anxiety in regard to the movements of our fleet down the river, which move no doubt reached you through the papers. The object of our expedition, I regret to say, was not accomplished, resulting from a series of misfortunes. The greatest of all was getting on shore the two most formidable ironclads, the *Virginia* and this ship, just above the enemy's obstructions and under the fire of their batteries. They pelted us for over six hours, doing little or no damage to this ship, but succeeded in cutting up the *Virginia* considerably. We were absent a little over twenty-four hours, leaving here the evening of the 23d and returning here the morning of the 25th, during which time I was on my feet day and night, so you can imagine my extreme fatigue. God's mercy and your constant prayers call for my gratitude in largest measure! The weather is intensely cold, ice forming in the river in great quantities. How must our poor soldiers suffer in the trenches! I have sad news to give you, which has just reached me officially. Eaneas Armstrong was drowned to-night at 8 o'clock while on picket duty down the river, being run over by the flag of truce boat. I saw him two hours before in the commodore's office, and looking so well. He went to ask a permit to go to Richmond to see Richard, but the commodore told him "the Squadron was under sailing orders;" so of course he could not get the permit; and his brave young life went out a sacrifice upon the altar of his country! The bleeding hearts of wife and mother, brothers and sisters, will surely find pity and love from Him who does not leave us comfortless, for the death of one who dies nobly, in the path of duty and of right.

This is my birthday. Need I say it has been a sad birthday to me? But one has no right to think of birthdays in such times!

The report read as follows:

"C. S. IRONCLAD *Fredericksburg,*
"JAMES RIVER SQUADRON, *January 27th, 1865.*

"COMMANDER KELL.

"SIR: It becomes my painful duty to report, that while the steam Torpedo Boat *Hornet* was proceeding down the river last night upon her first tour of picket duty, she was run into and sunk by the flag of truce Steamer *William Allison,* and First Lieutenant Eaneas Armstrong, P. N. C. S., was drowned.

RECOLLECTIONS OF A NAVAL LIFE

"Lieut. E. T. Eggleston, C. S. M. C., who was in the *Hornet* at the time, reports the following facts in connection with this sad affair: About 7 P. M., and just after getting through the passage at the obstructions in Kingsland Reach, discovered the *Allison* coming up the river. Lieutenant Armstrong, to avoid a collision, ordered the *Hornet* to be steered to the south bank, and made every effort to attract the attention of the approaching steamer, but failed to do so in time and her bow struck the *Hornet* just abaft the smokestack, causing the latter to sink immediately. All hands were precipitated into the river, but all, with the exception of Lieutenant Armstrong succeeded through the exertions of the crew of the *Allison* in reaching the steamer in safety, she having stopped her engine just before striking. Lieutenant Armstrong was, unfortunately, drifted by the current so far below the steamer that no trace of him could be found after a vigilant search was made for him by Lieutenant Eggleston in one of the boats of the *Allison*. Owing to the excessive cold he doubtless soon became cramped, and in consequence sunk before aid could reach him. A search was made of the south bank of the river this morning with a view to the recovery of his body, but such was unsuccessful.

"The service has thus been robbed of an officer whose merits gained for him an enviable reputation; and during his service under my command in the recent trying operations of our squadron, it gratifies me to say as a slight token of my regard for his worth and an humble tribute to his memory, that he behaved with marked coolness and bravery.

"Very respectfully, your obedient servant,

"T. E. Shepperd,

"To Commander Kell,   *"Lieut. Commanding.*

"C. S. Ironclad *Richmond,* James River Squadron."

C. S. Ironclad *Richmond,*

James River Squadron, *February 1st, 1865.*

I am truly distressed that the mails fail to be carried through. I have written regularly three times each week. On our return from our most unfortunate trip down the river I made a visit of twenty-four hours to the city. I found Colonel S. and the baby all well and spent a long evening with Captain Semmes. I found him looking remarkably well. He delivered your package and told me of his visit to you. The Colonel and T. were very anxious for me to remain and have the captain to dinner with us, but I felt obliged to return on board ship, for I have a very severe cold, and I am sorry to say that drinking the James River water is affecting my health very much. I went to bed and took some medicine the surgeon gave me, and hope to feel better in a day or two.

RECOLLECTIONS OF A NAVAL LIFE

February 3d.

Just received two letters from you fifteen days on the journey. Had just sent a letter to you by private hand, the mails seem so unreliable. Though I am only nine miles from the city I have only been up once, and then on a special visit to see Captain Semmes. I am glad to see him looking so improved in health since we parted in England.

February 16th.

Glad to hear you received four letters from me at once. You must be very anxious at the news we have of the road being cut by Sherman. I send this by private hand. I rejoice with you at the mention of "gallant conduct" of your one dear brother. There is a rumor to-day of Hampton defeating Kirkpatrick, and I hope the next news will be that Johnson has defeated Sherman, upon which so much depends. If Sherman marches victoriously into Virginia, Richmond must be evacuated. Every precaution has been used for the immediate removal of all papers of the different departments of the government, but it is understood that General Lee will hold the city to the very last moment that prudence will admit. It will be impossible for you to get a package or small trunk through to me from Macon while Sherman holds Branchville. The weather is so cold and the river so frozen over, the steamboats cannot run. The river water and the intense cold together are making me ill, so being utterly disabled and unfit for duty I came up to spend a few days with the Colonel and your sister, to see if I can get better without going into the hospital. I met our old friend and groomsman Gailliard. He has just gotten twenty days' leave of absence to go home and get married (he tells me) to the daughter of the Member of Congress from South Carolina, Mr. Ker. Boyce. I told him these were very troublous times for getting married in, but he was too radiantly happy even to regard an allusion to the present times. I suppose you have seen through the press that Captain Semmes has been made admiral (an honor richly deserved) and is to take command of the James River Squadron.

RICHMOND, VA., *March 17th, 1865.*

I am still here with your dear sister and the Colonel. They are very kind to me. The doctor forbids my return to the ironclad till I have quite recovered. I suppose you hear all sorts of rumors about the evacuation of Richmond. Orders have been given for the removal of the different departments; the work-shops, too, all of which is precautionary. Should Sherman be successful in his march through North Carolina it may become necessary to give up Richmond, and our ironclads will share the same fate as those off Charleston, while we fall

272 RECOLLECTIONS OF A NAVAL LIFE

back with the Army. Bob puts his horse at my disposal, so I get a nice ride on horseback every day, and think I am getting a little stronger. To-morrow I will go to Greensboro, N. C., with your sister and the baby. It is best for them to be out of Richmond till matters are more settled. I do hope the little change will do me good and that I may return in a week or ten days quite restored to my post of duty.

March 18th.

Yours of the 15th of last month, which you gave to Mr. and Mrs. Clement Clay, reached me to-day, relieving me of much anxiety. They did not come further than Augusta, owing to the bad condition of the road. I have written by every opportunity going south. So much depends upon our holding Richmond,—if that is given up gunboats and ironclads must all be destroyed. The naval forces will fall in with the Army. Our Navy has been destroyed by piece meal by the evacuation of first one and then another of our seaports. However, confidence is being restored in our holding this city within the last few days. I send you in a little package twenty-four dollars in gold. It is now worth seventy for one, and is a balance paid me upon rendering my account of traveling expenses home from the *Alabama.* I send package and letter by one of the Colonel's clerks going direct to Macon.

DANVILLE, VA., *March 20th.*

I am getting very much discouraged! I gain no strength at all, even with the change and the very desirable good weather. The news is very cheering—General Johnson's army victorious several times with severe loss on the enemy's side. Mrs. General Hardee and her daughter are our next-door neighbors, so we get the latest news by telegraph direct from the General. Affairs around Richmond in *statu quo,* much depending on Johnson's success. [Which hoped-for success, alas, never came!]

No improvement in health coming to me, of necessity I gave up my command, and on sick leave came home to Macon, and was in Macon, broken completely in health and spirit, when news reached us that General Lee had surrendered. The dreaded blow had fallen! The South had fought the world and might had overcome! When news of the armistice was carried out to meet the incoming army of General Wilson to Macon they at first refused to credit it. Knowing that the army was approaching, through the advice of my physician, with high

RECOLLECTIONS OF A NAVAL LIFE 273

fever upon me, I left Macon, taking a favorite servant with me, whose parents and grandparents had served my family for generations. I found friends and a warm welcome with Colonel P. M. Nightengale, near Hawkinsville, he having moved his family there from the coast for safety. They cared for me as though I were a younger brother. The evening of the day after our arrival the temptation was too great for my servant Henry, and he took "French leave," carrying off my pistol, a fine navy revolver, with him. I forgave the departure more readily than I did the theft. I have never seen him since, but his old grandfather served me fondly and faithfully till death set him free a few years ago, his last hours made happy and peaceful by the love and care of my family for him in old age, and he died giving us all his blessing and farewell.

In due time I was paroled as a common soldier, and passed through Macon to Spalding County, Georgia, to sojourn with the uncle and aunt of my wife, where (though I did not dream of it then) I was to make a home and spend the rest of my life. In three weeks my wife and little son joined me in this quiet country home for a short visit. After this, for a long while, with broken health and penniless, for, as Admiral Semmes said of himself, like him "I had the honor to come out of the war without a dollar, life seemed to me full of chaos and destruction. I had not the health at the time to seek to take up my profession or work in another country. Many of my friends and brother officers went out of the South—some to South America, some to Egypt to serve the Khedive, quite a colony took refuge in Nova Scotia, and some remained in Europe where the collapse of the Confederacy found them. We passed a quiet summer. In July a son was born to us, whom I named for the admiral, his dear name being associated with my last dream of glory. In the fall of 1865 I made up my mind to start a little farm, to "turn my sword into a ploughshare" and "sit in peace under my own vine and fig tree." The Confederate banner having

274   RECOLLECTIONS OF A NAVAL LIFE

been furled to live only in the faithful hearts of the South-land, the banner over me should henceforth be that of love and home. Next door to our uncle and aunt, they having given us a double log cabin, and my wife's father adding to it and making us very comfortable, we began life anew as Spalding County farmers, and no palace ever held such joy and content as ours. We made a fine vegetable garden, on which I took several prizes the following spring at the "Middle Georgia Fair." Our flowers were the admiration of all beholders. For a year or two I refrained from reading the newspapers, unless something special was brought to my notice, but I took a number of agricultural journals, the *Southern Cultivator* and *Maryland Farmer* specially. I tried to be practical, but having no experience, my neighbors often laughed at my theories and book-learning, though I sometimes astonished them in a race for success. I only knew by hearsay who was President or governor, and my wife and the two happy little boys forgot all city ways and fashions. As I look back upon those days they seem to have been very happy, except that my restoration to health was very slow; and the loss of health will mar the happiest surroundings.

In the winter of 1865 Captain Semmes was arrested—I think it was on the 15th of December; Mr. Davis was in prison; General Lee had an indictment of treason against him, and but for the interference of General Grant would no doubt have been tried; Wirtz, the commandant of the Southern prison, though a paroled prisoner, had met death by execution; Madame Surratt, an innocent woman charged with being an accomplice in the assassination of Mr. Lincoln, had been hung; Mr. Clement Clay suffered imprisonment, though guilty of nothing more than being a Confederate Cabinet officer, so the arrest and imprisonment of Captain Semmes assumed a very serious aspect. A squad of soldiers took him from his home in Mobile to Washington, where he was kept a close prisoner for four months. Out of this dilemma he helped himself in

RECOLLECTIONS OF A NAVAL LIFE

his able and powerful defense, which was of course the theme of the daily press at the time. His appeal to the Chief Executive closes with these words:

> I have thus laid before you tediously, I fear, yet as concisely as is consistent with clearness, the grounds upon which I claim at your hands, who are the custodian of the honor of a great nation, my discharge from arrest and imprisonment. I have spoken freely and frankly as it became an American citizen to speak to the Chief Magistrate of the American Republic. We live in times of high party excitement when men, unfortunately, are too prone to take counsel of their passions; but passions die and men die with them, but after death comes history! In the future, Mr. President, when America shall have a history, my record and that of the gallant Southern people will be engrafted upon, and become part of, your history, the pages of which you are now acting, and the prayer of this petition is that you will not allow the honor of the American name to be tarnished by a perfidy on those pages. In this paper I have stood strictly on legal defenses, but should those barriers be beaten down, conscious of the rectitude of my conduct throughout a checkered and eventful career, when the commerce of half a world was at my mercy and when the passions of men North and South were tossed into a whirlwind by the current events of the most bloody and terrific war that the human race has ever seen, I shall hope to justify and defend myself against any and all charges affecting the honor and reputation of a man and a soldier. Whatever else may be said of me, I have at least brought no discredit upon the American name and character.
>
> I am, respectfully, etc.,
>
> RAPHAEL SEMMES.

WASHINGTON CITY, *January 15th, 1866.*

I believe the alleged object of the arrest of the admiral was "his illegal escape off Cherbourg harbor," with added charges of "cruelty to prisoners," etc. As soon as he got to Washington (or very soon after) he wrote to ask me to hold myself in readiness to come to him at any day, which I did not need to be asked to do; but his case never came to trial—his able self-defense proved sufficient.

It was the cause, however, of my losing a very valuable correspondence—many of the admiral's letters, several

276 RECOLLECTIONS OF A NAVAL LIFE

from Commodore Tatnall, and very many from my brother Navy officers. Thinking it safest in those troublous times, I made a large package of them and let them down by a cord between the wooden walls of the farmhouse in which I was then living, waiting for our log castle to be finished. The following spring or summer, when I went to liberate my valued correspondence from its concealment, the enemies of man—mice or rats—had cut the cord, and upon removing the plank where they had fallen I found my letters in mincemeat! A ruin of great and beautiful thoughts and sentiments, a noting of deeds grand and heroic, so much that would have been a precious heirloom to my children.

A few years after the war my dear senior officer honored my humble domicile by a visit of some days. Meeting my wife at the door he took both her hands in his and said: "How safely you have anchored my friend Kell; I am glad to have a welcome in his port." She smilingly presented the children, saying, "These are the anchors, Admiral." Our manly boy John, Jr., came to him; then his little namesake, who from that time during his visit took a seat as of right on his knees, and then our baby girl Marjory had her full share of his caresses. He took a deep interest in all around me, and said, "Kell, you must plaster this house," which I afterward did, at least a part of it. My wife told him she "would give him leave to lecture me on my sectional pride and prejudice; that she thought him an example to me of conservatism," etc. He replied, very gently, "He has fifteen years (or more) longer to live to feel as I do; I am at least fifteen years his senior. Give him that long to grow reconciled to things as they are." During the visit we discussed the past a great deal, and on one occasion the old Confederate scrap-book was brought out, containing many pictures from the English papers of the *Alabama's* cruise, officers and career. My picture being first, my wife said, apologetically, "Admiral, you will easily see who is the hero of the ship to me." He

RECOLLECTIONS OF A NAVAL LIFE 277

smiled and said, "And so he is to me my right hand, and I knew he would be ready when I called him." That he should have been satisfied that I had done my duty was very dear praise to me, and I here record it, not from vainglorious pride, but the desire that my posterity may know that I did my duty. Though Captain Semmes lived several years after this I never saw him again; but his pleasant, cheerful letters came sometimes to brighten us, specially to his little namesake and godson, in whom he showed an abiding interest as long as he lived.

Of the many fine tributes to the bravery of Captain Semmes and his ship I have seen none finer than the following, sent to me by Armstrong, our second officer—and, as he remarks, it is the tribute of an enemy!

[From the *Toronto Leader*, July 8th, 1864.]

BRAVERY OF CAPTAIN SEMMES.

[From the *New York News*.]

The *Alabama* cannot be captured. No beam or plan or spar or rope or sail of the far-famed sea-rover will ever be a trophy in the hands of her enemies. The ocean that has been the scene of her career protects her now forever! She seemed fated to battle and defy in disaster as well as in success. There is sometimes glory in misfortune and triumph in defeat. The words of the dying Laurence urging resistance against hope are more memorable than the records of his victories. The fate of the *Alabama* will be a theme for admiration with friend and foe, and we venture to prophesy that many a pen that has been active in denouncing her career will acknowledge a certain sublimity in its close. The commercial welfare and the naval reputation of the North are certainly most beholden to the commander of the *Kearsarge* and his subordinates for their successful efforts to destroy this formidable enemy, but they have "scotched the snake, not killed it." All accounts state that the *Alabama* had suffered severely by the wear and tear of her active existence. She had lost much of her capacity for mischief and her speed was reduced, and she was in fact worn out with hard service and in absolute need of such repairs as no neutral port would furnish. It was the indomitable spirit, the untiring zeal, and the splendid management of Captain Semmes that still rendered her formidable. That spirit, that zeal, and that capacity for management are yet in the service of the Confederacy. The happy star of Semmes watched over

278 RECOLLECTIONS OF A NAVAL LIFE

him after the last plank sank beneath him. He, too, escaped capture. The romantic attributes of the fight off Cherbourg harbor, and its thrilling denouement, will but serve to add to his renown and popularity with friends of the South. There is more éclat attached to his name by the circumstances of his defeat than by the long list of his successes. A public dinner was tendered him immediately upon his arrival at Southampton after the engagement. Captain Semmes will be lionized, fêted and encouraged. We doubt not that before long a second *Alabama* will be at his command. Meanwhile her commander has lost no prestige. He has sacrificed perhaps a little of his reputation for sagacity in risking an encounter with an opponent far his superior in speed, armament and strength of build, but human nature is more apt to sympathize with reckless daring than to condemn it. He has saved a handful of his men, who will serve as a nucleus for another crew, and there will be no lack of adventurous characters ready to serve the man who fought his ship till her guns were under water and then committed her to old Neptune's eternal embrace, leaving no vestige behind but the record of her deeds.

[From the *South Atlantic Magazine*, November, 1877.]

CAPTAIN JOHN N. MAFFITT, ON LIFE AND SERVICES OF RAPHAEL SEMMES.

On the 29th day of August last the startling intelligence was announced by telegraph that Admiral Semmes, the Bayard of the late Confederate Navy, had calmly "welcomed the peaceful night of long repose" and ceased to be numbered among the living. This sad annunciation affected every Southern heart with melancholy and grief, intensified as memory's panoramic review of past events pictured to the mind's eye the battle and the storm, the daring seaman and incomparable Viking of the ocean. Raphael Semmes was born in Charles County, Maryland, on the 27th day of September, 1809. At the age of sixteen was appointed midshipman by President John Quincy Adams. In October, 1826, on the Sloop of War *Lexington*, sailed from New York for Port Spain, Island of Trinidad, to convey to the United States the remains of the lamented Commodore Oliver H. Perry, the hero of Lake Erie, who, while attending to important diplomatic duties, died of yellow fever in the town of Angostura, on the Orinoco River, August, 1819.

The young midshipman from the time of entering the Navy was remarkable for studiousness. The board of examiners awarded him the first honors of his class. His active mind was never "off duty." While a passed midshipman on leave of absence he entered the office of his brother, a distinguished lawyer, and began with avidity the study of law. At the conclusion of the Mexican War (in which he took an

RECOLLECTIONS OF A NAVAL LIFE

active part) he was ordered to command the Ordnance Transport *Electra*. He occasionally practiced at the bar. In 1858 he was ordered to Washington city to assume the position of Secretary to the Light-house Board, upon which duty he remained until February, 1861, when, following the fortunes of his adopted State, Alabama, he severed his connection with the United States Government. Raphael Semmes for thirty-five years in the United States Navy had enjoyed an unblemished reputation as an officer and high-toned gentleman. His attainments were of the highest order, not only professionally, but also from a scientific and literary point of view. Later, he developed his master genius in the great arena of national strife, and displayed a chivalry that crowned him in the estimation of the unprejudiced world, Viking of the Seas.

He had ever

> "The keen spirit—seizes the prompt occasion—
> Makes the thought start into instant action
> And at once plans and performs, resolves and executes!"

Captain Semmes fitted out the little *Sumter* and unfurled the first Confederate flag upon the ocean. [The story of his many captures and grand successes has already been told.] * * * In the history of the world there is no record of the existence of so terrible a cruiser as the *Alabama,* the proud ship that met her doom in the historic British Channel. Over the taffrail rolled the waves, as deeper and deeper the noble craft settled. Raising his sword with affectionate solicitude, he gently placed it on the binnacle, sorrowfully exclaiming, "Rest thee, excalibar, thy grave is with the *Alabama!*" Giving one last sad look from the stem to the stern of his lost ship, a thousand glorious memories flashed proudly through his mind as accompanied by his first lieutenant he sprang into the sea. * * * England received him kindly, a beautiful sword replaced the lost one, and a lady of high rank made for him with her own hands out of richest silk, a mammoth Confederate flag. Returning home his government commissioned him admiral, his being the second promotion to that position that had occurred in the Confederate Navy. After the defeat of the cause he served so nobly he edited a daily paper in Mobile, and subsequently a daily journal in Memphis. Later, he returned to his first love and resumed the practice of law in Mobile, where he achieved a high reputation as a constitutional lawyer and an earnest practitioner at the bar. Modest and unassuming, his dignified deportment won for him the respect and confidence of the community in which he lived. * * *

On the 17th of August, 1877, Admiral Semmes complained of feeling ill and the resident physician at Point Clear, Alabama, was summoned.

280   RECOLLECTIONS OF A NAVAL LIFE

After repeated visits he became anxious, and expressed a desire for a consulting physician. The admiral objected, saying to him, "I know my race is run; there is not sufficient vitality in my old and worn-out frame to battle successfully with the disease that grapples me unto death." Four days before he expired he received the last sacrament of the Romish Church, of which he was a devoted member.

Gently, calmly, this chivalric king of the sea surrendered to the great conqueror—King Death. His body was carried by steamer from Point Clear to Mobile, attended by his family, the clergy and a large number of citizens. The pall-bearers, consisting of members of the First Regiment of Alabama State Troops and many of Mobile's most distinguished citizens, under the escort of the Mobile Rifles and the members of the bar, conveyed the remains to the cathedral, where Father Ryan, after the celebration of mass, delivered an eloquent oration on the character of the deceased. Bishop Quinlan concluded the services at the cathedral and the hearse, drawn by four white horses, was escorted by the various civil and military associations and a general gathering of the people through the solemn streets of the city to the Catholic Cemetery, where, in the language of the *Mobile Register,* "all that was mortal of one of earth's greatest heroes was left to that sleep that knows no earthly waking."

During the day all official places, stores and business offices were closed and draped in mourning. From sunrise to sunset, at intervals of half an hour, funeral guns were fired, and every mark of honor, esteem, and sympathy was exhibited that seemed appropriate to the melancholy occasion. "Yesterday he was ours: to-day he belongs to fame and to history." A fame that is not the exclusive endowment of the South. It enriches the world, the pages of whose history confess no truer gentleman, no more stainless hero in all the illustrious catalogue of the dead. Without fear and without reproach he may appeal to history. We can say with the poet—

> "Nor wreck, nor change, nor winter's blight,
> Nor Time's remorseless doom
> Shall dim'one ray of holy light
> That gilds thy glorious tomb."

Chapter XIX

The solitude of our country home was often broken in upon by friends, who sought us out with unforgetting love. My dear Robert Minor walked in upon us unexpectedly one day, and oh! the joy of that meeting! that reunion! Our eldest son, John, Jr., was having a birthday party with his little friends and schoolmates. Bob was the happiest of the lot. He entered into all the youngsters' games and mirth, nearly hugged the breath out of little Semmes, and held the baby girl Marjory with patience unrivaled, telling us all the time about his own loved ones and home. Bob was an embodiment of bravery and tenderness—all children loved him. That my posterity may value this friend of my youth and my life, I here insert some extracts of letters, and his graphic account of the battle between the *Monitor* and the *Virginia*, or *Merrimac*, in which he took an active part, and volunteering to fire the *Cumberland* was wounded. The following letter was written to my wife soon after the battle:

Naval Hospital,
Norfolk, Va., *March 8th, 1862.*

My Dear Friend: The Yankees have shut me up for a while with a ball through my side, but with the blessing of God and the aid of a strong constitution I hope to be up and at work again before very long. The papers have no doubt told you all about our terrible conflict and subsequent victory, and I can add but little to that you already know, save to tell you that we went into battle to do our best, trusting in Almighty God to guard and protect us, and most signally has His Merciful Providence been extended over us, for which in my heart I try to be thankful; but I fear that I am not sufficiently so, nor can I ever be for sparing me to meet again those so inestimably dear to me. Kell's old friend, Captain Franklin Buchanan, of the *Susquehanna,* of East India celebrity, was our flag officer, and most bravely, most nobly

282   RECOLLECTIONS OF A NAVAL LIFE

did he take us into action, right up to the enemy, and exposing himself entirely too much for his own safety and the ultimate good of our country. He did me the honor to appoint me flag lieutenant of his squadron, consisting of all the vessels in the waters of Virginia, and as you would no doubt like to know who the other officers were, I annex a list of them, among whom you will find some of your old acquaintances—

Flag officer, Franklin Buchanan; 1st lieutenant, Catesby Ap. R. Jones; 2d lieutenant, Chas. C. Simms; flag lieutenant, Robert D. Minor; 3d lieutenant, Hunter Davidson; 4th lieutenant, John Taylor Wood; 5th lieutenant, John R. Eggleston; 6th lieutenant, Walter R. Butt; paymaster, James Semple; surgeon, R. B. Phillips; assistant surgeon, Algernon S. Garrett; captain of marines, Reuben Thorn; chief engineer, Ramsey; sailing master, Parish; midshipmen, Littlepage, Foute, Marmaduke, Rootes, Long, Craig; commodore's clerk, Arthur Sinclair, Jr.; secretary, D. A. Forrest.

Among our several engineers I found one originally from the vicinity of Macon, a young Mr. White, who told me that he knew your father very well. He did his duty well, and stood fire like a true Georgian. The crash into the *Cumberland* was terrific in its results, for in thirty minutes after the action commenced the ship was at the bottom with, I fear, hundreds carried down in her. Radford was her captain, but was absent. George Morris and Stribling are said to be her lieutenants, and have probably perished. Our cleaver fairly opened her side, and down she went, though fighting as long as she could. Her masts, inclined at an angle of forty-five degrees, now mark the remains of this once gallant ship. She will never burn another navy-yard on Southern soil!

The *Congress* engaged us a while, but soon knocked under, and Billy Parker, commanding the C. S. Gunboat *Beaufort,* was sent with orders to "let her crew go ashore, her officers to be brought on board, and to burn the frigate," then hard aground near the Point. While endeavoring to execute the directions of the flag officer the enemy opened on him from the shore so hotly that he was forced to retire, but the commodore and myself, not knowing this, and seeing that the *Congress* was not in flames, the old gentleman became very anxious to destroy her, which he could not do while she had the white flag flying, and though he had once declined my volunteered offer to burn her, he accepted it when I made a second offer. For this purpose I took some eight or ten men in our only remaining boat and pulled towards her, while the fight was going on between the James River Squadron and the *Minnesota*. The flag officer ordered Lieutenant Webb in the *Teazer* to protect me in my little boat, for as I drew near the *Congress* the soldiers on shore opened on me with artillery and musketry, and very soon two

RECOLLECTIONS OF A NAVAL LIFE

of my men and myself were knocked down. I was only down a second or two, and, steering my crippled boat for the *Teazer,* Webb took us to the *Virginia,* where it had already been reported that they were firing upon me, and the flag officer, seeing it, deliberately backed our dear old craft up close astern of the *Congress* and poured gun after gun, hot shot and incendiary shells into her, when the smoke began to arise from her. The fierce flames exploded her magazines a little after midnight with a shock so terrible that it shook the windows of houses miles away from the Point. The flag officer was severely wounded while this cannonading was going on, being struck in the left thigh by a minnie or musket-ball, which so disabled him that he was taken below, and Catesby Jones, our brave and determined 1st lieutenant, fought the action out, which on Saturday resulted in the sinking of the *Cumberland,* the burning of the *Congress,* the serious injury of the *Minnesota,* the defeat of the *St. Laurence,* the retreat of the *Roanoke* (all first-class, heavy ships), and the destruction of a tug and some schooners—a good day's work for the *Virginia,* ably assisted as she was by the *Patrick Henry,* Commander Tucker; *Thomas Jefferson,* Lieutenant Commanding Barney; *Teazer,* Lieutenant Commanding Webb; *Beaufort,* Lieutenant Commanding Parker, and *Raleigh,* Lieutenant Commanding Alexander. Saturday night the battle ceased, the wounded among the crews being sent to this place, while the flag officer and I remained on board till Sunday morning, the action re-commencing soon after we left between the *Virginia* and the *Minnesota,* hard aground in such shoal water that our ship could not approach her closely, and the *Monitor* (your old acquaintance, John L. Worden, commanding) coming to her assistance, a hard fight took place between these two ironclad batteries, which resulted in nothing but some little damage on both sides, and so the *Monitor,* clearing out towards Old Point, our squadron came up to Norfolk. As soon as the *Virginia* is ready (by Saturday, I hope) she will drive ahead at them again. Thus ended our first big naval fight, and I thank our Merciful Father for giving us the victory over our enemies. Our total loss among all the ships was nine killed, among them Lieutenant James Taylor, of Virginia, and Midshipman Hutter, also of Virginia; about fifteen or eighteen wounded, one of whom has since died. The flag officer is here and is doing quite well, though his wound is quite a severe one. The ball struck me in the side, glanced around, and came out near the heart, and though not serious, is a severe wound, one which the doctors say will keep me off duty for about two months. D. heard of it Sunday and came at once to me Monday. God bless the women! What would the world be without them? Our children are in Richmond with my brother, where we hope to rejoin them. And now I have done with self, except to ask you to

284   RECOLLECTIONS OF A NAVAL LIFE

pardon this ill-looking scrawl, as I write in bed and by "fits and starts," as I get a chance.

Julian Myers (brother of Purser Myers of the *Sumter*) told Parker and myself a few weeks ago that the *Sumter* had destroyed 109 vessels. and Lieutenant McCorkle told me that she had $1,400,000, most of which he supposed had been sent to England; but I am inclined to think from later and more direct news that this latter item is all a mistake, for Captain Pegram of the *Nashville* sent Captain Semmes some money at Captain Semmes's request to Gibraltar. The Yankee vessels taken by the little *Sumter* have not generally had much money on board, hence Semmes's request for funds. I do not believe the printed report that Semmes was arrested at Tangier; but even if it is true the Confederate Government would have in his successor as brave and gallant a captain for the *Sumter* (now far-famed) as ever trod a deck or struck a blow for his country's cause. I hope most earnestly, my friend, that you have had letters from him by the *Nashville* or the *Economist* at Charleston, Chas. Fauntleroy on board. D. and I think and talk often and often of both of you, and deep would be our joy to see you united once more in safety, which we pray God may soon be granted. Yes, my friend, I pray for him, for you, and your little children, and when this war is at an end, oh, how glad we will be to see you all in Virginia! Now our beautiful country is given up. "Linden," "Eastern View," and the "Grove" are between our lines and the enemy, and we know not what will be the result! I think the President was right in withdrawing our army from Manassas. How are the two little boys and the dear little girl, my godchild? Give my warm regards to your father, write me at Richmond, and tell me all you know about Kell, also of his mother and sisters. D. sends her best love to you, and I am affectionately and sincerely your friend,

ROBERT D. MINOR.

This devoted friend of my boyhood watched my movements abroad with loving interest, and always tried to cheer my family if unfavorable news of the *Sumter*, and later of the *Alabama*, was reported, and no brother could have been more faithful. Once he writes:

Of course it would be no use for me to write on any other topic till I tell you all about the little *Sumter* and her brave fellows. She is not "wrecked!" She has not "gone to the Pacific." She was heard from in September at the Island of Trinidad. The Navy Department wishes that she was now in some port of the Confederacy, in which I know you piously join! But to details. Early in September there was

RECOLLECTIONS OF A NAVAL LIFE 285

a report in circulation, originating somewhere in the fertile region of lies, that the little craft had been lost by running ashore at night, and for a while it was believed to be so, but seventeen days later than the date of her loss she was at the Island of Trinidad. She did not remain long, but continued her cruise in accordance with instructions giving her a "roving commission to go where she could inflict most injury on the commerce of the enemy." The latest news of her at the Navy Department is to the 16th of September. My impression is that after cruising two months or more off the coast of Brazil she returned to the West Indies to operate there, or else (as is barely possible) she may have relied on her sails to take her across to the British Channel; but the steamer is small and her capacity for storage of supplies so limited I hardly think they could have favored this step. I hope and believe she has "doubled" on her pursuers, the *Powhatan* and the *Keystone State,* and is once more on her "native heath" among the West India Islands. Although Kell is doing our country good and noble service, for your sake I do wish he was at home, for there is duty enough to be done here, and we want clear heads and strong wills to work out the problem of our independence, of which I have never had a doubt, so great is my reliance on the righteousness of our cause and the high protection afforded by Almighty God.

Of course I cannot conjecture when the *Sumter* will return to the Confederacy, but I think it cannot be long. She may from several causes have to discontinue her cruise. It would not surprise me if she were sold in a foreign port, and her officers and crew find their way home as best they may! So you need not be surprised to see him, and next to you and his mother there is no one who would hail his safe and speedy return more gladly than myself, for not only were we friends as boys, but our friendship has "grown with our growth and strengthened with our strength!" God bless the old fellow is my daily prayer. May He watch over and bring him back in safety to those who love him so well! I hope to pass many merry, happy days with him yet, and when he brings you all to see us one of these days I'll show the little boys "specimens of natural history," the like of which the broomsedge hills of Georgia never saw! Very, very happy days were those at the Pensacola Navy Yard, when Kell's was a charming home for us, on the little *Preble.* I felt very sorry for the ship when I read her fate, but not a whit of sorrow for those on board of her, handling *my* guns, sleeping in *my* room, and working the little ship I loved so well. I have lately been in a very perilous expedition planned by Commodore Mathew F. Maury. Some time since I had several shots at the U. S. Steamer *Pocahontas,* and two days after the Battle of Manassas I found the body of Lieutenant Douglas Ramsey, of the U. S. A., on the

286 RECOLLECTIONS OF A NAVAL LIFE

field and had it decently interred, as he was an old acquaintance of mine, and the son of Captain Ramsey of the Navy. Sometimes I have two or three men's work to do in Ordnance Department. Ɖ. is with me. Do you get Richmond papers daily? They will be full of interest for the next three months. Always let me know if I can do anything for you; it gives me such sincere pleasure to do it. Always write me when you have news of John. Give love to his mother and sisters. Kiss my little goddaughter and hug the little boys. Don't let them forget me, the devoted friend of their father and mother. Does "Mundy" still pray for "Bob?" I hope so! God bless you and yours.

Affectionately, your friend,

R. D. MINOR.

The loving brotherhood that existed in the friends of the old Navy is something dear and sacred beyond words to look back upon. He, my boyhood's friend, has long since preceded us to the "better land," and it is sweet to remember him as one who loved God and his family and friends with faithful heart, and served his country, doing his full duty with noble, patriotic fervor. God grant us a happy reunion beyond the Sea of Time!

Chapter XX

AMONG the pleasant things that came into my life about this time I will mention this little incident. I had occasion to go to the coast, and in crossing over in the little steamer from Brunswick to Darien the captain came to me and said, "Is this Captain Kell?" I replied, "Yes." "Well," he said, "Captain Kell, I am glad to see you, and you are expected. I promised to give a signal to the shore when you were on my boat when we pass Barratt's Island. You have an old comrade there, one of your men on the *Alabama.*" "What is his name?" I inquired. "Rawse, sir." I tried to think, but the name was not familiar to me. However, I knew that seamen seldom use their own names. In a short time we came in sight of the island, and soon quite near it, and the signal was given. Out came a man, whom I recognized even at that distance as our master-at-arms. I raised my hat, and he uncovered his head and proceeded to give me from a pile of muskets at his side, that he had arranged for the purpose, a commodore's salute of thirteen guns, deliberately one by one! I waved my thanks and the little steamer passed on. Loyal Rawse, he knew what should have been my rank but for ill fortune and defeat, and determined that he at least would recognize it! The next day he came up to see me, and was very happy at the meeting. I said, "Well, Master-at-arms, I am glad to see you once more; tell me all about yourself." I found he was a sort of sentinel guard, or watchman to the convicts, that island being worked by convict labor. While in the city of Darien, Dr. Duncan, one of the owners of the island and lessees of the convicts, came to me and said: "Your friend Rawse gave us a terrible scare yesterday. We thought

288   RECOLLECTIONS OF A NAVAL LIFE

at the repeated firing of the muskets kept for our protection that the convicts had risen in mutiny and our island was in a state of insurrection. We were rejoiced to find it was a salute to our Georgia commodore instead."

It has been a great pleasure to meet at times the loyal, brave fellows that served with us, and Savannah held quite a number—Brooks, one of our efficient engineers; Marmelstein, our young signal officer, who had the honor of unfurling the first Confederate flag to the breeze on the ocean; the brave seaman, Michael Mars, who picked up an unexploded shell during the action with the *Kearsarge* and threw it overboard, perhaps saving lives thereby, and who only a few short years ago passed away from earth. I love to meet the brave and gallant fellows who made the glory of our little ship and were so loyal hearted.

Three years after the Civil War closed a great sorrow befell my family in the death of my wife's father. Thinking it best to make a change for them, and hoping the change would benefit my still weak health, I took my family out to Nova Scotia for some months. Armstrong, who resided there, had long ago suggested it to me as a motive for renewing health. We sailed from New York for Halifax in one of the fine English steamers, and I had four days of pleasure on Old Ocean again. We had a very pleasant season in that unrivaled summer climate, spending some weeks in the city of Halifax. Commodore Tatnall's family, Captain John Taylor Wood, the Wilkersons, the Sinclairs, ex-Governor Charles J. Jenkins and family, Lieutenant Hoge, my friend and comrade Armstrong, his young wife and child, and many other Southerners formed a delightful society for us. We went into the country for a couple of months, to Petpeswick Bay, Musquidoboit Harbor, where the fishing was fine—mackerel, cod, herring and salmon, fresh from the water, making a wholesome diet, and all so great a change to us from our sunny Southern home. I do not think there can be in the whole world anything more beautiful than this Arca-

RECOLLECTIONS OF A NAVAL LIFE

dian country, where I have somewhere heard or read that Longfellow went to write his "Evangeline" or others of his poems, where one can readily imagine the task could be made easy in the sight of the limpid streams and little miniature lakes, a chain of which we passed in our thirty-mile drive from Halifax to the bay. Our beautiful evening walk was usually to a small church, beside which was the manse embowered in vines and flowers, all so suggestive of the "Lights and Shadows of Scottish Life," the stories so enchanting to youths in days gone by. It is the land of mosses and lichens, where one scarcely sees the face of the earth for its beautiful adornment of green, and the deep blue sky above is heavenly in its color (like October skies at home); and gazing into its depths of ether one must be drawn away in thought and made for a time, at least, to forget earth's desolate unrest. The summer was blessed to us in the re-establishment of health, and we returned in the fall to the dear old "red clay hills" of middle Georgia, quite invigorated. I had no complaint of invalidism thereafter, and with my active outdoor life and constant exercise soon did credit in health and strength to the blood of my Highland ancestors.

In the fall of 1873 a message came over the wires to me from Selma, Alabama: "The doctor has been very ill; is convalescing; will come to you for a change." Back flew the answer: "Rejoice to hear it; come at once." One of the beloved friends of my life, Dr. Charles Frederick Fahs, of the United States Navy, with whom I spent the cruises to China and Japan in our youth, and whom I had not seen for seventeen long years, came to my home to die. With his wife and brother they left Selma, and he seemed to improve each mile of the way, till nearing Atlanta a chill of congestive nature set in, and his condition became alarming. Upon arriving in Atlanta Dr. Westmoreland and other physicians were summoned, who urged delay, and that he should remain there; but he steadily refused, saying, "If I must die, I would rather die

19

290 RECOLLECTIONS OF A NAVAL LIFE

with Kell." The cars brought him to my door at nine o'clock in the morning. On a bed he was brought into my house, but growing weaker each moment. Before the sun set, nine hours after he came, his noble spirit departed unto God who gave it, as he leaned upon my breast to die. His triumph in departing (though he had so much to leave in lovely wife and children) was beautiful to see, and something never to be forgotten, increasing our faith, enlarging our hope, telling us, "It is not all of life to live, nor all of death to die!"

Dr. Charles Frederick Fahs was a man of science and learning, who adorned his profession, and who, like the great Maury, was a man of noble simplicity of character and childlike faith in God. He wrote the flora and fauna for the Japan Expedition, which added much to Commodore Perry's published volumes for the United States Government of that very interesting period. Peace to the ashes of one so noble and beloved.

> "Friend of my early days,
>   None knew thee but to love thee,
>   None named thee, but to praise."

In the year 1886 I was invited by the *Century Magazine* to write an article on the historical fight between the *Alabama* and the *Kearsarge*. The use of the pen has always been a burden to me, and my life has been one of deeds, not words. I at first declined. I thought Admiral Semmes's book was enough for history and the world. I had been solicited by many leading journals, and the press of the country often, to write, but my farming life left me little time, and I had always declined. After a second invitation, yielding to the earnest entreaties of my home circle, who considered it a duty I owed to the "Lost Cause," I wrote the historical article embodied in their "Battles and Leaders of the Civil War." It was really amusing and interesting to see my mail for some time after. I felt offended that the lying sailor yarn preceded my arti-

RECOLLECTIONS OF A NAVAL LIFE

cle, and that the "hearsay," though able, article of Dr. Browne followed it, but I made up my mind to take no notice of it, when to my great pleasure I found Galt could not stand it, and emerged from the solitude of his country home to defend the truth of history.

CIVIL WAR HISTORY.

To the Editor of the Sun.

SIR: In the April number of the *Century Magazine* appeared the long-looked-for articles on the *Alabama,* which attracted notice rather from the expectation of their containing new developments of an already well-understood story of the war than from any hope that what was already known would be correctly stated by Northern writers. As one of the *Alabama's* officers, who served on board her whole cruise, it is not out of place for me to correct some of the gross errors which the sailor's story wilfully, and the doctor's through hearsay, are more or less full of, and between which Captain Kell's direct and truthful narrative was sandwiched and shrouded by some curious stories and pictures which have amused those who were present on the scene. The story of the sailor is such a vulgar misrepresentation of the history of the ship that it has excited surprise that a reputable journal like the *Century* should permit such a tissue of statements worse than errors to have a place in what is supposed to be history, even though pictorial, of the Civil War. The man's name is unfamiliar to me, but if it be a *nom de plume* he has done the most decent thing he could to hide his identity when telling such stories about his ship. If he was a sailor on the ship his account at once convicts him of a treacherous record, and if he has been writing from hearsay he has simply been paid for an elaborate series of forecastle inventions utterly without truth. Nor can my memory refer me to any one on board whose career was so bad (except the man Forrest) as to have tried to traduce the record of the ship. The article would not have been considered worth notice had not the *Pall Mall Gazette* judged from that account harshly of the discipline on the *Alabama,* and thus tried to injure the reputation of as fine a crew as ever served, whether English or other. The stories of mutiny and want of subordination are such absurd exaggerations that one hardly knows how to deny them, and the well-known record of the *Alabama's* work in every phase of her career is the best commentary on such trash as the sailor has put forth. It is difficult to understand why such accounts were published, except on the ground of enduring malice on the part of some writers and readers owing to the great damage done on the high seas by the *Alabama,* and when it is known that the editor of the maga-

RECOLLECTIONS OF A NAVAL LIFE

zine desired Captain Kell in his article not to let the bitterness of the past be introduced, it is somewhat singular that this narrative should have been flanked by a series of statements which the merest tyro in criticism must have seen to be gross exaggerations. The loyalty of the crew of the *Alabama* to the flag they served under, the cheerfulness with which they stood up to the varied emergencies of her career, and the gallant fight they made at the last against their invulnerable enemy could not have been surpassed! The greater part of the crew were English, and they behaved with the customary bravery and fortitude of their race. If Haywood was of that race he has certainly managed to distinguish himself, nor has the *Century* added much to the character which it has striven for as a pictorial recorder of the late Civil War. Among the items in the sailor's account as especially absurd is the idea of Captain Semmes being thought by the crew to have been a parson! While that would have been no discredit, it is however the case that he was a consistent member of the Roman Catholic Church, and there was nothing in his bearing to indicate that he was anything but what he looked and acted—an officer of great determination, with intelligent direction of resources in peace and war; an admirable judge in managing his crew with a high appreciation of the great responsibility of his position, which he worthily maintained under all circumstances.

Other misrepresentations are the stories of the conduct of the boarding crews on prizes. Notwithstanding the very great temptations to pillage, I cannot recall any complaints made by the boarding officers. Nor do I remember complaints on the part of masters of prizes about the undisciplined conduct of our men. The account of the conduct of the crew at Martinique is a pure fabrication, especially the story of the "connivance of French Naval officers and shore authorities" to assist us in getting clear of a supposed United States man-of-war. There are scattered through the whole of this sailor's story these repeated accounts of the crew which are totally unworthy of credit, such as the smuggling of liquor from prizes, wholesale desertion at the Cape of Good Hope, and in fact almost his entire narrative shows a hopeless want of regard for the truthfulness which is just as becoming in the forecastle as elsewhere. Dr. Browne's article is a very much more creditable contribution to the Northern side of the question, as was to be expected. The doctor very naturally, from his position on board the *Kearsarge*, must have written most of his piece from hearsay. As both his commander and executive officer were dead, he probably thought himself, as an old Navy man, better qualified by observation and experience to give a correct account of the fight with the *Alabama*, as the other line officers, he says, were mostly from the merchant marine. His only error of any consequence is in reference to the *Alabama's* firing after her surrender. This is simply not correct! The fire of the *Ala-*

RECOLLECTIONS OF A NAVAL LIFE

bama was suspended for awhile, as Captain Kell says, "owing to the shifting of her battery," but after the flag was hauled down there was no shot fired from that ship. The story the doctor tells as heard from the "prisoners" about the junior officers of the *Alabama* firing after the surrender is entirely without foundation, as was also the report that additional men were taken on board the *Alabama* at Cherbourg. It is very probable that the firing from the *Kearsarge* after the *Alabama's* hauling down her flag was the result of flurry and doubt on the part of Captain Winslow, who perhaps felt himself surprised into a victory over a vessel which had been so conspicuous during the war and had hitherto eluded the best efforts of capture.

The doctor would have shown better taste if he had omitted his opinion of a rather murderous kind about the *Alabama's* deserving to be sunk with all on board for her supposed firing after surrender! The hesitancy of the *Kearsarge* to send boats after the fight, was no doubt owing to that same doubt as to whether the *Alabama* was really sinking or not, though it seems that it might have been noticed, or the captain might have imagined that the *Alabama* was about to take a dive under to reappear as a submarine torpedo to effect against her enemy what her shot could not against the enemy's well-cabled sides. This delay to send boats to the sinking ship very naturally determined the officers and crew of the *Alabama* to look out for themselves, and thus deprived the enemy of the great satisfaction of getting Captain Semmes and others. The results of the fight of the *Alabama* were adverse for very simple reasons, as stated by Captain Kell, the damaged condition of the powder, the efficient plating of the *Kearsarge* and the foul bottom which injured the *Alabama's* speed. In fact, like all other important disasters to the Confederacy, it was the result of want of resources in material which the greatest skill and heroism could not cope with.

There is nothing but favorable report to make of the condition of the *Kearsarge* after the fight, and the treatment of prisoners and wounded men taken on board was all that medical attention and courtesy could have desired.

FRANCIS L. GALT,
Surgeon of C. S. Steamer Alabama.

UPPERVILLE P. O., FAUQUIER CO., VA.

May, 1886, the *Century's* editor wrote me:

DEAR SIR: By an oversight this copy of a letter received by us from Mr. Walt Whitman goes to you rather late, for which we apologize:

294   RECOLLECTIONS OF A NAVAL LIFE

"CAMDEN, NEW JERSEY, *April 3d, 1886.*

"My reading for the last two or three days (limited) of the articles in Century about *Kearsarge* and *Alabama,* which I have just finished. They form by far the best contribution I know to the literature of the Secession era, and are full of realism and thrill. The pictures are masterly. I only wish we could have accounts of all the swell episodes of the war in the same way, or approximately to it. I want personally to thank you all, writers and picture-makers.

"WALT WHITMAN."

I had scores of letters from personal friends, whose approbation and appreciation of my contribution to history gave me much pleasure.

Chapter XXI

Many years ago, when Mr. Davis was invited to make his tour of triumph through the South and be present at the unveiling of the monument to the gifted son of Georgia, the Hon. Benjamin H. Hill, I received a letter from Mr. Henry W. Grady—generous, noble Grady!—always on the alert to honor and give pleasure to an old Confederate, asking me to accompany the escort of veterans that were to meet Mr. Davis at Montgomery, Alabama. His letter read as follows (I accepted the invitation of veterans):

My Dear Sir: I inclose you a ticket to the platform next Saturday to witness the unveiling of the Hill statue. It is an appropriate compliment that you should be here to meet Mr. Davis, and it is my personal request that you come. Mr. Davis will be glad to see you, the people will be glad to see you, and I will be glad to see you, for I have always admired you and loved you for your gallantry in the cause for which my father gave his life, more than you have ever suspected! I shall look for you on that day.

Yours very truly,
Henry W. Grady.

I gladly accepted these kind invitations, and it was the first time in many years that I had left the seclusion of my country home (I enjoyed every moment of the time) to take part in any public occasion. The glad exultations of the Southern people to greet the patriot who to them embodied the dear "Lost Cause," to say nothing of the magnetism of his own personality, was beautiful beyond words to express. I hope and believe the shouts of welcome and words of love of that time and tour lived and re-echoed in his heart and memory until the unseen angels came to carry his great soul beyond the shores of time,

RECOLLECTIONS OF A NAVAL LIFE

where loyalty and patriotism (though but human virtues) may count for their true value before the Judgment Seat of Him who made our human hearts, and who has promised after death's long sleep that those who love and serve Him shall "awake and be satisfied!"

I have been asked many times in my life how I bore the quiet of a farmer's life after such activity as I had always known, or how I existed without a sniff of salt air and sea breezes? Man is the creature of habit. My habit of life changed and gave place to new tastes and experiences. This being a history of my public life and services, I will not intrude upon my readers, friends and posterity much of the home and farming life, combining so much of "the joy and sorrow with which the stranger may not intermeddle." While I made a support for my family, I never found anything remunerative in farming. I suppose I was too much of a sailor to farm well, except in enthusiasm. It has often been an amusement to myself to see how far away my thoughts sometimes were from my work. I was obliged once to let the family enjoy with me a joke upon myself. I was seated in my two-horse wagon and had a new darkey alongside of me driving, my thoughts of Spain and a famous fox hunt I once enjoyed there, when looking up I saw the boy was going in the wrong direction. Quick as lightning I called out, "Port your helm!" The darkey evidently thought my nautical language a majestic swear, and called out in a startled tone, "Sah?" I laughed in spite of myself—and he never understood why—and I said quietly, "Drive to the right, boy," and we continued our journey.

Among the happy summers of our life I recall the one of 187—, when we had as next door neighbors the family of the lamented, gifted Lanier. His wife and mine had been loving friends from the cradle of Mrs. Lanier, my wife being her senior several years—their mothers loving friends before them. Mr. Lanier was just then going on to Baltimore to join the orchestra with his magic flute.

RECOLLECTIONS OF A NAVAL LIFE

Such music I believe the world will never hear again, when the very soul of the master seemed to breathe out in its heavenly cadences, and the rapt listeners scarcely realized their mortality, so strong were the spiritual affinities at work within them. The very air of home seemed blessed in the happy evenings in which he made music for us. One morning he walked into our little sitting-room, and with a wearied look on his face threw himself on the sofa and exclaimed, "Such a delightful walk as I have had in and out of the beautiful corn rows in the field next to us. I never saw such corn before. I luxuriated in the rustle of its leaves!" This walk was the inspiration of the poem, "Corn," among his finest—if one can discriminate among his soulful lyrics. Even the heathen said, "Whom the gods love, die young," and this true, pure, manly soul was early called to heavenly blessedness; but the world is better for his life lived here, his music, and his songs.

A correspondence (our only communication with the outside world) is a great pleasure in country life, and yet when letters come with such clippings as these, how stirred up I feel to give battle to the falsehoods that are supposed to make history. In a recent letter Armstrong writes me:

In my last letter I referred to the enclosed and promised to send you a copy when I came across it. It so happened that an old classmate of mine, owner of the Steam Yacht *Intrepid*, came into port and behold! my old antagonist (and friend) J. Schuyler Crosby, a guest on board. This brought to mind the incident of my letter to the *New York Sun* in reply to Colonel Crosby's speech, revealing this precious bit of history, and a search among my papers brought it to light. Crosby was a colonel on Sheridan's staff after the war.

"UNITED STATES CONSULATE,
"FLORENCE, ITALY, *September 4th, 1879.*
"HON. WILLIAM HUNTER,
"*Second Assistant Secretary of State,*
"Washington, D. C.
"SIR: Within the last few days the following circumstances came to my knowledge, and I deem them of sufficient historical interest for the subject of this dispatch. An acquaintance of mine, Sir John Burgoyne,

298 RECOLLECTIONS OF A NAVAL LIFE

in the course of conversation told me that a few hours before the engagement between the *Kearsarge* and *Alabama* he took the lieutenant of the latter on board the *Kearsarge*. He was dining at the Crown Hotel, Dover, and his neighbor at table, who turned out to be an officer of the *Kearsarge*, invited him to visit her. The next day at dinner at the same hotel, another stranger, who got into conversation with Burgoyne, asked him what was the war vessel lying off Dover, if she was ironclad, what her armament was, and to what country she belonged? Sir John found him an agreeable and intelligent companion, and on his saying he was going aboard the *Kearsarge* acceded to his request to permit him to accompany him. On going aboard the next day the officer who had invited Burgoyne was not on board, but the officer of the deck, on seeing Burgoyne's card, invited him and his friend on board and showed them every part of the vessel, in which inspection the stranger showed a marked and intelligent interest.

"When Sir John and his companion returned ashore his unknown acquaintance said, 'Thank you so much; you little know what a service you have rendered me, Sir John, for I am the first lieutenant of the *Alabama.*' The subsequent meeting of these two vessels took place with the result all the world knows.

"I have the honor to be, etc.,

[Signed] "H. E. Huntington,
"Vice-Consul."

Copy of dispatch to State Department, Washington, furnished me at St. Augustine, Fla., by Colonel J. Schuyler Crosby.

R. F. Armstrong.

"Oh, how this world is given to lying," and never since Ananias was so suddenly silenced was a more absurd lie given to history! I never was at Dover in my life, I never made the acquaintance of a Sir John Burgoyne, and I never set foot on the deck of the *Kearsarge!*

Armstrong's able and caustic pen saved me the trouble of refuting, and the *New York Sun* soon published the following:

THE SECOND MATE OF THE "ALABAMA" REPLIES TO COLONEL CROSBY.

To the Editor of the Sun.

Sir: In your Washington correspondence of December 6th there appears an article headed "Lord Burgoyne's Remarkable Story Concerning the *Alabama's* Last Fight," in which Mr. J. Schuyler Crosby, recently appointed First Assistant Postmaster General, relates some very interesting incidents for the edification of the Loyal League. The only

RECOLLECTIONS OF A NAVAL LIFE

single fact in the whole story is that off Cherbourg on a certain day in June a fight did take place. The English yacht which rendered such efficient service in saving life on June 19th, 1864, was the *Deerhound,* whose owner was Mr. Lancaster—not *Greyhound*—and if Lord Burgoyne was on board the *Deerhound* it is the first time that any one has ever heard of the fact. The *Kearsarge* did not come to an anchor before the fight, and the only communication had with her from the shore was by the United States Consul in carrying to Captain Winslow the challenge of the *Alabama.* The only other craft, besides the *Kearsarge,* which shared the honors of saving life on that occasion was a French pilot-boat, and the writer asserts most positively that Lord Burgoyne was not on board of her. Our first lieutenant, Kell, was saved by the *Deerhound,* and I think I can trust my memory so far as to state that Lieutenant Kell did not leave the side of the *Alabama* from the day she entered Cherbourg until she steamed out of the port—in fact, was not on shore at all—and therefore could not have met "Lord Burgoyne" at a hotel, or elsewhere.

But, Mr. Editor, the necessity given for such a visit is the unkindest cut of all, and the reflection cast upon the officers of the *Alabama*—of not being able to locate the boilers of the steamship without a personal inspection—is such a slander upon our *Alma Mater,* the United States Naval Academy, that I feel called upon to resent it. But where is the use of further proving the romance of Lord Burgoyne's remarkable statements? But, then, Colonel Crosby has had but little experience of the sea, and of those who navigate thereon, and it is but charitable to presume that this "slip-over" effort of the gallant colonel was in the nature of one of those yarns we always tell to the "horse marines."

[Signed]   THE SECOND LIEUTENANT OF THE "ALABAMA."

ST. AUGUSTINE, FLA., *December 26th.*

Armstrong in his youth found home and happiness in another country; he never lived in reconstruction times, and I am afraid I shall have to give him thrice the fifteen years of additional age the admiral allowed me in which to become conservative. I am in receipt of an amusing article of his, as yet unpublished—

THE "ALABAMA'S" CROCKERYWARE AND FLIGHTS OF FANCY IN CONNECTION THEREWITH.

Editor Art Interchange.

In your September number appears an article entitled "Ceramic Relics of the Confederate States of America." One would judge from viewing the cut of the only article which properly can be classed under

RECOLLECTIONS OF A NAVAL LIFE

so pretentious a title, the hospital and ante-bellum hospitable jug, that these people could hardly claim distinction in ceramic art. Perhaps in their semi-barbarous and unæsthetic condition they laid more store by their military prowess than their manufacture of pottery. *Ars est celare artem*, and in the little brown jug the maxim is fully accomplished—in fact, in simplicity of design and finish this example of fine art makes towards pure æstheticism, and distinctly makes an evolutionary period in the history of a hitherto rude and uncultured people.

Mr. Edwin At Lee Barber, who, from his præcognomen, I should judge to be of the Flowery Kingdom, and consequently an expert in pottery affairs, shows a commendable spirit in delving into the hitherto unexplored field of Dixie, and it is to be regretted that his search for objects *d'art et virtu* of the Confederate period has been so barren of results. In fact, his search for these ceramic art treasures has apparently been so disappointing as to force him to draw upon the crockery establishment of Messrs. Badley & Co., of Staffordshire, and bring into the service of his article the crockeryware supplied by that house for the alimentary comfort of the officers and crew of the *Alabama*. *Mirabile dictu!* the plates, cups and saucers, and perhaps other pottery vessels, have been invested with miraculous flotative power, and with the factor of avoirdupois eliminated, like the wonderful borrowed axe of Elisha, have been made to rise from full fathom five to supply relics of "the famous sea-rover." I have heard of this putative *Alabama* crockeryware before, and in point of fact have in my possession a rather hefty specimen of it, no doubt obtained from the same source as those in the treasured keeping of the "daughter of the Confederate officer in Georgia" and the "lady in Florida." Hitherto I have attached but little value to my soup-plate, and as a specimen of fine art it is considered hardly up to some of the productions of Sevrès or even those of Mr. At Lee's own country; but now the case is entirely different, and in so well authenticated a relic "recovered from the vessel after she had been sunk" and *ipso facto* necessarily invested with miraculous power, I consider that I have a treasure which it is my duty to transmit as a valued heirloom!

'Several years ago in St. Augustine, I was asked by the Rev. Dr. Prime, of Holy Land memory, to authenticate one of these plates as a genuine relic of the *Alabama*. I asked the reverend gentleman if he had ever read of the little *affaire à deux* off Cherbourg? He replied that he had. "Then, Doctor, would you not think that at that time we were otherwise engaged than in saving crockery?" I must confess that the miracle theory had not occurred to me at that time, and I have probably prevented this particular plate from appearing in the lists of the genuine relics no doubt obtained by the gentleman in Palestine and

RECOLLECTIONS OF A NAVAL LIFE

301

other Eastern countries. Perhaps there is no more cause to doubt that the crockeryware of the *Alabama* bobbed up serenely from the bottom of the English Channel, and ergo, that the "plate, cup and saucer; said to have been recovered from the vessel after she had been sunk" are as genuine as half the Christian relics that we swear by, and far better authenticated! As time passes we shall, no doubt, hear more of these *Alabama* relics, so for the nonce I shall assume the rôle of "the bull in the china shop" and put a quietus upon the crockery part. Therefore, relic hunters, give ear to my story and attention to my relation.

The contract with Messrs. Laird Bros. was for a ship of certain dimensions and power, furnished complete with everything for the voyage. This, of course, included crockeryware, and accordingly four sets of this ware (with designs as shown in the illustrations) were put on board of the ship before she left Birkenhead. The designs in all were the same, only the colors were different—that for the captain being gold; for the wardroom, blue; for the steerage, green, and for the crew, brown. This latter set had short shift on board, and as its disappearance from the present investigation of Confederate ceramic art treasures constitutes the first crockery smash-up of a series. I will adorn my tale and perhaps point a moral by relating the circumstances. In those days—1862—of square-rigged ships and sail power it was essential that the crew of a man-o'-war should be sailors—it is not so necessary now, when artisans, mechanics and soldiers compose the personnel of a modern fighting machine, and the old-time shell-back has been educated out of existence—and the crew, according to immemorial custom, was divided into convenient messes, each in charge of one of its numbers, designated mess cook. The deck served for a table, a tarpaulin for a cloth, and the table furniture consisted of tinware—in not too excessive quantity. Each sailor was entitled to a pot, pan and spoon, and these, with his sheath-knife, comprised his whole mess outfit. The swinging-table and crockeryware abominations are of later introduction into the Navy, and it remains to be seen if such enervating luxuries have improved the morale of man-o'-war Jack.

Well, the *Alabama's* crew started on a crockeryware basis, and these emblematic plates, cups and saucers were a source of constant trouble. Shortly after going into commission, and while we were gradually but surely bringing our Liverpool packet material up to the standard of man-o'-war discipline, the complaints against these mess cooks were loud and frequent. This one did not wash the plates, that one failed to polish the cups, and they were altogether a bad lot! Finally, the patience of our executive officer, being wholly exhausted, and perhaps thinking it about time to give the disciplinary screw another turn, he ordered the whole of the men's crockery to be brought up from below. Jack was jubilant at the prospect of punishment being meted out to the

302   RECOLLECTIONS OF A NAVAL LIFE

delinquent cooks, but his joy was short lived, for as soon as the master-at-arms reported "all up, sir," overboard went about half a ton of Confederate States ceramic art, and perhaps it is now under the æsthetic arrangement of sea naiads' hands embellishing the abysmal caverns of sunken Atlantis. Jack's service thereafter was of bright tinware, and as this was what he had been accustomed to, he soon forgot his prized crockeryware and borrowed no further trouble about his mess arrangements.

There is a moral in this plain tale of the sea, but I shall leave it to the perspicacity of the reader to pick it out. I remember on one occasion chasing a vessel throughout the midwatch and turning the chase over to my successor of the deck. About daylight the chase, having been brought to and proving ripe for destruction, i. e., of the proper nationality, with no neutral cargo aboard, she was accordingly despoiled and fired. The captain and mate of the prize were assigned as guests of the midshipmen's mess. At breakfast, when coffee was served, the captain, examining the cup with far too critical an eye for a guest, blurted out, "Wall, look-y-here, Mate, I'll be goldarned if this here ain't one of our own cups and sassers." And no doubt the captain was right, for in those halcyon days such was the easy transfer of property on the high seas, that it was quite possible for this captain to have sipped his tea from his own cup on his own ship in the evening, and taken his coffee from the same cup on board "the pirate" at eight bells on the following morning.

It would appear from this anecdote that wear, tear and breakage had so diminished the midshipmen's stock of "this famous crockery" as to render it necessary for them to "draw upon the enemy for a further supply." Having thus disposed of the brown and the green, an indignant posterity must hold the *Kearsarge* responsible for having played the devil with the rest of it!

Chapter XXII

One day in the summer of 1886, coming in tired from my work, my wife, at her sewing on the porch "behind the morning glory vines" that shut out the world, called out to me, "Here's a letter for you from the *Constitution* office," but none can imagine my surprise at its contents! It seems that my friends had been thinking of me, and resolved to do something for me. The kindly thought originated in the mind of Col. L. N. Whittle, but it only needed to be suggested to others. Judge Richard H. Clark, Col. L. Q. C. Lamar, Hon. David J. Bailey, Sr., his sons, and my friend Frank Flint and my kind neighbors at Sunnyside, and Griffin, the county seat of Spalding, where I came to abide, and where my children were born, all lent a helping hand. Colonel Whittle wrote my wife and said: "Your husband must have position under the incoming administration. General Gordon will be Governor. Captain Kell, I know, will solicit nothing, but his friends will do it for him." Fearing some disappointment to me, knowing I had never taken part or interest in politics, my home circle kept very quiet and waited events. The suggestion reached the ears of Mr. Grady in connection with the place of Commissioner of Agriculture, and his letter to me read as follows:

Atlanta, Ga., *July 27th, 1886.*

My Dear Captain: I write you at the suggestion of my partner, Evan P. Howell. He and I were talking things over to-day and I suggested that you had been mentioned as a possible candidate for Commissioner of Agriculture, and that you ought to have something from the State. There are certain difficulties in the way of that office, but Evan then suggested that you apply to General Gordon for the position of Adjutant-General. I think the place pays about $2000 and is a good

304   RECOLLECTIONS OF A NAVAL LIFE

place. It is in the Capital, near the governor, and is a place of dignity and such work as would come to your inclination. In making such application you will have the earnest support of both Mr. Howell and myself and Mr. Hemphill, and indeed all of the *Constitution.* This I am sure will give you the place. Your application would be kept quiet, and if anything should go wrong would never be known. I am *sure,* however, it will be right.

Yours with high regard,
H. W. GRADY.

In August he wrote me again:

MY DEAR CAPTAIN KELL: I feel sure that the matter I wrote you about will be settled satisfactorily. I have spoken to General Gordon, and his views coincide with mine entirely, and there is no reasonable doubt that the appointment will be made. In giving you this news, I congratulate the State and General Gordon very much more than yourself. It is but small returns for the great debt that Georgia owes you; but I am grateful at being the humble instrument by which even so small a part of the obligation may be rendered. It will be well to say nothing at present. With high regard,

Yours very truly,
H. W. GRADY.

To this I replied:

SUNNYSIDE, SPALDING CO., GA., *August 22d, 1886.*

H. W. GRADY, Esq., Atlanta, Ga.

MY DEAR SIR: Yours of the 20th is received. Need I assure you of my sincere thanks for your interest and service in my behalf. I am pleased that General Gordon has been so kind as to consider my claim with the same generous feeling that prompted you. The complimentary manner in which you have been pleased to convey to me this news is appreciated with that warmth of feeling which can be experienced only by one who has served his country and tried to do his duty. Permit me again to assure you of my gratitude, and with sincere regard remain,

Yours very truly
JNO. MCINTOSH KELL.

The Atlanta correspondent of the *Macon Telegraph* gives the following information of a movement in this line:

The *News* (Griffin) has long advocated giving some appropriate recognition by the State of the past distinguished services of one of the

RECOLLECTIONS OF A NAVAL LIFE

most noted citizens in its borders. As modest as he is brave, Captain Kell has refused to seek any office, and it is all the more reason one should be given him, and we heartily endorse the present move of our distinguished Representative, Hon. D. J. Bailey, toward such an end.

Again the *News* says:

There is a movement on foot in connection with this office which will meet with warm endorsement throughout the State. The movement is to urge Governor Gordon to tender the appointment of Adjutant-General to Captain John McIntosh Kell, of Sunnyside. I do not know that he is in any way an aspirant for this office, but there is a strong feeling among his friends that he should get it. The head and front of the movement is Hon. David J. Bailey, the Representative from Spalding, the "grand old Roman" of the House.

He prepared the petition to-day, asking Governor Gordon to make this appointment. It was one petition that all seemed to sign with sincere pleasure. Such appointment will give a higher honor to the office and be a happy tribute to a gallant gentleman.

In November I received this letter from Governor Gordon:

STATE OF GEORGIA, EXECUTIVE DEPARTMENT,
ATLANTA, *November 16th, 1886.*

CAPT. J. McINTOSH KELL:

MY DEAR SIR: Your friends throughout the State have urged your appointment to the position of Adjutant-General. The office is not at this time vacant, but the present able and efficient incumbent, Colonel John A. Stephens, informs me that failing eyesight will make it necessary for him to surrender his post at the end of the present year. It affords me great pleasure to tender that position to you, and to express the hope that it may suit your views to enter upon the discharge of its duties on the 1st of January next. I would be pleased to receive notice of your acceptance at an early day.

Very truly yours,
J. B. GORDON.

To this I replied:

SUNNYSIDE, GA., *November 17th, 1886.*

To HIS EXCELLENCY J. B. GORDON,
Atlanta, Ga.

MY DEAR SIR: Your esteemed favor of yesterday is received. I am extremely gratified for the compliment paid me by my friends

RECOLLECTIONS OF A NAVAL LIFE

throughout the State in requesting of you the appointment of Adjutant-General in my behalf. I regret sincerely the affliction "of the present able and efficient incumbent," Colonel John A. Stephens, and in accepting the appointment to fill the position he will be necessitated to surrender at the end of the present year, I can assure you that my earnest desire will be to sustain and advance the interest of the military under your command, and all other duties pertaining to the office. Thanking you for your kindness in so pleasantly tendering me this office, I am, with high regard,

Very truly yours,
JNO. MCINTOSH KELL.

The outcome of these letters and the deep and abiding interest of my friends has brought about the congenial work of the later years of my life. I trust I have not disappointed them in the fulfilment of my duty in the high position they tendered me, for their approbation and kindly feeling is very dear to my heart. Among my greatest treasures are the many kind and loving letters of congratulation received upon my appointment to office. The first to reach me was the following:

U. S. POST OFFICE,
MACON, GA., *November 19th, 1886.*
CAPT. J. MCINTOSH KELL.

DEAR SIR: You will pardon an humble individual like myself for expressing his great gratification at your appointment to the position of Adjutant-General of Georgia.

I care not how many worthy and graceful acts Governor Gordon may do, he can perform no one that will strike the heart of all Georgians with more real joy than the one of your appointment. Accept the congratulations of one who professes to be your friend and admirer.

THOMAS HARDEMAN.

AUGUSTA, GA., *November 19th, 1886.*
MY DEAR CAPTAIN: Permit me to congratulate you and the Commonwealth upon your selection for, and acceptance of, the office of Adjutant-General of the State of Georgia.

Very truly yours,
CHARLES C. JONES, JR.

RECOLLECTIONS OF A NAVAL LIFE

There is little more for me to tell in these annals of my life. Since this appointment, for more than eight years past, through the love and respect of my fellow Georgians and the courtesy of succeeding Chief Executives, I still hold my honorable position. I have reached three-score years and ten (the allotted life of man). My life has been long, happy and eventful. Of course it has been checkered with the griefs and sorrows that fall to the lot of all, but nearing the sunset of my days, beyond which are the "hills of light," I can look backward into the past of holy memories without regret, and hopefully into the future, my lifeboat gliding on, no anchor dragging, Christ's love at helm, and God aloft!

The Neale Company's New Books and New Editions

Autobiographies and Portraits of the President, Cabinet, Supreme Court and Congress. Edited by WALTER NEALE. The first two volumes, now ready, contain the biographies and portraits of President McKinley, the late Vice-President, the members of the McKinley Cabinet, and of the Supreme Court of the United States, and all of the members of the Senate and House of Representatives of the Fifty-fifth Congress. It is the purpose of the publishers to issue supplementary volumes with each incoming administration and Congress, which will embrace the autobiographies and portraits of each of the new officers of the government.

Two vols., 9½ x 6½, pp. 1,140, illustrated by 471 engravings. Price, in cloth, $7.50 per set; half morocco, $10.00 per set.

Coin, Currency and Commerce. An Essay in Exposition of their Natural Relations, and containing Outlines of Monetary Theory. By PHILIP A. ROBINSON.

278 pp., 5¼ x 7½, cloth. Price, $1.00.

The Southampton Insurrection. By WILLIAM S. DREWRY, M. A., Ph. D. A complete history of the great slave insurrection of Virginia in 1831.

5½ x 8, cloth, illustrated by 36 full-page demi-teintes from photographs by the author, from Daguerreotypes, Drawings, etc., 236 pp. Price, $2.00.

History of Slavery in Virginia. By JAMES CURTIS BALLAGH, Ph. D., Associate in History, Johns Hopkins University. An exhaustive history of the theory and practice of slavery and of the treatment of negroes and other dependents in Virginia from 1607 to 1865.

5 x 7¼; cloth; 250 pp. Edition limited to 500 copies. Price, $2.00.

Niagara: Its History, Incidents and Poetry. By RICHARD L. JOHNSON. Illustrated by fourteen full-page photogravures in tints, from original photographs by Soule, twenty-four full-page demi-teintes and many half tones.

12½ x 8½; 115 pp.; red cloth binding, on which is mounted a reproduction in color photograph of the painting by Church. Price, $1.50.

Early Days of Washington. By Miss SALLY SOMERVELL MACKALL. The most authoritative history of the National Capital. Illustrated by 75 engravings and reproductions of old drawings and prints.

Cloth; 5½ x 8 inches; 328 pages; profusely illustrated; large, clear type; hand composition; gold top; stamping in gold; heavy enamel paper. Price, $2.50.

The Novels of Honore de Balzac. Including Scenes of Parisian Life; of Private Life; of Provincial Life; of Military, Political, and Country Life, etc. Complete in twenty volumes of over eight hundred pages each, and is the only English Translation of Balzac which is complete and unexpurgated. *The works are illustrated with 41 etchings, printed on Japan paper, and 180 demi-teintes; after drawings by Adrien-Moreau, Toudouze, Cortazzo, Robaudi, Vidal, Cain, etc. The volumes are printed on wove paper, antique finish, handsomely bound in linen.*

Complete set, $59.00.

Joan of Arc. A drama in verse by CHARLES JAMES.
5½ x 7½ inches; illustrated; 81 pages; printed from new type on Strathmore deckle-edge paper. *Price, $1.00.*

The Last Man. A novel by N. MONROE MCLAUGHLIN.
Cloth, 222 pp.; 5x7½. *Price, $1.00.*

As It Happened. A novel by JOSEPHINE WINFIELD BRAKE.
"* * * I have no hesitation in saying, I believe it to be the strongest exposure of modern masculinity the generation has produced. It is as intense in climax as 'On the Heights,' by Auerbach." DEWIT C. JONES, *Columbus* (Ohio) *Record.*
Bound in cloth; size 5 x 7½. *Price, $1.00.*

The Regeneration. A novel by HERBERT BAIRD STIMPSON, author of "The Tory Maid," etc.
Cloth; 5 x 7½ inches; illustrated; 181 pages. *Price, $1.00.*

Complete Poems of Colonel John A. Joyce. Author of "Peculiar Poems," "Jewels of Memory," etc. Compiled and arranged by the author. Illustrated by PAUL D. SULLIVAN.
Price, $1.00.

American Statesmen. Being many yarns and good stories gathered here and there on our public men—on those who hold office, those who hope to, and those who never will. Collected and edited by WALTER NEALE. Illustrated in caricature by FELIX E. MAHONY, C. T. BERRYMAN and PAUL D. SULLIVAN.
Cloth; 6 x 9; 500 pp. *Price, $2.50.*

Waifs of the Press. By HARRY L. WORK.
Cloth; 5 x 7½; 200 pp. *Price, $1.00.*

Vade - Mecum to the Dinner Table. By EDMUND, BARON WUCHERER VON HULDENFELD, formerly tutor to the ARCHDUKE EUGENE. Invaluable to Americans going abroad.
Cloth; 5½ x 8; pp. 154. *Price, 80 cents.*

Mr. Billy Downs and His Likes. By Col. RICHARD MALCOLM JOHNSTON. Includes the stories, which by many are regarded as Colonel Johnston's best work, *A Bachelor's Counselings, Parting from Sailor, Two Administrations, Almost a Wedding in Dooly District, Something in a Name,* and *Townes and Their Cousins.* In *The Conservative Review* for February, 1899, Mr. Bernard M. Steiner, his biographer, said, " Colonel Richard Malcolm Johnston was often called 'The Nestor of Southern Literary Men,' but the idea of old age never seemed to be a proper one to associate with him ; he was so full of life, so keenly interested in all that went on * * * American literature (at his death) had lost a noted writer without doubt, but, most of all, the world had lost the present influence of a noble man."

Cloth; 5 x 7½; 232 pp.; illustrated.   *Price, $1.25.*

She Cometh Forth Like a Flower. A series of washdrawings by Miss F. L. WARD, illustrating young girlhood just at the dawn of womanhood. This is Miss Ward's first appearance in the art world in book form, but we believe that the unusual ability shown in these drawings will place her in the front rank of American artists.

Half cloth binding; 9 x 12 inches; 8 full-page drawings and 8 pages of text. Makes an unusually handsome gift. Price in a box, prepaid, $1.25.

Cupid and Creeds. A novel, by W. J. NEWTON, In this delightful story a quartette of lovers hold the attention, and will delight those who like a good old-fashioned story, as well as readers of other tastes. The various experiences and troubles of these lovers make such varying situations that the book is of absorbing interest from the first page to the last.

Decorated cloth binding; 5 x 7½ inches.   *Price, $1.00.*

Brambleton Fair. A comedy in three acts, by W. J. NEWTON. Third edition includes a new one-act farce-comedy entitled *A Double Divorce,* by the same author.

Cloth; 5 x 7½ inches.   *Price, 80 cents.*

PATRIOTIC SONGS, BY W. J. NEWTON.

The Columbian Anthem. Music by E. BERLINER.

This anthem was first sung by the Daughters of the American Revolution at the National Council, February 22, 1897, and on Flag Day celebration of the same year was presented with the full Chorus and Orchestra of the Castle Square Opera Company at the Lafayette Square Opera House in Washington, and by a number of Public Schools in Washington and in New York.

At a concert given by Prof. Fanciulli with the full Marine Band at the White House Grounds in the presence of President and Mrs. McKinley, on Saturday, September 18, 1897, the *Columbian Anthem* was selected as the opening number.

The *Baltimore American*, commenting on this concert (compositions by American composers having been exclusively selected) under date of September 19th, 1897, said : "Among the compositions rendered was the *Columbian Anthem* by E. Berliner. Considering that this country has not a National melody, other than those borrowed from Europe, the *Columbian Anthem* has a good chance to be some day selected as our National Melody."

Songs From Brambleton Fair. Words and music, including *Love Needs No Language; Say Yes, My Darling; The Best of Friends Must Part; Wait For Me, Dearest*, and all choruses.

Price, in paper, 50 cents.

Old Glory. The Blake School Flag Song, music by E. A. VARELA.

Gloria Old Glory. The Brent School Flag Song, music by F. GAISBERG.

The Flag of Washington. The Abbot School Flag Song, music by W. J. NEWTON.

Songs For Sale by Music Dealers Only.

THE NEALE COMPANY, Publishers,

431 Eleventh Street,   WASHINGTON, D. C.

Printed in Great Britain
by Amazon.co.uk, Ltd.,
Marston Gate.